Once Below a Time

I0821300

SUNY series in

Psychoanalysis and Culture

Henry Sussman, editor

Once Below a Time

Dylan Thomas, Julia Kristeva, and Other Speaking Subjects

EYNEL WARDI

STATE UNIVERSITY OF NEW YORK PRESS

Published by
State University of New York Press, Albany

© 2000 State University of New York

All rights reserved

Printed in the United States of America

No part of this book may be used or reproduced in any manner whatsoever without written permission. No part of this book may be stored in a retrieval system or transmitted in any form or by any means including electronic, electrostatic, magnetic tape, mechanical, photocopying, recording, or otherwise without the prior permission in writing of the publisher.

For information, address State University of New York Press,
State University Plaza, Albany, N.Y. 12246

Production, Laurie Searl
Marketing, Michael Campochiaro

Library of Congress **Cataloging-in-Publication** Data

Wardi, Eynel, 1956–
Once below a time : Dylan Thomas, Julia Kristeva, and other speaking subjects / Eynel Wardi.
p. cm. — (SUNY series in psychoanalysis and culture)
Includes bibliographical references and index.
ISBN 0-7914-4559-3 (alk. paper) — ISBN 0-7914-4560-7 (pbk : alk. paper)
1. Thomas, Dylan, 1914–1953—Criticism and interpretation.
2. Psychoanalysis and literature—Wales—History—20th century.
3. Kristeva, Julia, 1941—Contributions in criticism. 4. Subjectivity in literature. 5. Semiotics and literature. 6. Myth in literature. I. Title. II. Series

PR6039.H52 Z94 2000
821′.912—dc21 99-089097

10 9 8 7 6 5 4 3 2 1

To the memory of my father

In the name of the fatherless
In the name of the unborn
And the undesirers
. . . .
O in the name
Of no one
. . .
No
One to
Be I pray

—Dylan Thomas, *Collected Poems*

Contents

Acknowledgments		xi
1	The Genesis of the Speaking Subject: Fantasies of Origins and their Realization in the Poetic Text	1
2	Poem on his Birthday	35
3	Incarnate Devil in the Garden of Eden	61
	The Possibility of the Real	61
	"Incarnate Devil"	66
4	Under the Sign of Loss, a Recuperation	93
	The Double Determination of Repetition	93
	The Princedom of the Apple Towns	101
5	The Lover, the Poet, and the Lunatic	131
	Oedipus and the Problem of Boundaries	131
	"A Prospect of the Sea"	135
	"The Mouse and the Woman"	150
Conclusion:	A Confession of the Speaking Subject (*or* Who Is Afraid of Dylan Thomas?)	171
Notes		191
Works Cited		221
Index		229

Acknowledgments

I am grateful to Shlomith Rimmon-Kenan and Julia Kristeva, the supervisors of my doctoral dissertation which was the basis for the book. I especially thank Shlomith for her teaching, which consolidated the theoretical basis for my work, and for her committed guidance and true friendship. Her attentiveness and lucidity, as well as a happy combination of rigor and open-mindedness, were an invaluable source of intellectual challenge and encouragement. Without them I believe my project would not have reached articulation. Julia Kristeva's writings and teaching stimulated my thinking over years. I am also indebted to her for making it possible for me to study in Paris. The time I spent there was extremely enriching and fruitful.

My deepest thanks go to Baruch Hochman, who midwived this book with boundless generosity in every stage of its creation. With his wonderful gift for active and activating listening, Baruch often freed my thoughts from murky entanglements, drawing out of me a crystallization of what I actually had to say. He read and commented on every draft of this project with his keen sense for the essential and his stylistic sensibility, and gave freely of his time and energy as well as his wisdom to help me in the process of submitting the book for publication.

I want to thank Henry Sussman for reading the manuscript and for his pertinent suggestions for improvement. I am grateful to David Harel for his earnest encouragement and gentle prodding at various stages of the work, and for his valuable technical help with the manuscript. And I thank Eli Weisstub for helping me to deepen my knowledge of what I was writing about.

I am grateful to Shimon Sandbank for his helpful comments on parts of the manuscript. Hearty thanks to Ayala Amir and Gadia Zrihan for editorial assistance and for their patience under pressure, and also to Hanna Ovnat, Rivka Miller and Maya Barzilai for their help with the bibliography. I am grateful to Raanan Kulka for pointing me to intersubjective psychoanalytic theory and for facilitating my access to relevant material. Ephraim Gerber I thank for his help in dealing with copyright permissions and other tasks. Finally, it has been a pleasure to work with James Peltz and Laurie Searl of SUNY Press throughout the editorial and production process.

I would like to thank the various institutions that have contributed to the entire effort, throughout my doctoral studies and the subsequent work on the book. First I thank my home institution, the Hebrew University of Jerusalem, for providing a most encouraging environment, for financial help and for easing my teaching load to enable me to pursue the project that became this book. Parts of the work were carried out during hospitable stays at Paris University 7 and Cornell University. My thanks to Cynthia Chase for making the visit to Cornell possible, to the Olin Library for providing an ideal work environment, and especially to Mary Jacobus for her inspiring seminar on "The Object and the Abject." I also enjoyed the hospitality of the libraries at the Van Leer Institute and the Israeli Institute of Psychoanalysis in Jerusalem.

I received generous financial support from the Wolfson Fund through the Israel Academy of Sciences and Humanities, from the Israel Council for Higher Education, and from the French government, the C.N.R.S., and the Rothchild Foundation.

I wish to extend my gratitude to the following authors and institutions for permitting me to use copyrighted material: The David Higham Associates and New Directions, who kindly allowed me to reprint Dylan Thomas's poems "Fern Hill," "Incarnate Devil," "Poem in October" and "Poem on his Birthday" and to quote from other poems from Thomas's *Collected Poems 1934–1952* (London: J. M. Dent & Sons, 1973 [1971]), as well as lines from *The Collected Letters of Dylan Thomas* (edited by Paul Ferris, Dent, 1985) and from his short stories, "A Prospect of the Sea" and "The Mouse and the Woman," published by J. M. Dent in *A Prospect of the Sea* (1979 [1975]); New Directions, for allowing me to quote from *The Notebooks of Dylan Thomas* (1967 [1966]); Faber & Faber, and Harcourt, Brace & Company, for permission to quote from T. S. Eliot's "Burnt Norton," published in *Four Quartets* (1959, copyright 1971 owned by Esme Valerie Eliot); Stéphane Moses and Les éditions du cerf, for permission to quote from Stéphane Moses's essay, "L'idée d'origine chez Walter Benjamin," published in *Walter Benjamin et Paris,* edited by Heinz Wismann (1986); Donald Davidson, for permission to quote from his essay "What Metaphors Mean," published in *Philosophical Perspectives on Metaphor,* edited by Mark Johnson (University of Minnesota Press); and David Holbrook, for permission to quote excerpts from his book, *The Code of Night,* published by The Athlone Press (1972).

Abbreviations

CP *Collected Poems: 1934–1952*, by Dylan Thomas, (J. M. Dent & Sons: London, 1973).

PFL *Pelican Freud Library* (vols. 1–14). Translated by James and Alix Strachey and edited by Angela Richards, Albert Dixon, Alan Tyson, Joseph Breuer, and James Strachey. Hardmondsworth: Penguin Books, 1976–85).

CHAPTER ONE

The Genesis of the Speaking Subject

Fantasies of Origins and their Realization in the Poetic Text

As its title might suggest, this book has a double focus: it presents a reading of Dylan Thomas, and a subjectivist poetics that is guided by contemporary psycho-semiological theory. The proposed poetics is formulated through dialogue with works by Thomas. My reading of Thomas at once illustrates and further informs an attempt to understand the dynamics of poetic language from the point of view of the subjective, and the *subjectifying*, experience of its articulation. In its to and fro movement between theory and textual analysis, this book traces the textual—linguistic as well as psychic—processes that generate the experience of subjectivity undergone in the course of poetic signification. Its concern is thus the genesis of the speaking subject as the simultaneous effect of the poetic text in the actuality of its realization—in writing and in reading alike.

The affinity between writing and reading, and between writers and readers, is established through analysis of the generative properties of the poetic text in its relational, intersubjective dimension. This dimension encompasses the dialogical and the transferential identificatory relations that animate both textual communication and intertextuality. The working of these relations are central to the shape and substance of this book. While its main focus is the dynamic correlation between meaning and subjectivity in Thomas's poetic writing, it also displays how that correlation figures in the reading process, both through its reflexive unfolding and through direct analysis in the concluding chapter.

My attempt to understand the subjectifying dynamics of poetic language is largely inspired by the work of Julia Kristeva.[1] Its point of departure is a dynamic conception of the poetic text as a performance, or act, and as a process of signification that generates, or rather re-generates its speaking subject in the course of its realization.[2] The textual genesis, as I understand it, consists in the positioning of an initially split subject in a meaningful symbolic relation toward an other, a relation which facilitates a momentary sense of internal unity. This generative dynamics is viewed as a repetition of early integrative processes that constitute the subject's "original" advent—as imagined by psychoanalytical theory.

The psychoanalytical approach informing this generative hypothesis synthesizes various Freudian and post-Freudian notions of the subject and his or her advent.[3] The latter pertain, by and large, to French Lacanian and British object relations theories (Klein, Winnicott, and others) and to syntheses of both, notably Kristeva's. Though often irreconcilable in their basic orientations and in their definitions of the subject, these different schools nonetheless seem to share a semiological perspective which, as Kristeva has so effectively shown, provides a basis for understanding the link between meaning and subjectivity in the matrix of the literary text. From this perspective, the subject is, by origin at least, a *signifying subject*, namely, a subject constituted by psychic processes that are essentially semiotic, or *semiological*, and by acts of symbolization that activate or enhance these processes. The subject's psycho-semiological being is founded on a lack that is associated with the archaic separation from the maternal. This lack—ultimately of a secure sense of being—propels and animates the subject's constitutive significations. Motivating his conscious as well as his unconscious representations, it gives rise to fantasies of origins that are projected back onto the subject's immemorial beginning. The representation and enactment of these fantasies indeed constitute the origin of the subject both in his "original" advent—and in the actuality of its reconstitution in the poetic text.

Underlying poetic signification there seems to be a nostalgic fantasy of prior identity, of a lost unity of being, which motivates the text as an act of nostalgic recuperation. Seen in the light of Kristeva's *Black Sun*, this fantasy is the idealized figuration of the object of *melancholic loss*; an affective representation of the paradisal plenitude of a maternal symbiosis that has been lost in the course of a more or less traumatic separation.[4] The loss of the maternal object—or "pre-object," for it is the configuration of the mother before she becomes distinguished as separate from the infant—is, according to Kristeva, the origin of all symbolization. It is thus that the origin of the signifying subject's psychic life—as a recuperative motion of displacement of loss by imaginary representation. And it is through poetic symbolization that the nostalgic original integrity is most effectively restored—or rather *originated*: for the "melancholic imaginary," as Kristeva calls it, is a fantasy which neither had nor has a conscious perceptible reality outside its symbolic representations. The enchanting suggestiveness of poetic rhythms, sounds, and semantic polyphonies invokes, or indeed, re-presents, as it were, the plenitude of the archaic object, to the effect of actually realizing its speaking subject's fantasy of origins.

But this realization is not only fantasmatic; it is also real, in that it sets in motion an integrative process in which the melancholic fragmentation that splits the subject gives way and begins a momentum towards a unifying desire. The subject's split is a psychic mark of the separation, manifested in affective, "psycho-somatic" dissociation and primary conflictual structures. As such, it is ultimately a defensive, *ambivalent* response to the loss of the maternal. In the simplest, Kleinian terms, the archaic object is both "good" and "bad," a polarization that configures the nostalgic idealization of satisfying aspects or experiences of the maternal object, and its resentment for being lost or experienced as rejecting or, alternatively, persecuting, devouring, or castrating. In its association with the (rejected) somatic aspect of the symbiotic object and its symbolic sublimation, the ambivalent polarization of these terms becomes a psycho-somatic split, that is, a dissociation between the body as the center of experience and a repressive mental consciousness. The melancholic effect of this primary, splitting ambivalence is that it suspends the articulation of affect, thus preventing the symbolic sublimation of the longing for the lost object in meaningful sign and object relations. Ambivalence is melancholic, in other words, in so far as it suspends the symbolic thrust of desire. Poetic texts enhance desire in the dynamic course of their articulation: the expressive and the relational (cohesive and communicative) properties particular to poetic language heal the melancholic split, as it were, by facilitating a process of "binding" otherwise loose and conflicting drive-energies into a unifying other-oriented, or other-bound, disposition. This accounts, I think, for the sensation of vitality and relatedness that "regenerates" the speaking subject of effective poetry—effective, that is, as the *topos* of desire and integration which realizes the subject's nostalgic longing for an original integrity of being.

In tracing the dynamics of the genesis of the textual subject as a repetition of his "original" advent, I have tried to remain as faithful as possible to a notion of the subjective experience of that repetition in the actuality of the textual performance, while taking into consideration its aesthetic and cultural dimensions. Therefore, in keeping with Kristeva and others, notably Winnicott, the book's psychoanalytical approach is existentially and phenomenologically oriented. Far from seeking to reduce poetic signification to a schematic psychological model and its speaking subject to a narrative of origins or a semiological formula, this writing seeks to maintain a double perspective. While tracing the psycho-symbolic mechanisms that realize the poetic text and its subject from the outside, "objectively," as it were, it also considers, and in principle prioritizes, the internal texture of their affective and imaginative experience. Central to this consideration is an emphasis on the poetic imaginary, whose fantasmatic *topoi* are valorized for their aesthetic effect per se, as well as in terms of their providing intriguing and stimulative spaces for the experience of subjective "being." I use the word "being" to suggest, precisely, a subjective ontology that seems to be at the heart of the aesthetic experience and hence of the poetic event. It refers, quite simply, to the sense of being—alive or real—in the time-space of the text. Indeed, it seems to me that the textual effect of the subject's integrative positioning in relation to an other corresponds, precisely, to the sensation of vitality and "thereness" generated by effective poetry, which places us in a state of *inner and outward relatedness*, or, alternatively, of being *wholly* "there," both body and mind, in the imaginative vitality of desire.

This internal relational perspective essentially coincides with current psychoanalytical approaches which are *not* part of the dialogue between literature and psychoanalysis conducted in this book. Of special relevance is the theory of intersubjectivity introduced by Stolorow and Atwood, which proclaims an existential-phenomenological orientation and an affinity with modern hermeneutic traditions.[5] Some of the intersubjective notions with regard to both the psychoanalytic subject and hermeneutics may help clarify my own, subjectivist perspective, especially as regards the indeterminate question of the identity of the subject I am writing about: who is it, ultimately or predominantly, the poet or the reader?

Intersubjective theory is defined by its authors as "a field theory or systems theory that seeks to comprehend psychological phenomena not as products of isolated intrapsychic mechanisms, but as forming at the interface of reciprocally interacting subjectivities."[6] Underlying this approach is an intent to avoid reification of the psychoanalytic subject. Originally introduced as psychoanalytic phenomenology,[7] intersubjective theory defines the subject in terms of his particular *lived experience* of himself in particular relational contexts.[8] Its concern is with affective meaning and its articulation rather than with objective mechanisms and forces—with the significance of the subject's interactions with the world for *him*, as, one might say, their signifying subject. The intersubjective relational model accounts for the recurrent and the changing "configurations of self and other in the person's subjective universe" which are manifested and perpetually generated in the course of his human interactions. Therefore, "it is not the isolated individual mind . . . but the larger system created by the mutual interplay between the subjective worlds of patient and analyst, or of child and caregiver, that constitute the . . . domain of [intersubjective] psychoanalytic inquiry."[9]

The methodological implications of all this for psychoanalytic interpretation are the need for empathic attunement to the analysand's articulation of his affects and, correlatively, reliance on the subjectivity of the analyst as an involved participant as well as an observer in the analytic situation. In the psychoanalytical encounter as an intersubjective "field," where analyst and analysand are engaged in a mutually effective relation of transference and countertransference, the analyst's subjective perspective is necessarily central, more central than in more traditional schools of psychoanalysis. But just as the subjective bias, or "prejudice" is seen by modern hermeneutics as a prerequisite to understanding,[10] so is countertransference a principal tool, rather than an obstacle, in intersubjective hermeneutics, where it is conceived of as a necessary condition for empathy. Empathy is a central term in self-psychology, which is a major influence on the intersubjective approach. But if empathy, as Kohut saw it, is what facilitates one's "attempt to enter another's subjective reality,"[11] it is by no means—from an intersubjective perspective—a matter of neutralizing one's personal psychological prejudice. The rationale for this is pertinently formulated by Gadamer, in his insistence on the "positive concept of prejudice" in the hermeneutic process: "Prejudices are biases of our openness to the world. They are simply conditions whereby we experience something—whereby what we encounter says something to us."[12] The subjective investment in the empathic attunement to the other and his texts, though yielding, as Dilthey put it, a "rediscovery of the I in the Thou,"[13] also enables us to touch on what is essential to the other—precisely because it touches on what is essential to us. Therefore, I believe that the subject I have written about in my reading of Dylan Thomas is *both* Thomas and myself in a *particular* intersubjective encounter. The principal subject matter of this book is, therefore, a dialogue between two subjectivities, which have evolved in the process of its articulation.

❧

In light of the psychoanalytical fantasy of origins that is projected in this book, the articulation of the poetic text involves the reproduction of the onset of desire through the re-enactment of the subject's primordial separation and his integrative entrance into the symbolic order of sign and object relations. The subject's "original" genesis is effected by primitive processes of signification which facilitate the separation from the maternal symbiosis and its substitution by object relations and linguistic representations. Drawing on rudimentary acts of symbolization, these processes enhance the elaboration of the archaic loss of the maternal through its "primal" repression and sublimation, and through the partial integration of the intrapsychic schisms and conflicts that split the subject-to-be in defense against the separation. Though pre-verbal, the early integrative, sublimatory processes are essentially symbolic in that they involve differential and combinatory operations within a preexisting "oedipal" schema. Indeed, it is only within a ternary structure that the experience of the symbiotic dyad can be made sense of, or even cognized, affectively and imaginatively.

The original psycho-semilogical processes draw on imaginary functions of identification that mark the "oral phase" in the subject's development, in which his experience is expressed and organized in fantasies associated with the activity of nutrition and ingesting. That is, the form and substance of these fantasies is provided by the palpable experience of eating, chewing, sucking, swallowing, spitting, keeping something inside, etc., but also of being the object of these activities (being bitten, devoured, etc.). In effect, the identificatory dynamics at work in the emerging subject's archaic symbolic functioning—projection, introjection, incorporation, etc.—derive from the "oral" activities of expulsion, or "excorporation" and incorporation.[14] Initially organizing experience in terms of pleasure and unpleasure—"good" and "bad" (pre-) objects which are to be incorporated and expelled respectively—these imaginary functions provide the differential and identificatory basis for the relation between the discrete realities of inside and outside, me and not-me, I and other. These pre-verbal symbolic acts demarcate the boundaries of the subject as a *relatively* autonomous and integral being, constituted *in relation* to the otherness of the external world and its representations.

What sustains this transition from the symbiotic to the relational mode of being is, according to Kristeva's model of primary narcissism, a pre-verbal and pre-genital symbolic function that makes possible the psychic representation of the somatic experience of the symbiotic dyad.[15] Inherent in the terms in which the mother experiences and expresses her relation to the child, and inherited through primary identification, that symbolic function is always already there as a virtual other which mediates the symbiotic dyad, and thus opens the way for its eventual substitution by sign-relations and other object relations. Its virtual alterity is implied in the very articulation of maternal love, constituting the "third party" with respect to which that love is articulated as such (as distinct from a non-articulated, symbiotic attitude). In its ternary context and by its association with maternal desire, that mediating alterity figures as a *paternal* function that conforms, under the pre-genital circumstances, to the logic of a retroacted Oedipus complex. By projecting the oedipal structure back onto the mother-child bond, this logic accounts for the "semiotic leap" from the somatic to the psychic, as well as for the constitution of the archaic object relations as symbolic *relations* rather than a state of symbiotic fusion or defensive splitting. The symbolic mediation of the pre-oedipal "*imaginary father*" which fosters the narcissistic foundations of love and of subjective identity is primarily cohesive in its function.[16] It is thereby distinguished from the primarily differential function of Lacan's oedipal, "phallic" "Symbolic" father, who will enter the life of Kristeva's subject only at the later stage of sexual differentiation, to introduce law and prohibition and to be associated, in retrospect, with the archaic separation as "castration."[17] From that point on, the role of the more archaic, *maternal*, father will be to ensure imaginary and affective cohesiveness *within* the differential, symbolic systems of language and other social codes. Indeed, the archaic imaginary processes facilitated by this maternal-paternal function lay the foundations for these symbolic systems.[18]

Though the psychoanalytic notions of psychic origins and stages or phases of development may make it seem as if the primordial processes of emergence have a measure of finality in them, these generative processes are never quite completed. Hence the *inherent*, continuing split of the subject and his recurrent need for the corrective repetition of his unachieved advent in perpetual acts of symbolization that yield his always *provisional* being as a (perpetually self-) signifying subject. Thus, it is precisely the unfinished business of his genesis that motivates the subject of poetry to repeat it in and through the poetic text, which "identifies" him only for as long as it lasts. The speaking subject has "being" "only insofar as he speaks" (writes, reads), that is, speaks himself *toward* being what he *is*: "a subject . . . in process" of *becoming*—in and through the poetic text (Lacan; Kristeva).[19]

The dialectic of being and becoming summarizes, and perhaps also resolves, the apparent paradoxicality of the psychoanalytical synthesis which guides this book's generative hypothesis. That synthesis combines opposing positions regarding the controversial question of the subject's integrity of being. For clearly, the idea of integrative "being," which may be taken to correspond to the essentialist notion of identity or the "self," is antagonistic to Lacanian theory, which relegates the integrated self to the specular domain of the imaginary. Lacan's distinction between the subject and the self (*je*; *moi*) underscores the inherent condition of a subject split by a separation that can never be worked through, a subject who is therefore destined to repeated processes of "becoming" through symbolic expressions of his desire for an impossible integrity.[20] Lacan's notion of the self designates, precisely, the *illusion* of that integrity—a projective reflection as in a mirror, whose redoubling effect manifests the very split which it seeks to heal. As the metaphor of the mirror suggests, the self is always external to the subject; the narcissistic identification with it, which gives the illusion of integrity during the "mirror stage" and in the subsequent erections of the imaginary that repress, or "misrecognize" the separation as "castration," cannot be other than temporary and evasive: it is a dim mirror bound to be cracked before it clears up and to be displaced by an endless chain of inappropriate signifiers.

For the psychoanalytical theories that affirm a more continuous, stable notion of the self, by contrast, the imaginary is an actually formative force. The subject's identity is established by his identifications; the core of the self as "being" is constituted by the *introjection* of maternal love—an other's affect that becomes an integral part of the self, through and beyond the *incorporation* of her discourse, or parts of her, as foreign bodies within the self.[21] Such "appropriation" is denied Lacan's subject, who is no more than the *agent* of his impossible quest for identity. For him, seeing can never turn into being; taking something in does not make it part of one's *proper* self. And so, identified only with/by his desire, that would-be subject is forever destined to seek his original integrity in the perpetual erection and crumbling of his signs, doomed to an eternal split by the very medium of his quest.

A reconciliation of self and subject may be conceived, as it is in this book, as taking place during provisional moments of subjective "being," or integration, in the signifying process.[22] Essentially split, the speaking subject can nevertheless attain a real, if temporary, integrity in moments of meaningful relatedness in the process of articulating the text. In these moments, the transferential dynamics of signification enhance the introjection of otherwise split-off affects, through the incorporation of the textual or intertextual discourse of another. This issue is further elaborated on later in this chapter, in the discussion of Thomas's poetics.

To conceive the paradoxical coincidence of being and becoming in the textual performance takes some faith in the imaginary—more faith, at least, than Lacan has in it—and in the poetic imaginary in particular. And if that is not available a priori, then a little imagination will do, under the necessary condition of a provisional suspension of disbelief which makes possible the actual experience of being *in* the text. That experience may become clearer if we look at it from outside as well as from inside—from a semiological perspective, which perceives the poetic text as a *heterogeneous utterance*, and from a phenomenological perspective which sees it as a *chronotopos of wish fulfillment*.

The experience of being in the text is at the center of my phenomenological analysis, which is concerned with the situation of the subject as a *signifying body* in the spatio-temporal reality of the text, and with the correlative intensity or palpability of that reality. Such a "situation" implies, then, a view of the text as a *space* for being as well as a process of becoming, a space which, in order to accommodate the subject, must transcend the specular dimension of representation. It does so by dint of its heterogeneity and its dynamic aspect as a performative space. The textual space is heterogeneous in that it combines linguistic as well as trans-linguistic modes of representation. Kristeva calls the former mode *symbolic* and the latter *semiotic*.[23] The *symbolic* designates the determinate denotative signification of predicative language that is subjected to the differential and the combinatory laws of grammar and logic. The *semiotic* is the distinctive mode of poetic signification. It is operative in the symbolic indeterminacy of sound and metaphor which generates the translinguistic connotative element of poetic meaning. The latter is the imaginary-somatic (as distinct from symbolic) meaning-effect, irreducible to language, of affects, sensations, and sense perceptions. It is what yields the dynamic *topoi* of the poetic imaginary in the "aura" of poetic meaning. It draws on the materiality of language for its distinctively suggestive, connotative representation of the subject's signifying "body," and in doing so it signifies the subject's body deictically, or iconically, rather than by the symbolic conventionality of the arbitrary sign.

Thus, the heterogeneous text does not only reflect the subject, through a mediating symbolic representation (of a "world" as a mirroring other). It also signifies him as it were directly, metonymically (deictically): it contains, or "embodies" the subject in the translinguistic realization of the *semiotic* representation of his "body" in its affectively and imaginatively invested materiality. For while subverting the determinacy of the denotative, *symbolic* representation, the *semiotic* ("somatic") inscriptions of the signifying subject's body also charge it with the connotative—affective and imaginary—intensity that lends it its efficacy as a space for being. Indeed, it is the investment of the linguistic representation of the textual "world" with the subject's *intimate* relation to it that make the representational space real—real, that is, for the subject who responds to it with his whole, psychic-*cum*-somatic being, while at once constituting and inhabiting it, and being constituted by it. At this dynamic, temporal point of intimacy it seems as though the subject and the text are one; as if the textual time-space—a version of Bakhtin's *chronotopos*—and the subject who both realizes it and is being realized by it are united in the dialectic motion of mutual creation, as in Yeats's poem, where you cannot "know the dancer from the dance."[24] You cannot tell, because their common space is one that allows for positive being by controlling the negativity of *différance*: a performative space whose boundaries are delineated by the motion of dancing; a space spanned by the trace-work of the motion like the circular tail of a comet.

The logic governing this simultaneity is the logic of desire, realized in meaning as a creative intentionality toward an other. The textual space for *actual* being is spanned by way of *imaginary* wish fulfillment, that is to say, *by the way*, as it were, of the articulation of the desire for meaning, which is the desire for being *in* an intimately significant relation to the world's otherness. Such a meaning-full relation takes place—and *makes* a place for the subject—in the *transitional space* of the text.[25] Winnicott's term designates the experience of the self in its imaginative, projective relation to the external reality in the early, narcissistic stages of its development, as well as in adult life. Replacing the traditional psychoanalytical distinction between internal and external reality, this notion of intermediary reality reflects Winnicott's existential approach to the self in terms of the subjective experience of one's intimate and creative relation to one's environment. In this, Winnicott anticipates the redefinition of psychic reality achieved in the theory of intersubjectivity. In its application here, Winnicott's notion qualifies the heterogeneous space of the text as representing both me and not me; both my desiring body in its metonymical gesture of signification and its metaphorical object which, as it now appears, is not quite an other but rather the space of *transition*, of movement toward it; it is precisely where I *am*, where I am fulfilled. For the object of poetic representation is, so it seems to me, not so much (or not only) the world as other, but mainly the subject's relation to it—or rather his desire for such a relation, which is realized within the narcissistic bounds of the textual space.

❧

Winnicott's intermediary spaces illustrate the close connection between subjectivity and narcissism by foregrounding, like Kristeva in her analysis of primary identification, the relational aspect of narcissism as a symbolic (or proto-symbolic) disposition that adheres to an alterity. Winnicott's intermediary spaces—which, like signs, mediate, that is, both separate and relate the subject and his environment—are also called *potential spaces*, which suggests his emphasis on the role of creativity in the subject's "narcissistic" self-realization. Winnicott stresses the generative function of illusion and the experience of narcissistic omnipotence in the subject's "original" advent, as well as in the constant creation in adult life of intermediary spaces that realize his potential for relational being. As distinct from the subject of traditional psychoanalysis (Freud, Klein), who is immanently defined in terms of his separateness, as the product of "an ongoing process of rational coming to terms with the limits of his being, a kind of cumulative process of disillusionment and mature mourning," Winnicott's subject continually transgresses his "objective" limits by creating both himself and his world.[26] This transgression is part of the subject's constitution as such because it sustains his imaginative, desirous relation to his perpetually re-created world, a world which, however, does *not* thereby lose its effective otherness for him. This paradox may be formulated as follows: "I create the world and the world is me, although it is there before me and for itself, as it yields itself to me and for me, so that I may create it."[27] The reciprocal relation between me and the world suggests my awareness of the world's alterity as distinct from my imaginary re-creation of it—which is nonetheless necessary in order to make that otherness accessible to me, and me capable of relating to *it*. It is this dialectic which characterizes the function of the text as a relational space for being and becoming.

Within Kristeva's and Winnicott's conceptualizations, subjectivity is bound up with narcissism in its life-oriented—relational and desiring—aspect. This life-oriented, or "erotic" aspect is opposed to the unrelated, "autistic," or "autoerotic" aspect of narcissism, whose regressive, introverted disposition is melancholic and dominated by the death drive.[28] Kristeva, who sees narcissism as the foundation of the speaking subject's psychic life as well as of the poetic text, distinguishes narcissism from autoeroticism by its ternary structure, which is founded on the archaic symbolic disposition she associates with the mediating otherness of a pre-oedipal paternal function.[29] Drawing on Freud's essay "On Narcissism," she adopts the view of narcissism he proposes there, and affirms his notion that narcissism develops from the autoerotic state of the mother-child dyad, by dint of a "new psychical action."[30] This new action she associates with Freud's notion that the foundation of the ego lies in an idealizing "primary identification" with the "father of individual prehistory" who is conceived to be "the origin of the ego ideal."[31] She calls that paternal function the "imaginary father," distinguishing its particular function from that of the oedipal, "Symbolic" father. Assimilated through "primary," that is, "direct and immediate identification [that] takes place earlier than any object-cathexis" (Freud),[32] the imaginary father is not an object, but rather a model—an ideal otherness to *be like* rather than an object to *have*—set up by the symbolic adherence of maternal speech. The pre-objectal paternal model is a "simple virtuality, a potential presence, a *form* to be cathected"[33]—a relational pattern or metaphorical *schema* to be invested with affective or imaginary content.[34] Its assimilation facilitates the separation from the mother and the beginning of psychic life through the "primal repression" and sublimation of the separation and its maternal "object." It opens and sustains a psychic space—narcissism—which functions as a "screen": while at once performing and repressing the separation, its receptive emptiness is the "zero degree of the imagination" which, under the aegis of the cohesive paternal function, sublimates the object and its loss into nostalgic, affective, and imaginary plenitude. Thus primary identification opens the way for the imaginary and subsequent symbolic displacements of the autoerotic "object," establishing narcissism as an intermediary state of transition between autoeroticism, with its melancholic leaning towards death, and object relations, which hold out the promise of vitality and life.

In the textual context, such a transition occurs through the transformation of melancholy into desire, a *nostalgic* desire which sublimates its underlying melancholic loss. Although it is clear that it is the life- or Eros-driven thrust of narcissism that sets the poetic process in motion, textual desire is not self-evident. With a hidden or manifest melancholia as its point of departure, poetic signification is animated by a conflict which may be called "oedipal." While moving towards a symbolic displacement of the lost maternal object, it is also subject to a regressive, incestuous, and melancholic pull toward its silent materiality, that is, away from erotic difference towards the autoerotic return of, or to, the same. At the hesitant intervals of poetic indeterminacy, when the habitual meaning of signifiers is suspended to give way to new meanings, the silence of tautology and the prospect of further metaphorical displacement contend with one another. Their contention constitutes the text as a point of intersection between nostalgia and melancholia, between the erotic orientation of narcissism and its thanatic counterpart. The resolution of this tension on the side of Eros and metaphor is the effect of the binding motion of signification, which consolidates its initially weak disposition towards the other through the integrative reenactment of the pre-oedipal conflicts of an ambivalence that splits the subject and suspends both desire and signification.

The imaginative and emotional logic of this ambivalence can be elucidated in terms of Melanie Klien's conception of the subject's coming into being. Indeed, primary ambivalence is the predominant factor in Klein's psychoanalytical model. The Kleinian subject oscillates throughout his life between dissociative and integrative "positions" that perpetuate the economy of ambivalence which marks the early phases of his development.[35] In the first, pre-objectal, "paranoid-schizoid" phase, the ambivalence is not experienced as such, but manifests itself in the defense mechanism of splitting. This mechanism involves the polarized projection of ambivalence onto "good" and "bad" parts of the mother's imagined configuration. The projection of the internally threatening hate for the mother onto an objectified image perceived to be "outside" establishes it, in Klein's understanding of the process, as a persecutory object or "part-object," against which the subject-to-be defends himself by introjecting the "good" part-object, which is the image of his projected love. The predominant factor in this phase is aggression, displayed in the defensive projection (i.e. expulsion) of the "bad" object and in the "paranoid" experience of persecution by it. In the following phase in Klein's scheme, the "depressive" phase, aggression and fragmentation are displaced by guilt and the need for restoration. In this phase the subject-to-be comes to recognize the mother and relate to her as a whole object, assimilating rather than polarizing and projecting his ambivalence. It is at this point that he becomes an ambivalent *subject*—an event which generates the anxiety of facing his own conflicts and destructiveness, and gives rise to the "depressive" mourning of the object which he imagines to have destroyed in the previous phase. The anxiety is attenuated by the intensification of the introjective processes and the reinforcing, through idealization, of the introjected "good object" that constitutes, according to Klein, the positive (loving) core of the ego. The idealization of the maternal object, which reduces the conflictual intensity of the ambivalence, is a part of a sublimational process in the course of which splitting begins to give way to repression. Feeling a "depressive" guilt for his destructiveness and anxiety about its effect—the loss of his object—the subject represses his aggressive impulses in order to restore the integrity of his lost, fragmented object. This sublimatory work of *reparation* is, for Klein, the origin of symbol-formation. Thus, it is the earlier "schizoid" rather than the later "depressive" manifestation of ambivalence that corresponds to the notion of melancholia introduced earlier, where it is conceived as a disintegrative state in which one is subject *to* primary ambivalence rather than assuming it. The depressive position, as Klein suggests, corresponds to Freud's notion of mourning—as distinct from melancholia—as the working through of loss in a whole-object-relation. But "the depressive position is never fully worked through,"[36] and so the melancholic schisms keep surfacing to subvert the integrity of the subject and his symbolizations, alternating with sublimative reparations of the subject's nostalgically mourned and projected "original" integrity.

The integrative failure which impedes the full working through of the depressive position (and hence the stability of the subject's integrity and his symbolizations) is inherent to the mechanism of sublimation which facilitates that position. The idealization necessary for introjecting the "good" maternal object and the internal reparation of the mother's split image draw, according to Klein, on defensive mechanisms of *denial* that are in themselves "schizoid."[37] What is being denied is the psychic reality of the depressive loss and the related conflicts of ambivalence. The affective dissociation from them by the correlatives of depression, *mania* and *obsessional mechanisms*, permit at once a detachment from the affective meaning of loss and an illusory omnipotent sense of control over it.[38] While negating the negativity of loss and ambivalence—protecting the subject from the anxieties of dependency, his mournful sadness, and the fear of his own destructiveness—the manic and obsessional dispositions in effect enact that negativity in the form of an aggressive annihilation, or control over, the object, thus subverting, to a varying degree, the work of mourning and internal reparation.[39]

Kristeva applies Klein's notions of reparation and denial in her *manic-depressive* model of the advent of symbolization and of aesthetic sublimation. She thus sees poetic symbolization as often involving a cathartic (rather than integrative or elaborative) manic negation of depressive ("melancholic") loss within a representation which at once restores and annihilates the lost maternal "object."[40] Primary ambivalence is thus enacted here, as in the child's entrance into the world of signs, as simultaneous reparation and matricide.[41]

Kristeva's notion of sublimation differs, however, from Klein's, in the oedipal framework within which it posits the earliest phases of the subject's development. Her tripartite, narcissistic model condenses the processes of splitting and sublimation into the simultaneous occurrence of primary repression and sublimation at the originary moment of primary identification. Indeed, the presence of the paternal function in Kristeva's construct accounts for the differential distance that is necessary for mourning and sublimation in the "depressive position." Polarized accordingly, the projective correlatives of Klein's "bad" and "good" objects in Kristeva's model are, roughly speaking, the objects of primary repression and sublimation, namely, the maternal "*abject*" and the archaic "*Thing*."[42] The "abject" object of primary repression represents the negativity of the separation, including the defensive ambivalence in response to it, while the "Thing" represents the plenitude of the idealized symbiotic state in a nostalgic affect. Thus, the maternal abject represents autoerotic ambiguity and melancholic splitting, or fragmentation, whereas the Thing is the sublimative product of the integrative aspect of the *nostalgic* narcissistic imagination.

The maternal abject is the phobic imaginary figuration of the abhorred materiality of the *undifferentiated* somatic-symbiotic object, as well as of its traumatic loss, which is associated with maternal violence or *abjection*. Maternal abjection is anxiously associated with death and maternal castration, while the materiality of the maternal abject is linked with death through the fantasy of being devoured by the mother and then putrefying within her body. Hence the defensive need to abject (expel) the abject—the "bad" somatic-symbiotic "object"—a maneuver which gives rise to the unseparated subject's psycho-somatic split, as well as to his advent as a signifying being. Like schizoid splitting in Klein's system, abjection is the most archaic, defensive form of separation, whereby the subject-to-be delineates his boundaries against the maternal abject. But in order for it to delineate *something*, this act of negation needs to be complemented by some correlative of Klein's introjection. This is where the Thing comes *in*, literally, as the heterogeneous, *symbolic* sublimation of the ambiguous object. Like the sublimative, reparational "good object" which becomes "a symbol within the ego,"[43] the affective *representation* of both the object and its loss in the nostalgic Thing is both differential and recuperative. It serves both to differentiate the emerging subject from the threatening mother and to recover an imaginary representation of her, thus functioning as the prototypical basis for signification. In its heterogeneous, semiological function, it integrates primary ambivalence by subordinating the negativity of loss to an affirmative, recuperative displacement.

But primary narcissism is fragile. Its tension-film—the projective "screen" of primal repression—is easily broken, giving way to the negativity of abjection that subverts the provisional imaginary plenitude, and creates the need for its displacement by further sublimations. When abjection surfaces, it encroaches on the narcissistic assimilation, undoing the introjection of the affirmative maternal affect of the Thing. At this point affective dissociation abandons the subject to the throes of abjection and conflict, which constitutes the melancholic foundation of poetic sublimation.

Melancholia, as I understand it in the light of Freud and Kristeva,[44] is a fixation on the splitting loss of the ambivalent archaic "object," manifested in the withdrawal of desire from objects and signs into the autistic, autoerotic non-space of psychic fragmentation. In her book on melancholia, Kristeva associates this non-space with the "narcissistic emptiness" generated by the separation, and with Freud's notion of "open wound" which drains the melancholic subject's drive-energies, "drawing to itself cathectic energies . . . from all directions, and emptying the ego until it is totally impoverished."[45] This draining, which Freud terms "anticathexes," accounts for the dissolution of desire in melancholia, caused by the fragmentation of drives and the "disintegration of bonds" within psychic structures and their representation (Kristeva).[46] This disintegration testifies to the work of the death drive either in its archaic form, linked to the psyche's fragile constitution prior to its organization in relation to "good" and "bad" part-objects, or in its secondary, "schizoid" form of turning round upon the ego of the "paranoid" aggressiveness toward the ambiguous archaic "object," or in both. Kristeva is more interested in the manifestation of the first, Thanatic process, which characterizes what she calls "narcissistic melancholy." Her melancholic subject in *Black Sun* is immersed in sadness in the face of his narcissistic emptiness, seduced by his dissociated Thing—the unconscious representation of his lost object that beckons him to a lethal reunion in the bottomless pit of loss. Freud's melancholic, however, has more in common with Klein's schizoid subject and Kristeva's abject. The subject of introverted aggression, he is split by a fragmenting conflict of ambivalence. In a Freudian perspective, the fragmented non-space of melancholia is the site of identification with the ambivalent "original object."[47] Fusional and murderous, melancholic identification enacts the twofold negativity of its object. It perpetuates the cherished negativity of the object's symbiotic-somatic materiality, which the melancholic as it were preserves by embodying it—rather than representing it—in the space of his autistic silence. And he also perpetuates the negativity of its loss by denying it conscious representation. Thus, melancholic identification *enacts* the primal ambivalence by at once preserving and annihilating the ambiguous object. As Kristeva maintains, the subject of melancholia withdraws from the world in order to retain his original integrity (which never was) in the maternal Thing. In doing so, he clings to the affective idealization of the somatic-symbiotic fusion in an unconscious image of paradisal plenitude. But by denying his affect conscious articulation—which would betray its representational difference from the thing itself—he at once disavows the separation from it and repeats it. He repeats, that is, maternal abjection in the form of internal splitting, or affective dissociation, from what thereby becomes the abjected part of himself, namely, his disowned affect (the longing for recuperation) or desiring "body." For the melancholic subject, who is dissociated from his affects, the Thing is not an expression of his nostalgia, but rather a lost *object*. The split, introverted subject objectifies his affect, identifying it with the melancholic object with which he wishes to reunite. In other words, if, as Kristeva suggests, the melancholic is "a prisoner" of the affect, it is because in his unconscious, fusional submergence in it, he fails to contain, or to "own" it—by way of its imaginary or symbolic articulation.[48]

The manifest or hidden melancholia of the speaking subject of poetry accounts for his conflictual attitude towards language, which is reflected in the creative violation of its rules. At the onset of poetic creation there seems to be, alongside and in direct correlation with the pleasure of it, a frustration with language as an alienating symbolic order which distances us from the world, and which needs to be modified so that it corresponds to our unmediated experience of the world—as if such an experience ever took place. Poetic language is thus an attempt to force language to bring about, or restore the nostalgic intimacy of the Thing itself which, in our never-quite-separated, dissociated condition, we long to experience in our relation with the objectal world. From a Lacanian perspective, which associates the order of language with a paternal *law*, the speaking subject's conflict with language is an oedipal conflict with a "castrating" Symbolic father who separates him, as it were, from an "incestuous" maternal unity. A secondary, oedipalized version of primary ambivalence, this conflict is enacted in the poetic text as a tension between symbolic and subversive asymbolic dispositions, which are encoded, as Kristeva points out, in the heterogeneity of the textual signification. The dialectic between the *symbolic* and the *semiotic* modes of signification constitutes the text as a simultaneous movement toward the sublimation of the maternal object in the "Name of the Father" on the one hand, and, on the other, of regression towards the fusional silence—or silent tautology—of the self-signifying Thing itself.

The *symbolic*, in its propositional function and its denotative determinacy, conforms to the "castrating" law of differentiation and substitution. It displaces the materiality of the maternal object and of the objectal by the arbitrary sign, and disrupts its nostalgic symbiotic unity by syntactic relations that draw on categorical differentiation. The "castrating" arbitrariness of the *symbolic* sign is in effect a paternal, legalized form of abjection, in that it excludes the somatic, affective expression of the subject, and hence also precludes relation to the other as an object of desire. A "castrated" sublimation, it thus bars off both the nostalgic object *and* its effective substitution by an intimate, affective, and sensuous experience of the objectal world. The *semiotic* aims to undo the alienating effect of language, but it also threatens to annihilate the other from the opposite direction—by subverting *symbolic* signification through connotative indeterminacy. In drawing on the translinguistic materiality of language, it fulfills the Russian Formalists' "*poetic function*" of breaking and "de-familiarizing" the *symbolic* code.[49]

The *semiotic* is the wild, indeterminate associative aspect of language that is never totally bound semantically. It is perceived most clearly in the suggestive non-sense of poetic incantation or "music," as well as in the surplus connotative charges of poetic collocations, notably metaphor. The *semiotic* is operative where metaphor, like sound, signifies something beyond a specific cognitive content; where, as Donald Davidson puts it, "it does not say and it does not hide, [but] *intimates*"[50]—something intimate. A material gesture of indication rather than a representation, *semiotic* signification opts for transcending the *medium* of language through that very medium, by pointing directly to, or invoking something that resists the limiting and distancing confinement of *symbolic* mediation. The *semiotic* defies the paternal law of language by a "*direct semantization*" of the material signifier which, by subverting the signifier's symbolic determinacy, seems to retain the lost unity of its ultimate, nostalgic signified.[51] As a continuous material equivalent, the *semiotic* signifier functions as a "psychosomatic modality" that restores the affective and sensory traces of the somatic-symbiotic object by way of metonymic signification:[52] it functions, in its materiality, as a kind of *index*—instead of a substitutive sign—to the extralinguistic object and the objectal.

The tension between the *semiotic* and the *symbolic* foregrounds the "castrating" arbitrariness of normative language, which the melancholic subject fails to forget, or repress.[53] It challenges the solidarity between signifier and signified which, drawing on this repression, ensures the functioning of the sign and the subject's integrative, relational positioning. The absence of this solidarity—for the split subject—places him in the non-space between two equally negative dispositions which reflect his dissociated condition: a meaningless (affectively disembodied) relation to the alienated other of the (therefore) "empty" *symbolic* signifiers; and a death-bound, autoerotic movement toward a fusional, objectless intimacy. A third and more pleasurable option, that of an intimate relation to the other, is attained through the integrative, *dialectical* actualization of the heterogeneous modes in the binding dynamic course of the textual articulation. The articulation of the text "motivates" the arbitrariness of the sign by binding the *semiotic* traces to the "empty" *symbolic* signification, to the effect of "filling" it with affective significance.[54] What it fills it with, ultimately, is the initially unbound drive energy turned into an other-bound desire, a desire that is sustained by the twofold—symbolic and metonymical—functioning of poetic language. The dialectic of the *symbolic* and the *semiotic* superimposes their respective signifieds, the symbiotic object and the represented objectal world, so that the longing for the first is transferred onto the representation of the latter. The result of this transference is that the meaningfulness (or subjective significance) of the textual world is sustained by the looming of the *semiotic* signified in the suggestive horizon of its *symbolic* representation. In other words, the textual heterogeneity facilitates the simultaneous representation and realization of the desire for the intimate otherness of the world.

In light of the foregoing description, the speaking subject's constitutive reentry into the Symbolic order is almost literal. In motivating the arbitrariness of the sign, the subject introduces (the translinguistic representation of) his "body" into the differential space between signifier and signified, thus entering it, as it were, *in person*. But this is a transgression of the Symbolic law, one might protest in the name of the Symbolic father. Indeed, in the dialectics of the poetic performance one may detect the concurrence and the resolution of the conflictual motions of the oedipal narrative (and of its underlying primary ambivalence): murder and incest in the *semiotic* transgression of the *symbolic* toward the barred-off maternal object, to the effect of its re-naming in the *inherited* Name of the Father in the new code of the poem. In taking the law into his hands in order to adapt it to his needs, the poet indeed usurps the Symbolic father; but it is precisely through such murderous identification that he can realize the Symbolic function of the paternal order as such, that is, that he gives it its efficiency as an integrative, regulative order.

The imaginary motivation of that order—a transgression which poets perform each in his own *style*—draws on a regression, through and beyond the Oedipus, to the more archaic origins of language associated with the narcissistic "imaginary father." It is to that archaic semiological function that the transsymbolic cohesiveness of poetic language is owed, a cohesiveness that marks both the level of the signifiers and that of the relation between signifier and signified. That archaic semiotic function accounts for the alternative *orders* that constitute poetic form—the material patterns of repetition and the associative equivalences in phonic and rhythmical as well as figurative structures. These patterns and figurative transpositions provide alternative (*semiotic*) orders of material concatenation which both displace and complement the *symbolic*, syntactic, and logical order of predicative language, while naturalizing, as it were, the latter's alienating arbitrariness.[55] For the archaic paternal function ensures the imaginary cohesion—as distinct from the conventional symbolic relation—between signifier and signified. Repressing the negativity of both maternal abjection and paternal castration, it is what enables us to forget that poetry, like any discourse, signifies absence. It allows us to suspend our melancholic disbelief in language, or in its possibility to procure a sense of plenitude—a possibility which poetry realizes when it is effective. Beyond the paraphrasable sense of a poem, poetic meaning is primarily a matter of *meaning-fullness*, which has its origin in the wishful filling of the negative space between signifier and signified—between representation and its impossible object—with an affectively charged, wish-fulfilling fantasy. The virtual alterity of the archaic father as a "schema," or pattern, provides a gestalt of meaning as plenitude. Preceding sexual and linguistic differentiation, the paternal "schema" which gives meaning to the articulation of maternal love represents, as Kristeva proposes, a "conglomerate of the mother and her desire," and thus of the mother and the father in a wishful, narcissistic bi-sexual (or pre-sexual) plenitude. It gives meaning, and thereby constitutes maternal love as such by dint of the "oral" dynamics involved in its assimilation through "direct" and "immediate" primary identification. It is this oral assimilation that makes possible the introjection (internalization as identification) of the maternal affect through the incorporation (internalization of a foreign body) of its material articulation. The introjected affect is thus appropriated—made part of one's proper self—by dint of its rearticulation in the *form* of a narcissistic affect, or fantasy. Hence the symbolic origin of our "being" as the subjects of a love that is perpetually introjected, decentered or dissociated from, and then again reintrojected in "oral" acts of signification.

The oral dynamics of this perpetual genesis occurs, with its bilateral simultaneity, in poetic signification, in the *in-vocative* articulation of the dissociated affect within the incorporative rearticulation of the language of the Other—and of others. The subject of poetry reappropriates his dissociated affect by way of transferential identification, through the incorporation and rearticulation of other people's texts, in the *intersubjective* acts of writing and reading alike. Indeed, without their "oral," narcissistic relation to another subject—the subject of intertextual allusions and the poet respectively—the speaking subjects of writing and reading have no being, and it is precisely the psychic space between them, mediated by speech, that constitutes them as distinct integral identities: "When the object that I incorporate is the speech of the other . . . I bind myself to him in a primary fusion, communion, unification. An identification. . . . In being able to receive the other's words, to assimilate, repeat and reproduce them, I become like him: One. A subject of enunciation."[56]

❧

As I note at the outset, it was in the course of an extended dialogue with the work of Dylan Thomas that I crystallized my conception of poetry as a space in which both the poet and the reader of poetry reenact a primordial experience of coming into being as an emergent subject. It is surely no accident that my reading of Thomas, more than other poets, impelled me to ponder a variety of theories, chiefly psychoanalytic ones, which seek to explain the genesis of the speaking subject, and to try to formulate a coherent theory of poetry. Thomas's poetic practice is not only characteristically modern but also paradigmatically "poetic." In their marked emphasis on the materiality of language, his often opaque but forcefully suggestive texts draw on pre- or transverbal meaning-effects which contribute to the distinctive magic of poetry, while laying bare both the rhetorical and the psychological dynamics of their performance. The revealing self-reflexivity of these texts is the effect of a radically self-conscious deconstructive performance, as well as a mark of their thematic aspect, which facilitates access to their author's deeply thought-out poetics. Indeed, Thomas's highly relevant self-conscious poetics does not merely correspond to the theoretical notions put forward in the previous pages, but has in effect contributed to their development within a "dialogical" reading of the texts.

Thomas's predominant thematic concern is clearly his own creative practice, and the ways in which he introduces that concern foreground a desire for self-generation which motivates, I believe, any poetic text. His poetry presents itself explicitly as the wishful realization of that desire through recurrent motifs of genesis and regeneration. The literal images of birth and conception, the metaphorical allusions to various creation myths (biblical, Welsh, and others), and the myths of regeneration (Christ's, Noah's, Orpheus's) that fill his work all represent the creative process as the enactment of its subject's fantasy of his own advent. Though they are often nostalgic for lost "Edenic" origins, Thomas's works generally acknowledge their nostalgic dimension to be the wishful enactment of a *beginning that never was*, and they mourn the existential predicament stemming from the absence of such beginnings. They acknowledge themselves to be the plea, heard and formulated by David Holbrook, of "one of those persons, suffering from a dreadful feeling of never having been born,"[57] who sets out to begin, *once again for the first time*, by repeating his unachieved beginning.

The trials of the "unborn,"[58] or prematurely separated, subject of that repetition are depicted by Thomas in his famous visceral imagery, which corresponds to (and sometimes even anticipates) the psychoanalytical phantasmagoria in ways which are at times refreshingly illuminating and at times banal. Thus, there is the recurrent generalized image of an aborted foetus who gropes his way "In the Direction of the Beginning."[59] The direction of the beginning is both backwards and forwards, in accordance with the protagonist's ambivalent temperament: backwards towards a missed or miscarried beginning—to the melancholic site of "Before I knocked"[60]—and forwards, toward its corrective, nostalgic symbolization within the space opened by the regenerative poetic process, often figured in the image of the risen sun and Son. The latter pertains to the Christian *topos* of resurrection which, together with the myths of Orpheus and Noah, is employed by Thomas for effecting and dramatizing the psycho-semiology of the regenerative poetic sublimation of abjection and melancholia. His employment of Christian motifs confirms Kristeva's analysis of the Catholic phantasmagoria as an accurate representation of "the essential dramas that are internal to the becoming of each and every subject,"[61] whose symbolic—narrative and ritualistic—display, like many forms of art, perpetuates their dynamics to a sublimatory, cathartic effect. The motif of the Christian sacrifice, with its condensation of death and resurrection, serves in Thomas's poetry to elaborate melancholic loss and ambivalence within a "sacramental" articulation.[62] This articulation foregrounds, especially through the metaphorical evocation of the ritual of the eucharist, the oral subjectifying identificatory dynamics which it triggers,[63] and the pivotal role of imaginary narcissistic omnipotence in generating the evocative magic of poetry. At the same time, Thomas's way of handling the symbolism calls to mind the possible influence of the Christian arche-typology on the shaping of the psychoanalytical mythology, and particularly Kristeva's version of it.[64]

The regressive-sublimative movement in Thomas's poetry enacts the "essential drama" of its split subject's becoming. It does so through Thomas's deconstructive handling of oppositional images and schemes of imagery, a practice he called "my dialectical method,"[65] as well as through his metaphorical condensations and the narrative sequences that structure many of his poems. The latter often follow the cathartic, "manic-depressive" itinerary of Christian and orphic return journeys, which bind the ambivalence represented by their bilateral directions in their narrative course. The regressive destination of these narrated or implicit journeys—the melancholic non-space lurking under the ruins of empty, deconstructed signs and the see-through screen of primal repression—is configured in images of traumatic or aborted birth and of mutilated or dead bodies. Similarly, "devouring" spaces of maternal abjection and their correlative, affectively empty inside of the body represent the unseparated subject's fear of disintegration and his defensive dissociation. Thus, through "the cut in the heart" that grooved his narcissistic wound, the subject of these journeys "in the direction of the beginning" sees "the world [going] down through a siren's stranger's vision . . . sucked to the last lake's drop." There, "[i]n the exact centre of the enchantment," he sees himself as "a shoreman in deep sea, lashed by the hair to the eye in the *cyclop's breast*."[66] The condensation of the devouring breast and the cyclop's introverted eye (gazing blindly towards the melancholic site of the absent breast) concretizes the identificatory dialectics of abjection, whose not-yet, because unseparated, subject/object is the negativity of both the abjecting/abjected mother and the abjected/abjecting son. By the same fusional logic, "he marked *her outcast* [mirror] image . . . and heard the interrogation of the familiar echo [of his own plea]: which is my genesis . . . ?"[67]

His (as well as her) genesis is in the very articulation of the question, or appeal, which posits the redeeming otherness of its potential addressee. For it is by reference to that virtual alterity that the maternal/internal abjection is symbolized: "This was *the god of beginning in the intricate seawhirl*, and my images roared and rose on heaven's hill."[68] (All emphases in quotations from Dylan Thomas are the author's.) Facilitated by identification with that prehistorical "god of beginning"—"Windily master of man" that is "*my* ghost"—the production of the poet's images restores, by way of a retrospective idealization, the original integrity of the paternal *Word* of "the beginning."[69] That nostalgic Word is reproduced in the actual, heterogeneous space of the text by dint of the oral dynamics which unfolds that space: the prelapsarian psycho-somatic plenitude of the Word is at once voiced and introjected through its rearticulaion in a mimetic, harmonizing gesture of signification of the "*said world*"[70]—just as it was breathed into being in the first place, on "*H*eaven's *H*ill."

The oral dynamics of poetic signification is central to Thomas's "sacramental" poetics. Many of his texts depict their poetic performance symbolically as a Christian sacrament—a prayer, a sermon, the eucharist—which derives its invocative power from its "oral" dynamics of intentionality. Those dynamics govern the poetic text as an act of faith which draws on the "*magic function*" of language, whose "incantatory" enactment involves, as Roman Jakobson specifies, "some kind of *conversion* of an absent or inanimate third person into an addressee of a conative message."[71] As an *act* (rather than a statement) of faith, the poetic text generates faith—in the world, or words, or the Word which connects them—by summoning into presence the addressed object/signified of their invocative articulation. *Credo*: "act of confidence implying restitution" (Kristeva);[72] an obliging act of giving *credit* that must be justified (de Certeau)[73]—whereby the credited object is "charged" to exist or, alternatively, is charged *with* affirmative significance. This view of the poetic text as a devotional act explains the poetic credo which Thomas allegedly formulated in 1951, defining his poems as "poems in praise of God's world by a man who doesn't believe in God."[74] His statement suggests—and enacts—a rejection of the named "God" of the Scriptures, while implying, by the very speech act of praising and attribution, the restitution of its ultimate, nameless addressee, that is, the thing (or Thing) itself. In his works, Thomas's credo follows a deconstructive procedure of "negative theology" which conforms to the oedipal scheme presented earlier: the works lay bare the metaphoricity of the scriptural language—and thus subvert their Symbolic (paternal) authority—while applying to its *semiotic* materiality for the "magic" conjuration of the prelapsarian Word of the "god of beginning."

The oral magic of the *semiotic* is elucidated by Thomas's application of the incorporative model of the eucharist. This model marks the subjectifying identificatory relation—or intersubjective "communion"—depicted in and enacted by his self-reflexive, symbolically devotional poetry. Reflected in the poetic persona's intratextual, regenerative identification with the figure of Christ (his Passion and his resurrection), the eucharistic principle governs Thomas's intertextual relation to his Christian (scriptural) sources. Thomas's incorporation of the story of Christ through its rearticulation involves the transubstantiation of the sacramental materiality of its scriptural signifiers—to the effect of invoking and in-voicing their transverbal signified (the Word). Thus it is despite, or rather precisely through, his deconstructive appropriation of the discourse of the scriptural Other that Thomas communes with, or shares its pre-verbal, subjective meaning, namely, its underlying desire for Being.

Thomas's recurrent energetic—indeed, obsessive—preoccupation with the issue of his genesis manifests the crisis of subjectivity to which contemporary, post-Freudian literature and psychology testify with distinctive intensity, and vividly illuminates that crisis in its characteristic strategies and emphases. What predominantly determines the condition of the post-Freudian subject—or so it seems, at least, to his analyst's ear (Green)[75]—is no longer so much the vicissitudes of sexuality and repression which characterize Freud's neurotic, hysterical, or perverse subject, but rather conflicts of a more archaic origin which threaten the basic organization of the psyche and the very capacity for symbolization that sustains it. Mythologically speaking, it seems as though in the move from Freud to post-Freudianism, the prototypical hero of psychoanalysis has undergone a metamorphosis. Passionate Oedipus has been transformed into the self-absorbed figure of Narcissus in the melancholic phase of disillusionment. A Narcissus who has lost his identifying mirror-images and the erotic fascination with them, that melancholic subject is haunted by the problematics of his very being and by the threat to the desire that sustains it. Such melancholic narcissism is clearly perceived in yet another mythical figure, Hamlet, whom André Green identifies as the transformed, once-Oedipal hero of our times.[76] As Green understands him, Hamlet is unable to act upon his oedipal desires because he is haunted by the more pressing question concerning his very being as the agent of such action: how can he settle the question of whether or not "to do," when he does not yet know what it is and whether or not "to be?" And if this is an overdramatization of the modern subject's condition, and his ambivalence does not reach the acute state of a practical question—that is, whether or not to commit suicide—let us say that ontological ambiguity does haunt the self-conscious, decentered Narcissus, for whom a mirror is *only* a mirror, and therefore he must face the question: am I, or am I not? Facing the naked unreality of his representations, he now opts for the impossible real: for all his playful deconstructive irony, the contemporary subject is vigorously obsessed with the Truth—which annihilates him. The symbolic crisis of our self-reflexive culture manifests itself in the mistrust in the imaginary as it is projected by language, and which sustains the illusion as well as the reality of the subject.[77] The "subject never *is*," says Lacan, settling the existential ambiguity only to designate another: "this subject never *is*" anything but a "*want-to-be* (*manque à être*)" subject; a missing subject who, for want of being, wants to be.[78]

Such an ambiguous, melancholic "want" motivates the speaker in Thomas's "Vision and Prayer," who prays "In the name of the fatherless . . . the unborn / And the undesirers . . . to / Be."[79] The lineation suggests what the fulfillment of this prayer means. It means "*One* to / Be": a unity of being which inverts the "*No*" at the negative center of narcissism and of the poem by separating it out from the preceding "No / One," abjecting it, as it were, in order to subject it to the sublimatory motion of the "pray[er]" at the end. A prayer is, by its nature, addressed to someone (or some One), present or virtual, but the "fatherless son" has "no one" to pray to; the Name of Father is an empty name. So the speaker says to the negated One: "*Be*[,] I pray . . ."

Needless to say, the other side of the question of the subject is the question of the "other," which preconditions subjectivity and symbolization. For a decentered subject who is caught up with conflicts having to do with the very point of gaining—or losing—access to it, alterity is indeed an acute and slippery question, to judge by the remarkable obsessiveness with which it haunts contemporary discourse.[80] By invoking the absent alterity of the One/father, the praying subject-to-be transforms the negativity of non-being in abjection (the central "No") into being in the symbolic, *relational* motion of intentionality, the "undesirer's" newly other-bound desire: "One *to* / Be I pray . . ." His prayer is answered at the end of the poem, where its object/addressee is summoned into presence by way of implication in the final "I pray." It is the utterance of these words which constitutes the prayer's speaking subject.

❧

In the final analysis, nobody really knows what happened "[o]nce below a time,"[81] in the pre-verbal, pre-historical beginning of the speaking subject. One can only imagine, as do poets and analysts alike, appealing to those subjective sources of intuition which mythologize the desire for being and its underlying "memory" of death by separation. Both poets and analysts speak their "endopsychic myths," as Freud called those "illusions of thought" that are projections of "[t]he dim inner perception of one's own psychical apparatus."[82] Lacan's retroacted Oedipus, Christ's and Orpheus's adventures in Heaven and the Underworld, and Thomas's aborted foetus who drowns in the eye of the cyclop's nipple, are all truthful myths. The methodological implication of this has been formulated by Shoshana Felman who, pointing out the equal status of literature and psychoanalysis as both "bod[ies] of knowledge" and "bod[ies] of language," advocates a dialogical rather than applicative psychoanalytical interpretation of literary texts.[83] The present writing has followed this dialogical principle to some extent, perhaps less than I would wish, in the synthetic myth of the genesis of the speaking subject which it develops through a to-and-fro movement between mutually nourishing readings of Thomas and his sources on the one hand, and psychoanalytical and critical sources on the other.

But the more significant dialogue, from the point of view of the *subject* of this text, is that which follows Thomas's "eucharistic" principle. My reading of Thomas involved an exhaustive chewing over of a small number of texts which engaged me in an intense identificatory—and indeed subjectifying—com-union with what I believe to be their deepest subjective meaning. For to read Thomas as vigorously as possible, bringing all the tools of literary and psychological analysis to bear on him, is in the end not only to exhume their constitutive and subjectifying processes, but also to reenact them. My dialogue with Thomas is not undergone only, or chiefly, on the manifest, *symbolic* level of ideas, nor in the passive space of receptive reading, where my unconscious presumably communes with his. It also takes place in the active textual practice of interpretation, where the incorporative chewing on the "body" of his language activates in me the currents of conflict and desires which animate his poetic works—even as *his* texts, by their deconstructive intertextual incorporation of other discourses, mediate their intersubjective dialogue with the other of the discourse.

❧

As for the structure of the present study, it is as follows.

Chapter 2 offers an illustration and further development of the subjectivist poetics set out in the present introductory chapter. This is carried out in the course of a close reading of Thomas's "Poem on his Birthday,"[84] a reading which traces the event of the genesis of the speaking subject in and through the poem itself. This lucidly self-reflexive birthday poem celebrates its speaker's rebirth from melancholia to faith by dint of its own, transformative devotional performance. It follows the cathartic, depressive-manic course of an orphic return journey to the autistic site of traumatic origins, and back to the newly and vibrantly affirmed otherness of the world. The sublimative process that leads to the poem's celebratory ending corresponds to Klein's model of the "reparation" of a split maternal object and the integrative, introjective projection of its idealized gestalt, as well as to the Freudian oedipal model, as adapted and developed by Kristeva, of the subject's generative entrance into the paternal order of the Symbolic. My reading of the poem traces the psycho-semiological mechanisms whereby the poem's sublimative narrative journey effects the consolidation of the poem's other-bound disposition. In particular, it identifies the transverbal, *semiotic* forms of concatenation that support and even sustain the poem's cohesive narrative course to the effect of binding the desire which animates it, an effect which is thematized by the poem's reflexive dramatization of the viscissitudes of its conflicting drives. The poem elucidates the process whereby its animating desire, which is initially neutralized by melancholic conflict and fragmentation, is liberated by the provisional integration of that conflict within the time-space of its textual unfolding.

The major focus of the discussion in chapter 2 is on the oral dynamics of *semiotic* signification, whose sensual and imaginary aspects are foregrounded by Thomas's "eucharistic" poetics. The relation of those dynamics to the pre-verbal "oral" stage, and particularly to abjection, is suggested here by Thomas's blatant use of "psychoanalytical" anatomical imagery (engulfing/devouring womb/tomb, etc.). The poem elucidates the role of orality in the wish-fulfilling articulation of poetic images, as well as in the creation of the poem's performative space as the aural by-product of oral articulation. Finally, Thomas's eucharistic poetics throws an interesting light here on the role of orality and identificatory processes in *intertextuality*, showing the latter to be a subjectifying dynamics that draws on the incorporation of the material signifier of an other.

Chapter 3 continues to explore the psycho-semiological conditions and processes involved in effective poetic symbolization, this time through analyses of symbolic failures in the poem as poem, as well as through consideration of several self-conscious themes in Thomas's poetry. While accounting for failures that are characteristic of Thomas, especially through a close reading of his poem "Incarnate Devil,"[85] the chapter also relativizes and problematizes general claims made in the previous chapters concerning the generative potentials of the poetic text as a sublimatory, integrative process. Thus, in focusing on the phenomenology of the experience of subjectivity as a lived textual reality—"the possibility of the real" referred to in the title of the first section—the discussion touches on general questions concerning the pragmatic and the representational relations between language and reality. A central topic of exploration in this context is the correlation between subjective ontology and mimetic representation. The first is a pragmatic effect of ("being" in) the text, while the latter is what sustains the imaginary object in relation to which the textual subject's "being" is constituted or, conversely, what testifies to the intensity of that subjectifying relation. In light of the same relational perspective, the chapter proposes a new definition of *poetic mimesis* that accounts for the textual experience of subjectivity and explores the linguistic and the psychological conditions for its efficacy.

The "possible real" posited here—by significant distinction from Lacan's idealistic, "impossible Real"—as the effect of successful poetic symbolization signifies a notion of authenticity that is a function of affective relatedness. The question of its possibility emerges from a challenge of my earlier, celebratory reading of "Poem on his Birthday," which addresses the poem's somewhat forced, "manic" tone and the integrative failure which it seems to betray. This critical impression confirms Melanie Klein's observation concerning the often subversive effect of manic and obsessional strategies of "reparation" which involve, to various degrees, the denial of ambivalence or, in experiential terms, an affective dissociation. Such dissociation and its de-authenticating effects are also traced in other poems by Thomas, and especially in his distinctly obsessive poem "Incarnate Devil."

"Incarnate Devil," as I read it, is a hyper-self-conscious poem that mourns its own mimetic failure and the narcissism that causes it. The poem universalizes that narcissism into the solipsism of language as such, and tries to account for it aetiologically by reference to the biblical story of Genesis and the Fall. Thomas's various interpretations of the biblical story are read in a dialogue with Walter Benjamin's interpretation of it in his essay on the origin of language, and with my own, which is in turn informed by Freud's essay on "Negation."[86] The reading highlights the part played by the "Incarnate Devil in the Garden of Eden"—a title of a section in the chapter which refers to forked-tongued abjection when it ambiguates our otherwise nostalgic beginning, and thereby dooms us to innate exile from the *imaginary* grace of the real in a "fallen" language that dissociates us from experience. The "exegetic" dialogue, as well as the poem's obsessive deconstructive performance, foreground the ways in which abjection, as an ambiguating motion of ineffectual splitting ("border-lining"), undermines meaning and mimetic efficacy, as well as their would-be aetiological conditions of basic ontological faith and the correlative trust in language. And yet, a close reading beyond the poem's ambiguous symbolic argument and failed mimesis witnesses how abjection also facilitates meaning: in the fissures of the poem's threadbare mimetic texture, where the bare reality of the signifying process emerges as the object of a mimesis of a different kind, another, "antithetical" kind of subjectivity asserts itself in a negative relation—but still a relation—to its other.

Chapter 4, titled "Under the Sign of Loss, a Recuperation," considers the pivotal role of nostalgia in animating the poetic text as a signifier of loss as well as an act of recuperation focusing on Thomas's notably nostalgic poems, "Fern Hill" and "Poem in October."[87] Starting from an account of the symbolic inefficacy of "Incarnate Devil" in terms of the poem's failure to sublimate its underlying melancholia, the chapter's first, theoretical section distinguishes between melancholia and nostalgia. In light of Freud's "Mourning and Melancholia" and "Inhibitions, Symptoms and Anxiety," these psychic syndromes are respectively associated with the death instinct and the pleasure principle and with their manifestations in tautological and transformative repetition in less and more effective poetic symbolizations. Hence "The double—regressive and sublimative—Determination of Repetition" in the first section-title. My reading of Freud's essays indicates the role of nostalgia in the constitution of psychic life and symbolization, while its specific role in poetry is expanded upon with close reference to Walter Benjamin's essays on language,[88] Gaston Bachelard's *Poetics of Reverie*, and Winnicott's theory of the origins of creativity, with allusions to the great nostalgic masters, Proust and T. S. Eliot.

Drawing on Benjamin's historical conception of language, the chapter explains how nostalgia locates the poetic act and its subject in the dimension of time—how, by inciting the retrospective projection of idealized origins in the motion of a reparative memory, it constitutes the history of the speaking subject and his desire (for future recuperation of his "lost" origins). The second section, which returns with Bachelard and Thomas to the latter's childhood "Princedom of the Apple Towns," shows how that nostalgic memory marks not only the poetic present but also the golden moments of the longed-for past, which are thus links in a series of nostalgic recuperations of an atemporal origin. The analysis of childhood perception (as it emerges from Thomas's poems and from readings of Bachelard, Winnicott, and Proust) illuminates the phenomenology of metaphor which, in this temporal perspective, corresponds in its turn to Benjamin's notion of "translation." Finally, the analogy, in the way it emerges here, between the child's and the poetic modes of perception, with their analogous "transitional spaces," illustrates the function of benign narcissism and narcissistic (identificatory) processes in aesthetic experience and creativity. It also foregrounds the formative, subjectifying role of the imaginary under the aegis of the pleasure principle.

Chapter 5, titled "The Lover, the Poet, and the Lunatic," moves from childhood's Eden to the next, adolescent phase in the subjective history that emerges from Thomas's works. The period of adolescence, with its oedipal and narcissistic crisis, seems to constitute the determining, fixational point of departure of the textual history I am tracing. I show this by discussing Thomas's two short stories in poetic prose, "A Prospect of the Sea" and "The Mouse and the Woman."[89] Both stories dramatize a manifestly oedipal symbolic crisis in a way that illustrates, with remarkable insight, the relation between sexuality and textuality. Their analysis focuses on the problematics of boundaries—of textuality and subjectivity—as it emerges from Thomas's exploration of the border-line, as well as the relation of continuity, between poetry and psychosis.

In both stories there is a "lover" who is tormented by acute conflicts of oedipal guilt and a narcissistic crisis, both symptomatic of the adolescent transition from childhood latency and narcissistic omnipotence to adulthood. "A Prospect of the Sea" represents that transition as a conflictual point of intersection between the two, regressive and sublimative, "determinations," which are impersonated by the figures of the siren and the muse. The choice between these female creatures, who inhabit the two sides of the metaphorical shore-line, will determine the adolescent lover's fate as either a lunatic or a poet. "The Mouse and the Woman" is about a poet who attempts to write the woman of his dreams into existence and goes mad. His story is depicted as a Faustian drama of overreaching which links his "oedipal" transgression of the symbolic boundaries of language and sanity to the dynamics of narcissistic inflation. This perspective, which also emerges from "A Prospect of the Sea," highlights the narcissistic, *semiotic* dynamics of the "magic function" of language (Jakobson), as does the thematization, in both stories, of the *semiotic* dynamics of the poetic voice. The dramatization, in these stories, of the oral-narcissitic, vocal transgression, or blurring of symbolic boundaries—be it by the siren or the muse—yields some insight into the mystique of voice.

The final chapter, which is "A Confession of the Speaking Subject," concludes this book with a discussion of Thomas's poetry and its subjectifying dynamics from the point of view of the reader's response, and especially my own. My "confessional" response is located in relation to the distinctive approaches in Thomas's criticism, as these are alluded to by Thomas himself in a confessional letter written shortly before his death. The letter, in which he describes his creative process in terms of its communicative dynamics, elucidates the intersubjective dynamics of transference and countertransference, which seem to be activated by his texts so effectively that they actually account for the dominant attitudes critics have taken toward his work. Thus Thomas's letter also clarifies the dynamics of identification and resistance that determined the structure of my own response as a reenactment of the very ambivalence which I attributed to Thomas.

My response to Thomas's work as set in chapter 6 unfolds through engagement with the work of David Holbrook, who is the only critic who has offered a systematic psychoanalytic reading of Thomas's work as a whole, including an illuminating reader-response analysis. Holbrook's reading is very inspiring and boldly personal, but it is also very provocative in its intense, emotionally charged critical aspect. I see his approach to Thomas as a pathologizing one, whose defensive, controlling motivation is, as Holbrook himself suggests, common among Dylan Thomas's critics. My yielding to the provocation of Holbrook's negative judgement of Thomas has helped me to better understand and formulate my own ambivalent response to Thomas's poetic works. It has also encouraged me to touch on the rather murky question of assessing their quality in terms of the extent to which they sublimate their underlying psychological predicaments effectively, that is, into effectively aesthetic works of art—rather than mere confessions of a speaking subject.

❧

Indeed, I would hope that what I have been saying about the immanent logic of Thomas's poetics, and what has been clarified for me in the course of my engagement with Holbrook's reading of Thomas, will contribute to a renewed valorization of Thomas's work. Up through the mid-seventies, Thomas was one of the most celebrated and studied of poets among English-speaking critics of the midcentury; indeed, he may well have been "the most thoroughly and frequently explicated modern poet" in English.[90] Since then, critical interest in his work has waned. This is hard to understand, given the brilliance, the density, and the distinction of his best work. This is doubly hard to fathom, given his relevance to issues central to contemporary literary and psychoanalytic theory. Thomas's poetics and his recurrent thematic concerns constitute a treasure trove of insights and examples which illuminate the nature and origins of poetry, but also some of the most fundamental predicaments which beset us in contemporary life. I hope that my exposition of issues and my explication of texts will establish new and firm grounds for the estimation of Thomas, and for the enjoyment of his work.

My own sense is that Thomas never lacked *readers*; I assume that his "natural" readers need neither professional explication nor elaborate theorization. At the same time, since so much reading is now mediated through formal study, I would like to think that my formulation of issues and values will help to place Thomas on the literary and spiritual agenda of new readers.

As for the material on which I base my reading, and for my claims and aims in general, I should note that I do not presume to have embraced the entire body of Thomas's work, or to have propounded a universally applicable poetics. As should be clear from my outline of the book as a whole, my exploration of Thomas's poetics is undertaken through very detailed analysis of a very limited set of works. Nevertheless, I feel I have probed the essence of Thomas's achievement. Because of the narrow range of my chosen material, however, the subjectivist poetics I propose here cannot in good faith be offered as a comprehensive statement about poetry as such. Indeed, though the poetics I propose is informed by generalizing theories, it is not meant to be comprehensive, even though my theoretical discourse may make it seem that way. For this reason, too, I foreground the subjective aspect of this writing here (and still more in the final chapter). The subjectivist poetics elaborated in this book is *a* poetics that emerges from *a* reading and writing process—a particular event which entertains a specific encounter, or dialogue, between the subject of this writing (myself) and the subject of Dylan Thomas's works. Other voices echo in this dialogue, predominantly those of psychoanalytical theory but also of Walter Benjamin and Gaston Bachelard, and of biblical and other sources of Western mythology to which both Thomas and psychoanalysis allude. Despite the multiplicity of voices, however, it is clear that the applicability of the proposed "poetics of poetry" is limited in perspective as well as in scope. Just how limited it is, however, is a question which I leave open. I would argue that what emerges from my encounter with the texts considered in this book does apply to most of Thomas's poetic practice as well as to important aspects of modern poetry in general, and to some vital aspects of poetic language as such. My interest, however, does not lie in arguing this point. My intent is rather to *suggest* some notions about how poetic language "works" for and on the subjects who articulate it, in the hope that the formulation of these notions may correspond to and elucidate some readers' experience or intuitive sense of what poetry is about for them.

❧

One more word. Looking backward on the process of writing this book, I find myself somewhat surprised at my spontaneous identification with Thomas's male psychology and with the male-biased conceptual apparatus on which I drew for formulating my response to him. I now imagine that, being a woman, I might have responded otherwise. But the fact is that these identifications *were* spontaneous, and sprang from sources far deeper than mere intellectual adherence to theoretical preconceptions. A partial justification for the critical blindness emanating from this uncritical response may be found in the fact that this book is concerned, precisely, with the elastic system of identifications that generate meaning and subjectivity within the intersubjective space of the text—a space whose focal center happens to be occupied, in this case, by a male subject. However, I would hope that checking my response by taking into account the source and the implications of such identifications would broaden the applicability of my critical and theoretical claims. It is a question which I certainly do wish to explore, with the help of the material that has been written on it by feminist critics, but which is, for the moment, beyond the scope of my current project.

CHAPTER TWO

Poem on his Birthday

I pluck again
The sweet, steel strings
To bring the sun to life . . .
—Dylan Thomas, *The Notebooks of Dylan Thomas*

POEM ON HIS BIRTHDAY

In the mustardseed sun,
By full tilt river and switchback sea
Where the cormorants scud,
In his house on stilts high among beaks
And palavers of birds
This sandgrain day in the bent bay's grave
He celebrates and spurns
His driftwood thirty-fifth wind turned age;
Herons spire and spear.

Under and round him go
Flounders, gulls, on their cold, dying trails,
Doing what they are told,
Curlews aloud in the congered waves
Work at their ways to death,

And the rhymer in the long tongued room,
Who tolls his birthday bell,
Toils towards the ambush of his wounds;
Herons, steeple stemmed, bless.

In the thistledown fall,
He sings towards anguish; finches fly
In the claw tracks of hawks
On a seizing sky; small fishes glide
Through wynds and shells of drowned
Ship towns to pastures of otters. He
In his slant, racking house
And the hewn coils of his trade perceives
Herons walk in their shroud,

The livelong river's robe
Of minnows wreathing around their prayer;
And far at sea he knows,
Who slaves to his crouched, eternal end
Under a serpent cloud,
Dolphins dive in their turnturtle dust,
The rippled seals streak down
To kill and their own tide daubing blood
Slides good in the sleek mouth.

In a cavernous, swung
Wave's silence, wept white angelus knells.
Thirty-five bells sing struck
On skull and scar where his loves lie wrecked,
Steered by the falling stars.
And to-morrow weeps in a blind cage
Terror will rage apart
Before chains break to a hammer flame
And love unbolts the dark

And freely he goes lost
In the unknown, famous light of great
And fabulous, dear God.
Dark is a way and light is a place,

  Heaven that never was
Nor will be ever is always true,
  And, in that brambled void,
Plenty as blackberries in the woods
  The dead grow for His joy.

  There he might wander bare
With the spirits of the horseshoe bay
  Or the stars' seashore dead,
Marrow of eagles, the roots of whales
  And wishbones of wild geese,
With blessed, unborn God and His Ghost,
  And every soul His priest,
Gulled and chanter in young Heaven's fold
  Be at cloud quaking peace,

  But dark is a long way.
He, on the earth of the night, alone
  With all the living, prays,
Who knows the rocketing wind will blow
  The bones out of the hills,
And the scythed boulders bleed, and the last
  Rage shattered waters kick
Masts and fishes to the still quick stars,
  Faithlessly unto Him

  Who is the light of old
And air shaped Heaven where souls grow wild
  As horses in the foam:
Oh, let me midlife mourn by the shrined
  And druid herons' vows
The voyage to ruin I must run,
  Dawn ships clouted aground,
Yet, though I cry with tumbledown tongue,
  Count my blessings aloud:

  Four elements and five
Senses, and man a spirit in love
  Tangling through this spun slime

To his nimbus bell cool kingdom come
   And the lost, moonshine domes,
And the sea that hides his secret selves
   Deep in its black, base bones,
Lulling of spheres in the seashell flesh,
  And this last blessing most,

   That the closer I move
To death, one man through his sundered hulks,
   The louder the sun blooms
And the tusked, ramshackling sea exults;
   And every wave of the way
And gale I tackle, the whole world then,
   With more triumphant faith
Than ever was since the world was said,
   Spins its morning of praise,

   I hear the bouncing hills
Grow larked and greener at berry brown
   Fall and the dew larks sing
Taller this thunderclap spring, and how
   More spanned with angels ride
The mansouled fiery islands! Oh,
   Holier then their eyes,
And my shining men no more alone
   As I sail out to die.

A Prospect of the Sea: Synopsis

"Poem on his Birthday" not only commemorates, but also repeats—in an attempt to work through—the unfinished business of its speaker's genesis. The burden of its symbolic narrative (stanzas 1–7)—the protagonist's redemptive, Dantesque "midlife" journey to a visionary death at the bottom of the sea—is the speaker's corrective return to the traumatic site of an incomplete psychic birth in an oceanic, symbiotic womb-tomb, where pleasure and death are as yet undifferentiated. Within the manifest "full tilt river" of time that sweeps the sacrificial protagonist forward to a regenerative Christian death in the "bent bay's grave," a hidden undercurrent works to pull him backwards, to the site of his aborted genesis once upon a traumatic separation, out of which he will be born *again, for the first time*. Yielding to the gravitational force of the repetition compulsion, the speaker performs an orphic descent to the lethal site of his ambiguous maternal object so that he may turn his back on it and live. The purpose of the imaginary quest-journey is self-generation through the conquest of the death cocooned in that enticing abject site, and the consequent liberation of captive Eros. This is to be achieved through a process of separation and sublimation which constitutes the poem's performance. The speaker negates the maternal pole of the death instinct by symbolizing it, thus liberating himself from the deadening grip of autoerotic fixation into the possibility of love, that is, into a desiring affirmation of self and world.

This achievement is represented in the second part of the poem (stanzas 8–12), where the speaker surfaces from his cathartic underwater fantasy to a sea-borne reflection of the reality of the poetic process. Ascended from his imaginary, regressive-introverted death journey, he now sets *out* and *forward* on his real journey of life, voicing his affirmation of that life in the Symbolic light of a symbolic Christian revelation. This shift of vector—from *down* and *in* to *up* and *out*—signifies the Erotic ("phallic") binding of Thanatos, which involves the domestication of the maternal sea that is also imaged as a horse. Whereas in the first part of the poem the vitality of the depressive, death-doting protagonist was drained by the devouring "horseshoe bay"—the "bent bay's grave" which sucks up the river of life—in the second part it reemerges to animate the speaker, who now rides that "tusked, ramshackling sea" in manic exaltation, celebrating his regeneration as a desiring subject.[1] The advent of the speaker's subjectivity is distinctly marked by the shift from the third to the first person in stanza 9. There, the speaker abandons the protagonist—the "he" of the first eight stanzas who is his specular image—to the mute, morbid pleasure of underwater reunion with his lost object, and emerges as the *speaking* subject of a sublimated desire for the world: "though *I* cry with tumbledown tongue,/ [let me] Count my blessings aloud:// Four elements and five / Senses, and a man a spirit in love."

Introduction to a Genesis: Endopsychic Mythology

It is said that after his return from Hades and a period of mourning his twice-lost Eurydice, Orpheus abjured Dionysus and became the ascetic preacher of the cult of Helios, his father, whom he addressed as Apollo. At the last sight of him before the bacchants tore him to pieces in revenge for his defection, he was "hastening through the night [until] he reached the summit of mount Pangaeus and waited there to see the rising sun."[2] Although it did not save him from the claws of the bacchants, it was surely thanks to that affiliation—to Apollo's paternal order of aesthetic and religious sublimation—that the mythical poet came to be reincarnated, in the Christian centuries that followed, as Orpheus the legislator, civilizer, humanizer, theologian, and the religious teacher and prophet of love. For those who christianized him, he even prefigured the Logos, in having "predicted or spoken [the] truth of the Son of God or the Father" (St. Augustine).[3] What earned him all these titles (and granted him perpetual regeneration in the history of myths) was the magic power of his "sweet speech" to invoke, or create the/a harmony between all aspects and levels of existence. Relying much as he did on introspection, he invoked the harmony between the macrocosm and its animating astral spirits, notably the sun's, and the microcosm of the human spirit.[4] By his "comparative method" (metaphor, that is), he showed the "unity in [the] multiplicity" of things of different orders, invoking the "mystery" that unites them; and with the harmonies of his "beautiful voice" (sound)—a paradigm for all artistic expressions of "the music of the soul"—he tuned Apollo's song, to which, some say, the heavenly bodies still dance.[5]

It is by virtue of a similar solar affiliation that the poet "On His Birthday" is redeemed from his melancholia, and is regenerated as the subject of the Symbolic law of a sacred, though declaredly metaphorical Other. The speaker's orphic sea journey illustrates a process of rebirth from depressive anxiety into Christian or Gnostic faith (Burdette),[6] configured in the metaphor of the "*mustardseed sun*." The latter alludes to two metaphors of conversion in the New Testament,[7] which are symbolically enacted in the poem. The poem presents itself as a kind of Christian sermon, whose transformative cathartic effect is enhanced by the intertextual assimilation of the layered signifiers of the Christian other, namely, the scriptural word and its signified, the Christian Word, the ("mustardseed") "sun" and the Son. Such an assimilation is also suggested in the equally allusive image of the sea journey,[8] which illustrates the archetypal Christian myth. The symbolic dramatization of the myth of Christ's sacrificial death and resurrection brings about the actual realization of its psychoanalytic correlative, that is, the myth of the subject's genesis through the Symbolic sublimation of death (loss, "castration," etc.). The dramatization of the protagonist's conversion is thus a vicarious reenactment of Christian rebirth through identification with the Word, whereby the speaker enters the Symbolic order of language as it were via that of religion.

The poet's conversion is the cumulative effect of two transformative religious experiences, a vision and a prayer,[9] illustrated by the underwater and the surface parts of his orphic sea journey. These reflect the imaginary and the symbolic practices that constitute both the subject's entry into language and the psycho-semiology of the poem's performance. In the mystical, apocalyptic vision of the first part of the poem, the protagonist fantasizes his resurrection in Heaven's bosom (stanzas 5–7) after an imaginary dying process (stanzas 1–4). The *voiced* prayer or sermon, which follows that mute scene in the second part (stanzas 8–12), culminates in the poet's mystical communion with nature in a shared affirmation of life (stanzas 10–12). The first, visionary experience can be seen to represent the movement from autoerotism and melancholic fragmentation to narcissism, which sublimates the ambiguous maternal by dint of identification with the Imaginary Father (or the interchangeable Son). The sublimatory narcissistic act consists in the transposition of the ambiguous symbiotic Thing into a nostalgically idealized fantasy of mystical fusion. A similar transposition also marks the movement from the first to the second experience, where the fusional fantasy is displaced onto the speaker's sacramental relation with nature, and thus reflects a subjectifying transition from the imaginary towards signs and objects through language.

Each of the religious experiences consummates an apparently autonomous cathartic cycle of conversion within the poem's repetitive metaphorical structure. In both parts of the poem, the poet moves from agnostic darkness to the light of faith. In the first, visionary experience, the protagonist's doting upon "his crouched, eternal end" as it is seen from "Under a serpent cloud" of fallen imagination finally transports him into "the famous light of great / And fabulous, dear God" in a revelatory glimpse of "Heaven that never was, / Nor will be ever [for the faithless, but] is always true" for the enlightened (Burdette).[10] "There," in Heaven's baptismal light, "he might wander bare" of his mortal body, enjoying a communion of souls with his fellow "dead [who] grow for His joy." In the second part of the poem, the resurrection is brought down from Heaven to the "earth of the night," where the company of the dead is displaced by "all the living" with whom the poet "prays" (stanza 8). The poet starts off, once again, by "mour[ning] . . . The voyage to ruin [he] must run," and ends up "sail[ing] out to die" willfully, as his nocturnal mourning is transformed into an exalted alleluia that is echoed in the world's *actual* sunlit "morning of praise." Thus, the final experience of grace is the realization of the fantasy of heaven *on earth* through the language of the prayer (the earth being the self-reflected reality of the poem's devotional practice). The reflexive structure is already announced by the prepositional ambiguity of the poem's title, which suggests both the event represented in the "Poem *on* his Birthday" and the circumstances of the event of its performance. The symbolic meaning of these related events resounds in a metaphor embodying a similar symbolic ritualistic relation between performance and representation: the bell which the poet tolls to enunciate his birth-day is also the Angelus bell of the Annunciation.

The poem's reflexive structure projects Thomas's distinctive religious poetics, as well as his private fantasy of origins. It reflects his conscious sense of writing toward faith against a haunting absence of being which he associates, by his suggestive use of images, with an aborted beginning. Far from advocating Christian dogma, Thomas's birthday sermon manifests a poetic credo which affirms the pragmatic, sublimatory function of the poetic act of faith to draw its speaking subject (both writer and reader) into "being" in an intimate, affirmative relation to the world. The sermon foregrounds the strategies of enchantment whereby it fulfills this function, through the symbolic depiction of the closely analogous Christian sacrament. The generative process of the protagonist's conversion, which consists, essentially, in the eucharistic reception of the divine Word through devotional incantation and imaginary incorporation, illustrates the phenomenology of the transverbal magic of the poetic signifier. It thus displays the dynamics of *semiotic* signification in sound and metaphor, laying bare its constitutive "oral" aspect, namely, the processes of projection and identification involved in the articulation of the material language of poetry. The integrative function of these processes is elucidated by the symbolic as well as the practical reenactment, in the poem as eucharist, of the logic of the Christian sacrifice. The logic of sacrifice, as it is unfolded in the poem, reconciles the life/death opposition that splits the subject upon his ambivalent genesis, while the eucharistic incorporation of the divine Word activates the reintrojection of the nostalgic Thing, which sublimates—to the effect of integrating—the ambivalent maternal "object." Thomas's depiction of the Christian sacrifice, with its suggestive visceral images, vividly illustrates the melancholic regression of the poem's speaking subject to his traumatic origins, and the sublimation of these abject origins in the reconstituted Name of the Symbolic Father.

In the two sections that follow, I will analyze the generative event dramatized in the poem through two perspectives that foreground the oral processes involved in its articulatory and imaginative dynamics. In the first section, I will center the analysis on the eucharistic dynamics of enchantment as it emerges from the self-reflexive depiction of the poet's symbolic act of faith. In this context, I will try to show how the intentionality of that act is reinforced in the course of its performance, to the effect of binding the split subject's conflictual, ambivalent dispositions into a desire toward the world's otherness. In the second section, I will examine the aggressive oral dynamics of abjection as it is dramatized in the depiction of the motif of sacrifice in the first part of the poem. I will then move on to discuss the redemptive oral function of projection and identification that constitutes the poem as an integrative "transitional space," that is, as an integrative, narcissistic space of intimacy which sustains its subject's other-bound desire.

"The Sun Roars at the Prayer's End": A Poetics in a Mustardseed

What sets the poem in motion—and also threatens to subvert it—is the poet's anxiety about time and death and its correlative depressive predicament. The poem is informed by a sense of the futility and the emptiness of speech in the face of death and of time's corrosiveness, which threatens to condemn the poet to a premature "death" of creative impotence. This mood is expressed in stanzas 1–3, which dramatize the depletion of life and meaning in time. Time's coercive course is configured in the collapse or fall of the "mustard*seed* sun," through the analogous "sand*grain* day" setting in the "bent bay's grave," and in the sweeping of the seed/grain by the wind (the "wind turned age"; the "thistledown fall"), as well as by the "full tilt river" that rushes down the bent day's drain. The river of time sweeps away the poet's metonymical abode—the "long tongued room" in "his house on stilts." Both room and house suggest at once his own, birdlike (beaked and long-legged) person, and the emblems of his faith and his creativity, namely, the church steeple where he tolls his and Christ's "long tongued" bell.

The drowning of his metaphorical colleagues—the priestly herons in stanza 3 (who will be mourned in stanza 9 as the "shrined / And druid herons")—suggests the poet's sense of emotional death *by* the loss of faith. Indeed, despair hollows out the meaning of his Angelus bell chime and aborts the birth it announces—and so the seedlike herons, who have begun to "spire and spear," are "steeple-stemmed" as they drown. All this trouble is announced in the first stanza by the ominous "*palavers of birds*"—the dubious discourse of the poet's metaphorical neighbors. By their double connotation, the birds' "palavers" (which signify both parables and idle talk) represent the poetic signifier, which, at this desperate point, is insignificant empty prattle—the "empty signifier" that signifies the melancholic's sense of the futility of speech and the meaninglessness of words.

And so, to be born—to enunciate his birthday, that is—the poet must deliver himself of the predicament of disanimated speech. He does this by adhering to the redemptive Christian Word. Through the language of Christianity, with its suggestive, archetypal death-negating symbolism, the poet will replenish his creative word, which will become an inspired "full speech," invested with faith.[11] The assimilation of the Word will fulfill this task by redeeming time from its destructiveness, that is, by subjecting time to meaning *in time*.

The visionary experience annihilates time. The poet travels to the dead end of time, where the experience of its irrevocable course as a deterministic, gravitational force that impels violent "full tilt" and "switchback" movements is displaced by the bliss of contained, weightless free-floating in the absolute *space* of the eternal light of Heaven: "And freely he goes lost / In the . . . famous light." This experience of containment resolves once and for all the painful dichotomy posited in "*Dark is a way and light is a place*," by restoring the paradisal plenitude of the maternal Thing—or rather creating it, by way of nostalgic idealization. The vision transports its subject outside of time into a familiar, imaginary space, a "Heaven that never was," which becomes, however, "always true" thanks to the corrective mnemonic effect of the future-bound projective image: the vision at once invokes and idealizes the past by turning nostalgia into desire for future recuperation, thus consolidating, in retrospect, the archaic maternal sublimation. This intersection of nostalgia and desire in an image that superimposes the negativity of past and future within a heaven that "*never was nor will be ever*," yields a heaven that "*is always* true" in "a minute freed from the order of time" (Proust on time and metaphor).[12]

But the metaphorical meaning-space is soon violated by time's destructive movement. The timeless moment of the mystical experience is followed by a shattering disillusionment and a retroactive deconstruction of the visionary metaphor. The climax of the mystical experience of Heaven in stanza 7 is followed by the protagonist's fall all the way down the enjambment back to "the earth of the night" in stanza 8, where he is once again "alone" and faithless. The intensity of the fall and its terrestrial destination are prefigured kinesthetically by the violence of the oxymoronic "cloud quaking peace," which connotes an earth-quake by a suggested reversal or reshuffling of the syntactic positions of the elements of the phrase (peace-clouding quake or peace-quaking cloud). This reversal foreshadows the reversal of the meaning of the mystical experience evoked by the phrase, the illusory nature of which, as it turns out, clouds every stage of its self-reflexive projection. In stanza 6, God's hitherto "famous" but "unknown" light becomes known to the converted heretic as "fabulous" (= wonderful) rather than "fabulous" (= incredible, imaginary) while he positively "goes lost" in it. Its projective tropical, or helio-tropical nature is reassessed, however, in stanza 7, when the poet proceeds to penetrate it toward its absent source: "*there* he [only] *might* wander . . . With unborn God and His Ghost"—a wishful virtuality at the missing heart of the "mythos" at the white center of the *fabulous* "logos," or the once-again hollow "palaver."[13] And if one were to regard that blind spot as the appropriate non-representation of the eye meeting the source in the mystical gnosis of the Pure Light, as does Burdette in his introduction to his gnostic reading of Thomas,[14] then one would be as misled as the "*gulled* and *chanter*" poet at the climax of his professedly self-blinding mystical experience. The poet's performance as "chanter" (cantor, first singer) in the heavenly choir of God's feathered priests—implicit angels incarnated here in gulls sand chanters (hedge sparrows)—turns out to be that of a trickster ("gull"), who en-chants his *gullable* self into fantastic beliefs with his idle "palavers" (or, to stretch it a little further, into superstitious indulgence in "*wishbones* of wild geese"). The eventual explosion or evaporation of the nothing but "*air shaped* Heaven" is also predicted by the hollowing out ("gulling") of the chanter's bagpipe,[15] as well as by the connotation, again in "gull," of the Welsh "*gwyla^n*," which means to wail, or wailer (*OED*). And so, the enchanter who incantates himself into faith is also a desperate wailer of its underlying negativity . . .

This, however, does not stop him from praying "Faithlessly unto Him," and from setting off on the poem's second cathartic cycle, to realize the uncanny metaphor of Heaven on earth. To the contrary, it is the vision that inspires the prayer, which in turn inspires faith, as we discover in the temporal course of its unfolding: "He . . . *prays* . . . *Faithlessly* unto Him // Who is the *light of old*." The memory of "the light of old" turns out, in the syntactic sequence, to be at once the source of inspiration and the desired addressee of the prayer, an addressee who emerges, as if in response to its challenging negation, to inhabit its new signifier at the end of the phrase. Obviously, it is not the truth value, or the *symbolic* meaning of the vision that animates the prayer with meaning, but the affective value of its imaginative experience. Similarly, the reinvocation of the affect is brought about by the equally transverbal, sensory experience of the prayer's incantatory articulation: "though I cry with tumbledown tongue, [let me] / Count my blessings aloud:// Four elements and five / Senses, and a man a spirit in love." Here again, "love" comes in response to its invocatory, *semiotic* signification, which consists not only of incantation, but also of actually calling, or *naming*, it (in "blessings"), which is a renaming in the metaphorical sequence of "light of old" → "blessings" → "Love" that binds the desire for it. This time, then, the "light of old" is saved from extinction and is repeatedly reinvoked thanks to its projection in time, that is, on the temporal sequence of the prayer's articulation, which vanquishes time on its own ground by subjecting it to the associative chains of repetition in metaphor and sound. The incantation of the names that signify the nostalgic affect and ultimately its object reerects the "tumbledown" tongue and the tongue of the angelus bell, which join to *rhyme away the time* by *telling it* within a pattern of rhythm and rhyme that gives it meaning. Thus, the first, second, and fourth metrical units in the section quoted above are almost identical: *though I cry with tumbledown tongue/ count my blessings aloud/* four elements and five senses/ *and a man a spirit in love*: ^^-^-^^-/-^-^^-/ . . . /^^-^-^^-. The effect of this repetition is reinforced by the metrical repetition in the first two units of a separate scansion of the blessings in the counted inventory: four elements and/ five senses and a/ man a spirit in love: --^^^/ --^^^. Thus, the *semiotic* signification of the nostalgic affect invokes the displacements of its object—the old light, faith, love, meaning—which fills the poet's empty word with a desire for the recuperation of that object *in time*.

The binding force of such *semiotic* signification dynamizes the speaker's sermon as well. The causal relation between the protagonist's two religious experiences establishes a metonymical continuity within what is thus the poem's concentric metaphorical structure. This concentric structure binds the entire poem into a cumulative movement of signification, which as it were displaces the initially fallen spiring steeple and its indexed heavens by another spiral ascent, this time towards the poem's consummating, down to earth but higher apex. The entire process of the poem, as well as the self-conscious poetics that elucidates its psycho-semiological dynamics, are already encoded in the "*mustardseed sun*," the poem's opening key metaphor, which condenses two metaphors for the Logos ("the kingdom of Heaven") that were employed by Jesus to illustrate the *semiotic* dynamics of the divine Word. In his familiar parable in Matthew 13, Jesus says that

> The kingdom of heaven is like to a grain of mustard seed, which a man took and sowed in his field: Which indeed is the least of all seeds; but when it is grown, it is the greatest among herbs,

> and becometh a tree, so that the birds of the air come and lodge in the branches thereof. (Matt. 13:31–32).

Now once this seed of faith has grown in the fertile fields of their hearts, says Jesus,

> Then [on the Day of Judgement] shall the righteous shine forth as the sun in the kingdom of their Father. (Matt. 13:43)

The righteous are identified and saved on the day of judgement by the shining through of the seminal Word which they have swallowed, which germinates and grows to shine (only) *in* them. The Word, then, is an empty signifier whose potential meaning is realized by the receiver who incorporates it. The poet's synchronized—imaginary and actual—births are brought about by a similar incorporative process of initiation. The poem's germinal metaphor of the mustardseed, an incorporated scriptural word, or "palaver," that is initially empty, grows to mean in its new habitat by virtue of the growth of its semantic—organic, astral, and religious—branches. The poet's conversion begins in the darkness of "the mustardseed sun," that is, in agnostic despair at the dawn of his actual birthday, and culminates in a literal (optical), religious, and symbolic "clarification," when the germinal sun reaches its actual zenith and metaphorical blossom. At that moment of enlightenment, the converted speaker feels reconciled to time and even celebrates the now lit, rather than "dark" way to the grave: "the closer I move / To death, . . . the louder *the sun blooms*." The sun's loud bloom, or laudatory boom, is the lionized response to his initially muted speech-act: here, as in Thomas' "Vision and Prayer," "The sun roars at the prayer's end."[16]

The audio-visual metaphor of the loud sun configures the oral-aural nature of the Logos as at once Word and Light, which reverberates and shines through in Nature's alleluia for its Creator—as it is reorchestrated by the poetic word: "the whole world, then / With more triumphant faith / Than ever since the world *was said* / Spins its morning of praise." The converted poet's consummating experience of grace consists, then, in his initiation into the order of the Symbolic Other through a simultaneous incorporation and rearticulation of His Word, which yields the blissful experience of a creative participation in the Word: the poet finds himself (literally) in an intertextual Communion between the poetic and the divine words, between his *wreathed* prayer and the world's *spun* praise, which are spun together in the orbit of the mustardseed sun-flower.

Now the regenerative oral dynamics of projection and identification with the Word also marks the speaker's sermon, which generates its meaning and its subject by rearticulating the scriptural Word. In fact, the incorporative-eucharistic principle governs the poem as a whole, as well as the structure of experience on each of its metaphorical levels. The subject of every level in the mise-en-abyme structure as it were incorporates one or both of the two aspects of the psycho-somatic Word—that is, Christ's body or his speech—and transmits it to the protagonist of the next (outer) level, who incorporates him or his word. Thus, the projective protagonist of the vision is saved by incorporating Christ to the point of total identification. After the crucifixion scene in "the ambush of his [/Christ's] wounds"—the bloody, imaginary death in stanzas 4–5—the protagonist takes his/Christ's place in the Trinity "With blessed, unborn God and His Ghost" (stanza 7). The poet's "eucharistic" identification with his resurrected specular self impels in him a regenerative cathartic transformation, which in turn inspires his prayer. The prayer reinvests the deconstructed Christian metaphor of the vision with a new meaning, which turns the poet into the new subject of the scriptural metaphor. Indeed, the poet's becoming the explicit subject of the devotional utterance in stanza 9 (an appropriation which, as I mentioned earlier, is designated by the shift from third to first person), is related to his identification not only with Christ's fate, but also with his figure as a *preacher*. The speaker inherits Christ's position as a preacher by incorporating the latter's Word: "To his nimbus bell cool kingdom come" to germinate in him so that he may embody its meaning and its *inseparable* subject. Indeed, the event of subjectification taking place here is realized through the introjection of the divine subject's *meaningful being*, in whom the correlation between meaning and subjectivity is realized. The achievement of this introjection restores the original integrity of "the light of old" as it is envisioned by the Gospel: "In the beginning was the Word . . . and the Word *was* God" (John 1:1).

The poet's identification with the speaking subject of the scriptural Logos is also suggested by the narrative situation of his prayer, which is analogous to the circumstances in which Christ emits his parables in the equally self-reflexive chapters in the New Testament (Matt. 13, Mark 4). The poet departs for his nautical tour from his "house on stilts" by the "switchback sea" in the footsteps of Jesus, who, the New Testament tells us, "began again to teach by the sea side: and [then] . . . entered into a ship, and sat in the sea" (Mark 4:1). Like Jesus, he concretizes the contents of his cathartic sermon by a didactic ship-wrecking: when Jesus ends his lesson, the disciples receive the opportunity of a preliminary test of the extent to which they have incorporated the Word, as well as a taste of their eventual identification with the fate of their Master:

> And there arose a great storm of wind, and the waves beat into the ship, so that it was now full . . . and they [the disciples] awake him, and say unto him, Master, carest thou not that we perish? And he arose, and rebuked the wind, and said unto the sea, Peace, be still. And the wind ceased, and there was a great calm. And he said unto them, Why are ye so fearful? how is it that ye have no faith? And they . . . said one to another, What manner of man is this, that even the wind and the sea obey him? (Mark 4:37–41).

The analogous journey of the poet, "one man through his sundered hulks," to the "wynds and shells of drowned / Ships," has the similar function of a didactic simulation, or dress-rehearsal, of death, practiced in order to calm his anxiety before the *premiera* by way of a sea-pacifying identification with his master.

Jesus' teaching consists in transmitting his speech-act poetics by several parables which concretize the incorporative process of the reception of the divine signifier and refer to its rhetorical magic—but do not explain it. Thus he says in Mark 4: "So is the kingdom of God, as if a man should cast seed into the ground; And should sleep, and rise night and day, and the seed should spring and grow up, *he knoweth not how*. For the earth bringeth forth fruit *of herself*" (Mark 4:26–28). A clue, however, *is* provided by Jesus' reply to his disciples' question as to why he speaks to them in parables, which Kristeva briefly mentions in her reference to the Evangelic "story of grains and fertility":[17] "*Who hath ears to hear, let him hear,*" says Jesus (Matt. 13:9), and then, by synesthetic extension, also: he who has eyes and a heart will see and feel (see Matt.13:15). Beyond the political motivation of excluding unwelcome listeners from the secrets of the hermetic sect, the statement implies pretty much the same idea as the parable of the mustardseed, namely, that Jesus' parables have no meaning beyond their literal one. All the meaning is in the literalness of its signifier, "For there is nothing hid, which shall not be manifested; neither was anything kept secret, but that it should come abroad" (Mark 4:22). Those whose "heart is waxed gross, and their ears are dull of hearing, and their eyes they have closed" (Matt. 13:15) are deaf and blind and insensible to the Word because they miss its directness. Failing to take in (literally) their *immediate* effect, they look for hidden, figurative meanings beyond it, which places them in the face of an altogether fictitious enigma.[18] Those whose sense organs are open, however, can interiorize the divine signifier, and let its materiality impress its sensual effect on their imagination and ultimately on their hearts. The righteous disciples, in whose number you and I are counted by the Christ-poet ("And *my shining men* no more alone / As I sail out to die"), will share with him the *semiotic* delights of metaphor and sound—that is, the intimate sense of unmediated reality that shines forth in an aura of sense perceptions, affects, and sensations through the suggestive medium of his word.

This gives a general idea, I hope, of how Thomas makes the sun rise on his poet's birthday. Like the tuner of Apollo's song, who at once composed and invoked it, that happy poet at once harmonizes Nature's noise and discovers/reveals its immanent song. And it is this ambiguity—the "orphic mystery" of the "unity in multiplicity" or metaphorical "communion"—that fills the poet's empty signifier:

> I hear the bouncing hills
> Grow larked and greener at berry brown
> Fall and the dew larks sing
> Taller this thunderclap spring . . .

The initially cacaphonic "palavers of birds" are harmonized by rhyme and alliteration and metaphorical equivalence into the song of the larks, who now come to inhabit the sprouting mustard tree ("greener" and "taller" "this . . . spring"), matching their tune to the beat of the thunder's clapping and the bouncing of the hills that "skip like lambs" in complicity with the poem's rhythm and, as in Psalms 114:7, in awe of "the presence of the Lord." In other words, by and *through* his words, the poet takes himself (and those who are gifted with good eyes and ears) to an intimate encounter between the "*Four elements and [the] five / Senses*," which generates "*a man a spirit in love.*"

Lacan would locate that poet on "the trade route of truth [which] no longer passes through thought: strange to say, it now seems to pass through things. . . . Here, no doubt, things are my signs, but, I repeat, signs of my speech."[19] Speech, yes (not "writing"), but a speech which points *out*, as Donald Davidson would say, with words that serve as material indices to the world,[20] or to its inscription in the psychosomatic "logos."

The Tongue in the Bell: Psycho-Analysis

The dialogical Communion with the creation gives the poet being in/toward the world—in the *analogous* "transitional space" of the textual creation that mediates this dialogue. Like the narcissistic space of that mystical, or quasi-mystical Communion, the space of the text constitutes a kind of a receptacle which contains its subject, thus protecting him from the existential anxiety which marks his initial and motivating condition as an abject aborted foetus in search of a maternal habitat. That seedy condition, as well as its wishful redemption, are embodied by yet another handful of scriptural seeds, in the sower's parable to which I have been alluding:

> . . . a sower went forth to sow; And when he sowed, some *seeds* fell by the way side, and the fowls came and devoured them up. Some fell upon stony places, where they had not much earth: and . . . because they had no root, they withered away. And some fell among thorns; and the thorns sprung up, and choked them. But others fell into good ground, and brought forth fruit. (Matt. 13:3–8).

The first, unlucky seeds configure the devastating sense, expressed in the poem, of one—a "wind turned" mustardseed—who has no place to be, or to begin to be, because time keeps snatching the ground from under his feet. Such is the condition of the poet whose representations are perpetually subverted by the irrepressible melancholic negativity which underlies them; whose meanings—his signs and object—are unstable, constantly collapsing as time goes by; whose signifiers empty out as soon as he posits them, to confront him, time and again, with the horror of his aborted beginning.

What saves this poet, as we have seen, is his active entrance into time. The poet re-creates the world as a *place to be* through his poem as an *act in time*. That act is the repetition of his splitting beginning, as it emerges from yet another of Thomas's "seed poetics":

> Each image holds within it the seed of its own destruction, and my dialectical method, as I understand it, is a constant building up and breaking down of the images that come out of the central seed, which is itself destructive and constructive at the same time.[21] (Letter to Henry Treece).

It is by the active movement of his dialectic signification in time that the poet avoids gravitating into its underlying abyss, that is, prevents the premature "wither[ing] away" of the seed of meaning and subjectivity from which his poem will grow. And it is by that movement, too, that he creates, or demarcates, the dynamic space for the germination of his constitutive seed: at once a temporal event and its site, the poem serves as a *chrono-topos* for becoming/being which displaces the negativity of time and its correlative non-space of abjection. This negativity marks the poet's initially dissociative, antagonistic notions of time and space (epitomized by "Dark is a way and light is a place"). For him, it was *either* destructive time that destroys any representational space which he might inhabit, *or* absolute, utopian space at the dead end of time. The displacement of that negativity, which is reflected in the transformation of the poet's initial death journey, involves the reconciliation of the antagonistic terms within the symbolic space of the poet's verbal journey of life. The syntactic layout in the first stanza concretizes the way in which the poem spans and opens its chronotopical coordinates for the advent of its subject. We see this in the series of adverbial phrases of time and space (*in*, *by*, *where*, *in*, *among*, *this . . . day*) that herald the emergence of the speaker's persona ("he") in line 7.

The vicissitudes of abjection and their redemption are displayed in a particularly elucidating manner in the first part of the poem, in the evocation of the Christian sacrifice which summons the nostalgic "light of old" into presence. The emergence of the light in the visionary scene concretizes the archaic act of sublimation which represses and displaces the autoerotic object by the nostalgic, narcissistic Thing. The first, *ambiguous* maternal object inhabits the "abyss" of the poem's metaphorical structure: the imaginary resurrection into the light is preceded by a representation of an ambiguous maternal cavern—"In a *cavernous*, *swung* [=rocked] / Wave's silence"—which soon turns into a "*cage*," the *bolt* of which the foetus is to "rage apart."

The sacrificial price of the Christian sublimation of death foregrounds the psychic predicament underlying the speaker's compulsive need to return to the site of his aborted genesis. The metaphor of the crucifixion concretizes the double-binding drama of abjection which, undermining repression, suspends its subject on the psychosomatic threshold of his existence. The undifferentiated protagonist of that drama, the abject (who is "neither subject nor object" but the negativity of the symbiosis that precedes them),[22] emerges here in the form of "rippled seals [which] streak down / To kill and their own tide daubing blood / Slides good in the sleek mouth." The autoerotic sadomasochism involved in this murderous oral Communion (the seals, who are among the rare mammals in the poem's ornithological zoo, drink their own blood), manifests the fixation on primary ambivalence which at once defends its (pre-) subject from death in symbiotic fusion and prevents him from separating. The logic of this fixation is that, as he retains within him the nostalgic object, which is also the incriminating and persecutory "bad object" that constitutes him as abject, he cannot dispose of it without disposing of himself. This is, however, exactly what he does, symbolically, in the crucifixion scene. It is the eucharistic blood of the crucifixion, which "slides good in the . . . mouth," that, on the manifest symbolic level, delivers the protagonist to his birth in the next stanza: "And tomorrow weeps in a blind cage / Terror will rage apart / Before chains break to a hammer flame / And love unbolts the dark." But this birth scene is almost a repetition of the previous one, in terms of the dynamics of abjection and sacrificial sublimation. The protagonist extricates himself from the maternal cavern, that is, from the terror in the face of its loss and its impossibility, by raging against it—raging terror *apart*, or, alternatively, raging *to part* with it. What enables him to part from the cosy cave is a projection that turns it into an imprisoning and devouring oral cavity—the "sleek mouth"—a projection which defends the frustrated suckling from, ultimately, his own insatiable hunger.

But here again, the object of the rage is inseparable from its (undelivered) subject, who breaks his chains with the hammer that nails him to the cross. This catch, immanent to abjection, compels its subject-to-be to a perpetual return to his aborted genesis—in order to abort it. He must perpetually purge himself of his unassimilated, but stuck-in-the-throat, ambivalent object, by giving it meaning—or "christening" it (and himself), as he does here, in the Name of the Father—through a symbolic sacrifice: a sacrament, a prayer, or a poem.

The descent to the site of the abortion, in the crucifixion scene as well as on the way to its underwater scenery, dramatizes the speaker's symbolic sacrifice, and also the symbolic deficiency manifested in the vicissitudes of the empty signifier. An unseparated prisoner of his symbiotic longing, the abject can do little more than constantly ward it off—in order to survive. He can abject his ambiguous object, but he cannot sublimate it and displace it by actual objects and signs. In other words, he is stuck, suspended by the mutual neutralization of the contradicting forces of nostalgia and abjection, at the threshold of his being in desire for the other in time. The practical consequence of this condition is the fragility of the subject's sublimations, manifested in the devaluation or the deconstruction of signs as soon as they are posited. This, in effect, is the abortion of meaning which repeats the original abortion.

The abject's catch is also manifested in the protagonist's imaginary gravitation towards death in stanzas 1–3, which dramatizes the collapse of the poet's sublimations and its cause/destination. These verses concretize the correlation between the depletion of meaning (or emptying out of the poet's signifiers) and maternal devouring/castration in the configuration of the linked fates of the poet's tongue and the tongue in the bell. The metaphorical relation between these metonymical tongues is obviously suggested by the "rhymer[s']" "long tongued room" in the bell tower: maternal abjection as castration is suggested by the correlative phallic beaks of the birds, which represent not only the poet/"chanter," but also the maternal source of his own dangerous enchantment. The association of the separational trauma with a phobic mother bird calls to mind "the fowls [that] came and devoured" the scriptural seed, whose incarnation in the poem, the mustard-seed, is threatened by a similar fate.

The protagonist's metaphorical fall evokes a gradual yielding to the death instinct as a provisional resolution to his manifest ambivalence regarding his birthday, which he both "celebrates and spurns." Thus, a gradual devaluation of the meaning of the birthday bell chime is reflected in the syntactic and typographical layout of the inverted analogies. The poet

> . . . *celebrates and spurns* [his birthday because he,]
> . . . .
> *Who tolls his birthday bell,* [knows that at the same time he also]
> *Toils towards the ambush of his wounds*

following the "dying trails" of all flesh—and fowl, as evoked in the preceding inverted analogy, where

> *Curlews aloud in the congered waves*
> *Work at their ways to death.*

The ambivalence in the first stanza is resolved—in favour of spurning—by the negation of the articulation of signifying (celebrating) sounds ("toll," "aloud") in the second stanza, which lays bare the repressed notion of death's "toil" (and "work") which underlies them both psychically and typographically. By syntactic correlation, the initial balance between the oppositional terms of the ambivalence in the first, coordinate phrase is violated in the following subordinate phrases, where the curlews' cries and the poet's "toll" are suppressed, as it were, by the main "death-dealing" phrases that bracket them. The subordination of life and signification to death is completed in the third stanza. There, the oppositional terms are reconciled in "*He sings towards anguish*," which foregrounds the melancholic/compulsive aspect of the speaker's resignation to death and its instinct. This foregrounding is reinforced by the retrospective suggestion of the destination of the poet's song in its movement "towards anguish" by the anagram in the parallel and rhyming "towards the a*mb*ush of his *wo*unds." Once fallen in that ambush, the swallowed tongue sings no more: its "blood slides good in the sleek mouth"—that "cavernous wave's *silence*" which is the oral cavity where the sacred Communion with the devouring/devoured mother takes place. In the silence that consummates the Communion, the Trappist eunuch preserves his cherished object unsymbolized, that is, unseparated . . . until it starts to persecute him. Then the tongue is resurrected to toll him free: in the cavernous wave's silence, "Wept white angelus knells . . . And to-morrow weeps in a blind cage."

In view of the compulsive destination of the fall, the poet's creative impotence consists in the melancholic syndrome of the negation of the signifier, or the negation of the negation of death—that is, of the object and its loss—by language. The depressive resolution of the conflict is also reflected in the kinesthetic images in the section. There is a tension between the ascending spiring of the spearing herons, which dramatizes a combative attempt to resist death, and an opposite regressive, descending spiral movement, suggested by the juxtaposed "wind turned" and "sandgrain"—the poet's "age" in an hourglass and a sand storm—which concretize the passive, vertiginous gravitation toward death. This tension is resolved in the horizontal movement, in the third stanza, of the procession of fishes and shrouded herons at the bottom of the sea, and the parallel horizontal movement in the sky, in the once again circular "claw tracks of hawks." The "regressive" spiral movement is similarly suggested by the simultaneous connotation of spinning and turmoil in "the hewn *coils* of his trade."

The "coils of his trade," like their metaphorical equivalent, the spiring church steeple, configure the poetic and religious fetish, which is "*hewn*" by maternal castration, as is the phallic tongue (or beak) and the stemmed steeple in "Herons, steeple stemmed, bless." Indeed, the same herons have erected the poet's creative virility in the previous stanza, where they "*spire*[*d*] and *spear*[*ed*]": "spear side": the male branch of the family"; "spire"—

"*spirare*" (Lat.): to create or produce by the agency of the breath (*OED*). "Spire and spear"—meaning to sprout, germinate (*OED*)—suggests, by way of displacement on to the "mustardseed," the phallic potency that erects the symbolic fetish of the spiring steeple and the poem. If attributed to the "phallic," castrating, maternal, the spiring and the spearing correspond to the possibly connoted "thorns [that] sprang up and choked" the scriptural seeds.

The castrated herons' blessing suggests the poet's complete resignation to his "*thistledown fall*"—or thistle *downfall* (as in "steeple stemmed")—in the third stanza, where the dried petals of the prematurely decaying mustardseed sprout are scattered by the wind. The resignation is also suggested by the *slowness* of the thistledown fall and by its preceding preposition "*in*," which is contrasted with the energetic resistance of the "full tilt" sweep into the "switchback sea" in the first stanza, where the poet is still "*by*" them.

But the drama of abjection, or the fantasy of the abortion are defensive reactions, paranoic, no doubt, but still protective against the trauma of separation, since the ambivalent fixation on the lost object is ultimately a defense mechanism against its loss or impossibility. The symbolic dive in stanzas 1–3 goes even beyond the defensive conflict to its unbearable cause, the "first death" that constitutes the object of primal repression. Beyond their verbal metaphorical meaning, the kinesthetic images of vertiginous falling suggest the traumatic *sensation* of a nameless dread of dissolution "once below a time" upon the time immemorial of a premature separation. (This is an example of the *semiotic* signification in metaphor: the verbal signified of the image is the overwhelming passage of time, while its transverbal signified is the spatial sensation underlying that anxiety, which the image communicates directly.) This dread is symbolized as well, in the first stanza, by the disintegration of the poet's "house on stilts" into "driftwood." The intensity of this concretization is further reinforced by the phonic juxtaposition of "*stilts*" that support the poet's "slant, racking house" and the sweeping river's "*full tilt.*" Significantly, this cataclysmic image condenses the narrative course of the poet's downfall as it is gradually unfolded in the first four stanzas, and so does, even more intensly, "This sandgrain day in the bent bay's grave" which is embedded in the space between the lines that yield it. The sandgrain is the metaphorical equivalent of the mustardseed sun, which is setting into the bay—the basin of the river of life that runs toward the "grave." In this short-circuited span of a day there is no time left at all; there is not even a verb to designate it, only an adverbial of place, suggesting the collapse, in the speed of light, of dawn into dusk.

These synoptic images epitomize the destiny of the subject's sublimations—that is, sign and object *relations*—to be aborted in the short-circuited detour of desire "stemmed" by *fear*. The detour is perfectly collapsed, of course, in the poem's key metaphor, the "mustardseed sun." "*Mustardseed sun*" condenses the entire birth → day narrative in its movement from "seed" to loud "sun," leaving no detour time, or space for even a prepositional relation, such as maintains the syntactic distance between the "day" and the "grave," not to mention a predicate, as in its embedding sentence. The process of the negation of the signifier coincides here, then, with that of the collapse of metaphor. Here, the empty signifier and the full but opaque metaphor amount to the same thing, namely, the negation of the signifier, by either silence (or alienated or mechanical speech), or by the annulment of its relation to its signified and hence of its communicative function.[23] What saves the helpless mustardseed from the maternal "beaks and palavers of birds" which "spire and spear" him, as did the analogous "thorns that sprang up and choked" the unlucky scriptural seeds (phobic hallucinations are the most primitive representations of abjection, Kristeva says)[24]—is a little action. The symbolization of the maternal abject in time involves the *decondensation of the metaphor*, which spans the relational detour for both the metaphor and its subject. This obviously takes place in the growth of the mustardseed sun to its meaningful blossom in the loud sun which, together with other metaphors, sustains the poem's temporal, narrative unfolding. The projection of the metaphor on the temporal sequence of the articulation yields, together with sound repetition, an associative chain which sustains the *symbolic*, prepositional chain of the textual detour.[25]

We can see this in the language of the prayer in stanzas 10–11. The unfolding of the action in stanza 10—the process of inner revelation, or inspiration by the "cool kingdom"—is obviously not established by a prepositional syntax, but by an alternative, associative order. The cumulative anticipatory effect of the repetitive *and*s and the repetition of sounds in the rhyme scheme as it were pave the way for the coming of the "kingdom," which seems to be "Tangling through [the] spun slime" of the chaotic syntax. The ambiguity of the subject (the "man" or the "cool kingdom") of the ambiguous "tangling" (intertwining/entrapping or becoming intertwined/entrapped in a confused mass; dredging or scouring) in "*a man . . . Tangling through this spun slime / To his nimbus bell cool kingdom come*" is reconciled by associative links to words in the following stanza: the "spun slime" receives its meaning—of internal chaos organized by the spinning of the poem—by association with the metonymical "sundered hulks" in the bottom of the sea, and with the spun praise in the next stanza. By spinning his poem, the man dredges his way toward the "kingdom," which is the same as intertwining/entrapping it in the spun poem, that is, making it "come," by way of *in*-vocation, to disentangle the slimy confusion in which the man is caught up.

The decondensation of metaphor involves the realization of its metonymical potential, which is, in this case, threefold: the potential of growth between the mustardseed and the sun, the causal relation between the vision and the prayer, and the redemptive sacrificial logic folded in the arch-metaphor, or symbol of the cross. In themselves, neither the cross nor its metaphor can save anyone from death. The formula "death generates life" embodied in them remains inert, preserving the life-death yoke in a state of mutual semantic contamination. The result is neither life nor death, only survival on the borderline—that is, the abject's catch, as in the crucifixion scene. The solution for this is achieved through the unfolding of the myth embodied in the symbol in narrative as well as in the performative sequence of the poem, which brings back to life both the dead symbol and the speaking subject.

The narrative realization of the Christian myth is sustained more than it is subverted by Thomas's "dialectical method," which binds the movement of the poem toward the integrative cathartic sublimation of its underlying (and animating) conflict. The poem's "switchback"—dialectic, depressive→ manic—structure polarizes the antithetical metaphorical terms within two cathartic cycles of death and resurrection. The symbolic representation of the polarized death yields (or would yield) a cathartic "clarification," or clearing of a mental space for a reconciliation. While in the middle of the poem, it was either life or death (the first resurrection involved a semantic inversion— of the value of the mortal "ambush"— as did the ensuing "fall"), here the poet is able to contain both. He can contain death precisely because it is truly sublimated, that is, because it is subordinated to life and speech. The competition between life and death is clearly solved in "the closer I move / To death, . . . The louder the sun blooms" to light the world as *a place in time*.

The world as a place to be is preconditioned (again) by a clarification of an inner, self-containing space. The oral *semiotic* dynamics of projection and identification activated by the poem to the effect of constituting both of these spaces is dramatized as a dialectic between the inside and the outside of the poet's bell. The transformation that facilitates the poet's escape from an unbearable inner reality (fear of death, or the inner abject) to the redeeming projective space (of eternal heaven) is imaged as the turning inside out of the poet's bell. The initially paranoic space of the bell's inside (the poet's "long tongued room" which is at once his own and the persecutory maternal beak, the inside of the maternal body configured by the cavern and the tortured space of his skull in stanza 5) is displaced by the blissful space *outside* it, to which the poet gains access by striking its/his tongue on the walls of its "swung" body: "In a cavernous, swung / Wave's silence, wept white angelus knells./ Thirty five bells sing struck / On skull and scar where his love's lie wrecked / . . . And love unbolts the dark" to become the luminous containing space—"Light is a *place*" where the poet "freely . . . goes lost." The liberating effect of the tolling recurs in the second part of the poem as well, but with a difference: after the collapse of his projection (the breaking of Lacan's mirror), the poet reinvokes "the light of old" by "cry[ing] with [his] tumbledown tongue." This time, however, he needn't be transported away from the bell's inside to an imaginary elsewhere, because the resonance of the struck tongue fills the bell with a sweetness that redeems its space from its former unbearable quality: "To his nimbus bell cool kingdom come." Through the incantatory "[c]ount[ing of his] blessings aloud," the poet introjects the heavenly signifier, which now becomes an inner space, or "nimbus" where he is contained, or indeed, self-contained. That psychic space of the Thing reinscribed can now be projected into a relation to the world. The "whole world" which resonates with the poet's blessing—"I *hear* the bouncing hills"—is a kind of huge bell that contains the poet; a place in which he is "no more alone / As [he] sail[s] out [on life's detour] to die."

Conclusion

In view of the foregoing analysis, it is clear that the manifest predicament that motivates the poem, namely, the anxiety of time and its corrosive, nihilistic effect, is a symptom, rather than the cause of the poet's "birthday blues." Time annihilates, rather than endears the meaning of life when the latter is doubted anyway, overshadowed by the lost "light of old" which it fails to displace and by the terror of the darkness underlying it. For the nostalgic, unseparated devotee of his eternal and eternally lost object, time is the old thief that perpetuates the original loss, sweeping his fragile sublimations—signs and objects—along with the subject constituted by them, down to the promised drainland of ambiguous recuperation in the oceanic end of time, which, as it is unfolded in the crucifixion scene, is also the site of his first death . . .

. . . Unless he wakes up to the bewildering realization that while he wastes his time being hypnotized by "the clock that tells the time backwards," life moves on and passes him by. Time flies by those who don't live *in* it, in active relation to the world, but *by* its full-tilt current; and when they awaken to notice it, say, by the chime of their birthday bells, they are bewildered to discover that it is getting late, that life might end before it ever had a chance to begin. Then they might pull themselves together, literally, in order to begin. The act of the poem is such an integrative enterprise, whereby the speaker plunges into the order of time—by symbolizing the fixational conflict that suspends him on its threshold.

CHAPTER THREE

Incarnate Devil in the Garden of Eden

THE POSSIBILITY OF THE REAL

By thematizing its own evolution as an act of faith on the one hand, and through the use of archetypal imagery on the other, "Poem on his Birthday" foregrounds the twofold—inter- and intra-personal—dynamics of subjectification involved in effective poetic signification. The poem lays bare the communicative functions and strategies of textual symbolization which position the speaking subject vis-à-vis an other, and the integrative processes that organize his intrapsychic subjective space. As I hope to have shown in its analysis, these inter- and intrapersonal aspects operate dialectically: by addressing an other (the reader, the represented world, and its resident addressees), the symbolic act activates the internal processes of integration that constitute the agent of that act, and so on. In this chapter I will expand further on the interrelation between effective poetic symbolization and integration, this time with a focus on how it enhances the signifying subject's coming into "being in reality." This perspective centers on the correlation between the "reality" of the subject and that of the represented world to which he relates, that is, between a feeling of (one's) being real—"there," "related"—and the palpability of the world to which one is relating. These inseparable, interdependent aspects of "reality" account for the authenticity of tone in effective poetic texts, as well as for the "sense of reality" and the "sensation of life" (Shklovsky[1]) that constitute the aesthetic effect of *poetic mimesis* as conceived below.

The question of reality in poetry is a question of faith. As the objective of the poetic act of *faith*, the mimetic effect is a would-be restitution, or retroactive constitution, of the basic *trust* in reality which is correlative to psychic integration and which makes for the *credibility* of the textual discourse. It is the basic trust in the spatial and temporal continuity of reality, which may be traced back to the work of the "reparation" of the maternal as a gestalt. Founded on dissociative—manic and obsessional—strategies of denial, the efficacy of the reparation is, as has been noted, variably limited, which accounts for the perceptibility of the conflicts and ambivalences underlying poetic texts. This limitation manifests itself, in various ways and to various degrees, in the tone of the poetic utternace and in its mimetic texture. The discussion, in this chapter, of Thomas's "Poem on his Birthday" and "Incarnate Devil," which betray the respective predominance of manic and obsessional strategies underlying them, illustrates this point. The detailed analysis of "Incarnate Devil" provides the basis for the development of an "obsessional" model of poetry, as an alternative to the "manic-depressive" model epitomized in the reading of "Poem on his Birthday" in the previous chapter.

The "reality effect" of poetic mimesis is an effect of vividness or intensity of representation (as distinct from tone!) which, relying on a sense of affective authenticity rather than on plausibility or verisimilitude, makes present at once an imaginary world and the actual subject who relates to it. The sense of authenticity is yielded by the *semiotic* representation of the speaker's body in sensations, perceptions, and affects, a representation which establishes an as-if unmediated continuity between the subject and the represented world and thereby intensifies its symbolic gestalt. This notion of poetic mimesis, which focuses on the phenomenology of textual representation as world-making, differs from Kristeva's view, while sharing some of its major aspects. For Kristeva, poetic "mimesis" is not an imitation (in effective representation) but a reproduction of the conditions of representation. Its object is the reality of the signifying process laid bare by the poetic text, where *symbolic* world-making is suspended, to a degree, by the subversive eruption of the *semiotic*. In this situation, denotation and meaning as the "truth" basis for representational plausibility are suspended by pluralizing connotation.[2] The "truth" of the mimetic "veri-similitude" is, therefore, not the linguistically posited meaning that sustains the representation of an object or "world," but the reality of the subject (in the process of becoming) and of the linguistic process whereby subjective truths are posited. It is, in other words, the "real truth" underlying the imaginary truths posited by language, or, as Kriteva calls it, the "truth of the real" ("le vréel").[3] In poetic mimesis as I see it, the repetition of the subjective process is indeed the major component, but only insofar as it is actually subjectifyng, that is, that it facilitates inner and outer relatedness, in which case its perceptibility supports rather than subverts symbolization. This suggests a situation in which the dialectic tension between the *symbolic* and the *semiotic* is synthetic, a situation in which connotative multiplicity supports rather than subverts meaning and representation. This is achieved by the enchanting, suggestive effect of *semiotic* indeterminacy. Indeterminacy in its suggestive mode of vague resonance (by distinction from a clearly definable semantic ambiguity) leaves space for the subject's "presence" in the text, in the metonymical notations (by distinction from denotations) of his translinguistic responses to the represented world. That subjective presence generates an effect of intimacy which intensifies or "authenticates" the representation, and which depends, ultimately, on the integrative positioning of the subject in the course of the textual dynamics. The latter positioning can be traced in the textual dialectic: the interplay between the *semiotic* representations of the signifying body and the *symbolic* representations of their secondary processing by the reflexive "mind," reflects the achievement of psychosomatic integration and the correlative resolution of primary (pre-oedipal) ambivalence. Indeed, it involves the subject as a "whole"—body and mind complicitly other-bound. The (always provisional) actuality of integration achieved through such effective symbolization makes the text a relative realization of Lacan's ideal of the impossible "Real" (as I understand it, namely, as signifiable "being"),[4] or, alternatively, as a Symbolic constitution of the *possible real.*

This symmetrical opposite of Lacan's "Impossible Real"—which will be distinguished from now on by a demystifying lower-case *r*—is placed here in reality on the basis of a more relative notion of the role of negativity in the signifying process as a relational process. I also locate it in reality in view of the transformative role of the imaginary in the service of the Symbolic, which Lacanian theory seems to somewhat underestimate. To put it simply: sublimation, or symbolization, is not necessarily "inauthentic" in the sense of being a *mere* "misrecognition" (*méconnaissance*) of the impossibility of the Real,[5] which does nothing more (real) than enact this impossibility by "barring" off its imaginary representation (the evasive signified which is the unconscious signifier of the "Real"). Effective symbolization is also *really* productive in that, making cohesive use of the imagination, it changes the subject's inner reality by actually—even if relatively and provisionally—healing the primal split that makes him feel dissociated from his experience of reality. This integrative transformation implies an assimilation of the Symbolic function which extends beyond the "castrating" or alienating procedure of subjection to the "Law of the Father." The determining psychic action in *truly* assimilating the Symbolic is that of imaginative identification with the oedipal father and the appropriation of his rights not only to power—to impose order and be a subject to it—but also to pleasure. The denial, or "misrecognition" of "castration" permits, in other words, the creation of true symbolic links in and with the world on the basis of the "incestuous" imaginary gestalt. This is, obviously, no more than a restatement of the common (and sound) sense—which theories of difference sometimes tend to marginalize by their emphasis on negativity—that the ultimate function of the Symbolic order is to *relate* us to the world, and that separation and difference are means subordinate to that end. "The Greek word *symballein* means to unite, to connect, to bridge separate parts together. . . . Symbols arise from the wish . . . to reach what is directly unreachable"[6] and their role is, precisely, to fulfill that wish by making good use of the body and the imagination, precisely, in the Name of the Father. As a function of cohesive relations, the real is, then, essentially Symbolic—but not unreal, for that; it is a real, transsymbolic experience that is yielded within and through the Symbolic order that connects us to the world.

Kristeva's association of the Symbolic function with the bisexual "father of individual prehistory" is pertinent in this respect, in that it combines both of the operations involved in the creation of relations, namely, separation *and* unity. The same (dual) relational function has been schematized earlier in the notion of the nostalgic Thing which, as a re-presentation that is at once differential and recuperative (of the maternal "object"), in effect combines, or integrates both of the parental functions. Now, when it is unassimilated, the Thing becomes an *ideal*—a dissociated *fantasy* of the "Real" (the idealized original integrity of the lost object bearing the paternal mark of unattainability) which we have seen configured in the visionary Heaven in "Poem on his Birthday." As an ideal, the "Real" is "a non-effective *negation* of the real . . . [which is, in that case,] no more than the *unthinkable* [that is, "impossible"] product of its negation" (Francis Jeanson, about the "faith of a non-believer").[7] This oppositional pair—the ideal-real, or the "Real," and its negation—corresponds to the disjunctive terms of primary ambivalence, which expel the subject from the relational, or "conjunctive," Symbolic order of the real to the impossibility of the real in the no-man's-land of *negative ambiguity*. These terms are condensed in Lacan's ambiguous concept of the "Real": "*the real is the impossible*" implies at once the impossible object and its impossibility, both of which are impossible because, by distinction from their conjunctive relation in the Thing, they are mutually exclusive: *either* fusion *or* separation, says the uncompromising split abject, who, by that characteristic disjunctive logic, is condemned to the contaminated non-space of *neither* fusion *nor* separation.

Neither fusion nor separation, but a *relation* makes the real possible, and this by dint of a preliminary polarization of the ambivalent terms: "good [part-]object" and "bad object" are first separated out and then integrated to make a real object. The poet "On his Birthday" reenacts the separation by polarizing timeless fusion and time as a radical, all-destructive negativity. He does so in order to finally reconcile them by subjecting time's negativity to the real-ization of the ideal of fusion within a symbolic relation (the dialogue between the divine and the poetic words), which he experiences as an *as-if* unmediated relation (in a self-consciously dialogical, textual "communion") with the creation. His mystical vision of the impossible Real ("Heaven that never was nor will be ever"), projected as against its unbearable impossibility (in a state of radical dissociation manifested in the speaker's fear of disintegration), is made possible ("is . . . true") through his prayer, which fulfills its primary "phatic" function[8]—to place him in the real by virtue of a relation to an Other.

The "phatic" element in the protagonist's experience is the essence of Thomas's de-theologized notion of faith, which elucidates, in the context of his "religious" poetics, the nature of the poetic act and its mimetic efficiency or credibility. As it emerges from "Poem on His Birthday," the faith that redeems the poet-protagonist's "ontological insecurity"[9] at the dawn of his birth-day is not an imaginary creed. It is not a truth, dogma or doxa, since the metaphoricity of those has been laid bare by the deconstruction of the mystical vision. Rather, it is an imaginative and affective experience of relatedness, or of being in touch with his experience of reality, which enables him to believe, or trust, in *the reality of reality*. The terms of this twofold—internal and external—connectedness are "count[ed . . .] aloud" by the birthday poet upon the fulfillment of his prayer to be born: "Four *elements* and five / *Senses*, and a *man* a *spirit* in love." The concord between the "senses" and the "spirit" and between the whole "man" and the "elements" is the psycho-somatic and subject-object relation which makes the identifying unity of the subject and his identity vis-à-vis the other. It is, in other words, what yields the subjective sense of self-identity. What generates this concord are the complicitious, *semiotic* and *symbolic* representations of its terms—of the "senses" and the "spirit" respectively, which yield the credibility of the "elements" and the authenticity of the "man's" experience of them.

A little demystification is naturally called for. Aesthetic reality is, obviously, not exactly reality. The "epiphaneous" intensity of poetic mimesis generates a kind of a "super-reality" effect which feels somewhat dissociated, because it resonates the conflictual tensions stimulated by the attempt to resolve the split, or bridge the gap between the "super" and the "reality." This tension is the direct correlative of the hermeneutic tension generated by defamiliarization (Shklovsky),[10] the basic strategy of poetic enchantment. Poetic defamiliarization generates at once a sense of estrangement (by "making strange" *both* signifier *and* signified), and of captivating intimacy, which involves an as-if unmediated "vision" of the signified. This paradoxical coincidence of strangeness and familiarity is of course the distinctive feature of the "uncanny" ("super-real") nature of liminal experiences, and the aesthetic is no doubt such an experience: the intense "reality" or "strong gestalt"[11] of aesthetic objects or "worlds" is the result of the exploration of their relational "ground," that is, of the very foundation of the Symbolic order that constitutes them. They shine through—to pursue the epiphaneous metaphor opened by Shklovsky's "vision"[12]—on a dark background of negativity, the negativity of a past and a prospective loss which never ceases to haunt the front or the back of the dissociated subject's mind and outline his representations with a shadow of doubt.

This negativity in effect haunts to the point of somewhat undermining the mimetic credibility of some sections of "Poem on his Birthday," insinuating a difference between what the poet says and what he actually does in the way of begetting himself in and through the poem. This negativity reverberates in the manic tone in which the birthday-poet celebrates his faith at the end of the poem, which betrays his desperate attempt to be born into a world which is not quite real enough for him to fully believe in. The trajectory of his strenuous effort to re-create the world as a place to be can be traced in the polarized, depressive-manic movement of the poem. In order to reach the here-and-now of a present moment on earth he needs to make a world-encompassing detour through Heaven and Hell, past and future, birth and death. He needs to explore the extreme poles or boundaries of his existence in time and space before he can ever simply be, or begin to be, *in* the world. One gets the impression of some kind of a schematic outline of a world, invested with the intensity of the effort to master, to establish a coherence—indeed, to reestablish the Symbolic order of the world. It is as though the speaker is trying to grant what should have been taken for granted, had it been assimilated, namely, a basic trust that the world is there and real.[13] The same obsessive need to explore, establish, and maintain the order of the world that is to sustain him is also felt in the birthday-speaker's relation to language. Thomas must first explore the negative poles of non-sense—the empty-transparent, and the too-full, opaque signifiers—before he reaches the right balance between the *symbolic* and the *semiotic* that makes a place for both the world and the subject. In order for a convincing sun to flower at the end of his poem, the ambiguous terms of the initial "palavers of birds" must first be polarized—into the birds' meaningless twitter on the one hand (the "mustardseed sun" is rather opaque in the beginning), and the empty prattle in dead scriptural metaphors, on the other. The final result, or overall effect, is, for me, a moving tension between a wish and its fulfillment in a represented world that is, indeed, uncanny: real and unreal, magic but also a little disconcerting; a "loud sun" that is a little blinding and a little too loud.

The faith that constitutes the object of the poetic act (as an *act*, rather than a statement of faith) is, then, the primordial, ontological faith in the reality of reality, which is a precondition for meaning and subjectivity: in order to be we have to believe that we are in the world, and in order to communicate we have to believe in what we say. Poets break and reconstruct the symbolic laws of language not in order to create a new, alternative world, but in order to re-create *the* world—a more urgent mission for those who do not have it (that is, who do not believe in it). This objective and its urgency are manifested to various degrees in the quality of poetic mimesis and in its characteristic intensity. While in ordinary referential discourse the predication of a verisimilar world presupposes a pre-predicated world, whose truth, or the symbolic order by which it is constituted as such, is reaffirmed *by the way* of the discursive unfolding, poetic discourse paves the way for the as yet nonexistent truth that will sustain the (representation of) the world to be. The poetic text reinvents language in order to reinvent the world, and the traces of this effort account for the intensity of the poem as well as its authenticity, because they intimate the truth of the desire that makes the world intimately meaningful. To re-create the world ex nihilo, poets must establish the very conditions of language. They must procure the Other that guarantees the Symbolic order and the categories for symbolic predication. "Every morning I make God in bed, good and bad . . . everybody's earth," says Thomas in his poem "When I Woke,"[14] in which he wakens to the anxious impotence underlying this megalomanic task by the creepy noises of the waking town: "No Time, spoke the clocks, no God, rang the bells." This mechanism is foregrounded by the dynamics of the birthday-poet's prayer, whose invoked metaphorical Other (its simultaneous object and addressee: the longed-for "real" or "faith") is at first posited only conditionally: absent from its "empty signifier," it exists only "on credit," which it will eventually come to justify (more or less), as the invocative articulation of the poem will summon it to "inhabit" or "fill" the empty signifier. Put in general terms of poetic experience, the thrill of poetic "epiphany" is in the *re*-cognition of our more or less benumbed or repressed transverbal relations to the world—substantiated within a concrete, sharable form.

The faith that is the object of the poetic act is not, then, an illusion, but an imaginative *property* which that act sets out to reappropriate (as in "to *have* faith"). It is correlative to the "basic trust" generated by a "good enough" early parental environment, which, according to Winnicott, preconditions integration by dint of the *transformative* function of the Imaginary.[15] According to Winnicott, psychosomatic continuity is the result of the interiorization of the compensatory, "transitional" illusion of continuity between inside and outside—me/not-me sustained by the gradually and carefully weaning "good enough" maternal/parental environment, which provides the relational gestalt for subsequent symbolization and object relation. This projected-introjected continuity, whose gestalt corresponds to the concept of the Thing, is the cohesive, imaginary foundation of the Symbolic function. I have pointed out the process of its appropriation, or reappropriation and functioning in "Poem on his Birthday," in the poet's assimilation of the Thing in his mystical vision through a process of projection and identification, which provides the imaginative foundation for the following prayer and its meaning-effect of grace. This last, religious term is suggestive of the function of faith in maintaining the Symbolic order, for indeed, it is the pleasure-bound *grace* of faith that ensures the power of the reality-oriented *law*. In other terms—those of the dynamics of desire—it is the residual trace of imaginary wish-fulfillment that propels the thrust of desire and its subjection to its binding Symbolic law. And if faith is a pleasure-bound and binding function of the imaginary in the service of the Symbolic, its absence and the correlative psychic dissociation are a defense against unpleasure.[16] A "justified" mistrust of an abjecting environment, this absence suspends integration—or causing, in Winnicott's terms, non-integration as a defense against disintegration[17]—while a split-off "mind" inflates to negotiate mechanically (or intellectually) with an unreal, because emotionally uninvested, world (Winnicott[18]). The world is unreal especially in comparison with the fallacious ideal of the "Real" bred by the dissociated mind, which eroticizes the impossibility to connect so that, when sickened by the emptiness of its dissociated representations, it can indulge in a necrophilic nostalgia for its cut-off, unassimilated, and therefore dead source of vitality: the famous "lost object" or the correlative mystification of the "authentic self."

Dissociative dynamics are, then, a compulsive fixation of an integrative failure, whereby the split subject would master the irrepressible separation by reenacting it. The abject reenacts his abjection by breaking all relations which presuppose trust, including those of language which, on the basis of a "social trust," assume a common faith in the (otherwise arbitrary) relation between signifier and signified. This mistrust in language—the syndrome of the "empty signifier"—and the compulsive defense against its vicissitudes are manifested in poetry and theories of difference (particularly Deconstruction) alike; but while the latter fixate this mistrust by rationalizing it, the former is generally an attempt to overcome it, by motivating, or naturalizing the relation between signifier and signified. The poetic act of faith (which often moves contrary to its message, when it mourns, within a self-reflexive enunciation, the limitations of language), is an attempt to reestablish the solidarity between signifier and signified, and it is that, first and foremost, which constitutes it as a reentrance into the order of the Symbolic. The means to that end is, again, polarization-for-the-purpose-of-integration, which marks the essence of poetic defamiliarization as a simultaneous, two-phase procedure. (These phases may clarify further the aspects common to Thomas's, Christ's, and Davidson's respective theories of poetry and metaphor and "parable" alluded to in the previous chapter). One phase is the laying bare of language's inadequacy, and making up for the "mere" metaphoricity of the "empty signifier" by making it *too* "full." This involves emphasizing the materiality of language to the effect of suspending its metaphorical function, and thereby reducing it to tautological self-signification (or a metonymical signification of the speaking "body"). This polarization of the metaphorical and the material/metonymical properties of the sign accentuates the arbitrary "bar" between signified and signifier—but only to engage the reader's attention in an attempt to transcend it: the suspension of metaphorical signification "de-automatizes" (Shklovsky[19]) linguistic perception to the effect of creating a hermeneutic tension that makes the reader invest imaginative energy (and content) in making present the evasive signified, which the signifier connotes indeterminately by way of *semiotic*, metonymical signification. Following the indication of the metonymical transgression of the "bar," the perception of the poetic sign is experienced as an as-if unmediated "vision" of the signified, which feels particularly real because libidinally and imaginatively invested. Indeed, the presence of what has been lost or is evasive is particularly forceful when found. This is true especially in the intimate, projective light of an imagination which is given the time and space to participate in the re-creation of the thing lost by filling the denotative gap that is maintained by its indeterminate representation with personal meaning. Thus, the defamiliarization of the poetic signified is in effect a means for the *re-familiarization* of the signified (and not an end in itself, as the Formalists claimed, and Shklovsky contradicted in his very introduction of this claim).[20] By blocking it out and then revealing it again, defamiliarization intensifies the perception of the signified and endows it with a sense of an immanent, intimate reality: the world re-cognized . . . (not "recognized," as Shklovsky would emphasize:[21] the hyphen makes all the *différance*).

The success of the technique of defamiliarization (its mimetic effect, that is) depends on a specific balance between the the strange and the familiar—between the *semiotic* and the *symbolic*—which conceals its strategy of polarization and thereby maintains the tension between presence and absence that intensifies the reality of the signified. This balance, which is a mark of a certain degree of integration, is sometimes lacking in Thomas's poems, when his "dialectical method" rocks them too energetically between the unintegrated poles of non-sense: either (con-) fusion in opaque, too-full and unjustifiably difficult tropes, or dissociation in "empty" (un-invested) ones, such as "untranslated" dead metaphors or symbolic archetypes. A testimony of this problem is to be found in the performance of my tortured "switchback" analysis of "Incarnate Devil" in the second part of this chapter, which displays the extent to which Thomas sometimes leaves the task of integrating his poetic meaning to the reader.[22]

My discussion of "Incarnate Devil" will address the preoccupation of this torturously narcissistic text with its own, characteristic problem of symbolization. The self-reflexive poem worries about its own self-reflexivity, whose constitutive specular split confines its subject to melancholic solipsism. The narcissistic problem of solipsism is traced back to its archaic origin in the speaking subject's primary split, which is yielded by the poem's manifest concern with the problematics of abjection in its obsessional symptom of "negative ambiguity."

"INCARNATE DEVIL"

Incarnate devil in a talking snake,
The central plains of Asia in his garden,
In shaping-time the circle stung awake,
In shapes of sin forked out the bearded apple,

And God walked there who was a fiddling warden
And played down pardon from the heavens' hill.

When we were strangers to the guided seas,
A handmade moon half holy in a cloud,
The wisemen tell me that the garden gods
Twined good and evil on an eastern tree;
And when the moon rose windily it was
Black as the beast and paler than the cross.

We in our Eden knew the secret guardian
In sacred waters that no frost could harden,
And in the mighty mornings of the earth;
Hell in a horn of sulphur and the cloven myth,
All heaven in a midnight of the sun,
A serpent fiddled in the shaping-time.

Synopsis

The vicissitudes of ontological faithlessness and its manifestation in the mimetic failure of "empty" signification are the theme of "Incarnate Devil." The devil that haunts the poem—is indeed incarnated by it—is the devil of unsublimated negativity, which subverts the poem's desperate endeavor to overcome the consequences of the "primal sin" of negating the Symbolic predication of the world: the solipsistic predicament of "fallen" language which, despite its self-redemptive motivation, cannot help perpetuating Adam-the-poet's exile from the faith-full, unmediated Edenic knowledge of the creation. This linguistic catch is accounted for aetiologically, by a reinterpretation of the biblical story of Genesis, Eden, and the Fall. Humanity, and the world, too, according to that interpretation, were created "fallen," that is, split and ambiguous in the manichaeistic image of the "garden gods" who "Twined [both] good and evil" in "the shaping-time." But this predestination of the fall by an ambiguous progenitor (lost object/abject and their paternal incarnations in a bivalent super-ego), Thomas knows too well, does not absolve him of the primal "sin" (and punishment) of his aborted genesis—or at least from the task of redeeming it, for otherwise who will?

And so he sets out, through a laborious negative theological detour through the Christian phases of history (Eden, Fall, Redemption), to reconfirm, in retrospect, the myth of the original integrity in a Genesis that never was. At the outset, "Incarnate Devil" seems to follow the same trajectory of fall and resurrection toward a detheologized faith as "Poem on his Birthday." Here, too, a deconstruction of scriptural dogma—the biblical myth—leads to the evocation of a personal, unmediated experience of the un-named good One: the "*secret* guardian" incarnated in a new, poetic metaphor. The access, through the poetic word, to the nostalgic Word ("the secret guardian . . . in the mighty mornings of [his created] earth") requires the same sacrificial (Christian) procedure of sublimatory self-abjection, which polarizes the "cross" terms of the "primal split" (the "pale cross" and the "black beast") for the purpose of its subsequent re-integration within a new "testament."

But the new testament never really takes place in "Incarnate Devil"—a metaphorical metonymy of its speaking subject—as might be guessed by its name and confirmed by its nature: written in the abject, forked tongue of an abject speaker ("a talking snake") who can neither spit out nor swallow the "Beast" he incarnates alongside the Word, this cursed poem, like its biblical analogue, cannot rise from the dust to dialogue with its divine counterpoint, nor raise its speaking subject from the unborn. The speaker's original "dis-integrity" dooms his speech to inconsequential ambiguity or, literally speaking, to the double-bind which suspends his genesis: a Christ who cannot be "christened" in the Name of the Father—whom he fails to rename (effectively).

What subverts the poem's mimetic effect is its hyper-self-consciousness. Bearing the print of its subject's "cloven" hoof, the poem accentuates the poet's reflexive notion (which distinguishes him from the mystic) that he produces his faith; that his cloven foot is at once inside and outside the imaginary "*as-if*" space which sustains it. This self-consciousness is bound up, as the poem suggests, with the angry/masochistic abject's denying himself the "incestuous" pleasures of the Imaginary that is necessary for effective symbolization, or indeed, the reconciliation of Father and Son through the "sacrificial" transgression of the paternal Law embodied in the scriptural myths of Eden and Christ.

On the Symbolic Origin of the Real and on the Imaginary Origin of Language: Genesis 1–3, Freud, and Walter Benjamin

Contrary to what some might fantasize, the garden of Eden was a civilized place, governed by law and order, and it was this fact that ensured the Edenic quality of the place: the sense of the real guaranteed by the order of the *at once* creative and cognizing Word. The world felt so real because somebody else had already said it; *pre*-dicated by an Other, no solipsistic doubt haunted its reality.

The symbolic order of the creative Word guaranteed the solidarity between reality and knowledge. As long as he accepted its law, says Benjamin, "Man [was] the knower in the same language in which God [was] creator"[23] and enjoyed the Edenic bliss. That "perfect," Symbolic knowledge was mediated by the prelapsarian "language of Man," the Adamite language of *name*. Man cognized the divine Word embodied in things by giving them their "proper names," which were proper (identifying and appropriate) "*translations*" of the mute "language of things."[24] These "translations" were at once objective and subjective, in that they articulated a creative reception of the creative Word manifested in things. Their "objectivity" was "guaranteed by God," for

> the name-language of man and the nameless one of things [were] *related* in God and released from the same creative word, which in things became the communication of matter through magic communion, and in man the language of knowledge and name in blissful mind.[25]

The implication of "man's" subjectivity, that is, his creative (but not solipsistic!) performance was guaranteed, as Benjamin's texts permit us to conjecture, by the transformative aspect of the translation, which perfected the mute, nameless language of things by making it articulate and communicative to *man*.

The Symbolic law by which the world was created, separated out of the watery chaos of material symbiosis and then cognized in or by God's name (as *earth*: significantly, that place-for-being was named by God, not "man") was also imposed on "man," in the prohibition of the tree of knowledge. While the prohibition was a practical instance of God's law, the tree of the knowledge of good and evil was, in itself, an emblem of the very premises of that law, namely, the divine *pre-judgement* (pre-dication) involved in the Symbolic creation of the world. The creation into which Adam was born had been realized by dint of a twofold judgment, which constituted the Edenic grace of "our first world"—the "grace of *sense*" that made it real (T. S. Eliot):[26] an ontological predication ("let there *be* . . . and there *was*" [e.g., Genesis 1:3]), and an evaluative judgment of the creation ("And God saw . . . that it was *good*" [e.g., Genesis 1:4]). These two predications may be read as an objectification, in a reversed order, of the discriminatory process whereby, according to Freud ("Negation"),[27] the subject comes to cognize reality. Two acts of judgment, by the pleasure (/unpleasure) and the reality principles respectively and consecutively, are involved in this process: first, the "attributive" judgment of good and bad part-objects by the "pleasure ego," which is bound to the oral function of incorporation and expulsion that will eventually mark the boundaries between inside and outside and subsequently between self and other. The latter are drawn by dint of a judgment of "existence," or "reality testing," which concerns whole objects in which the "reality ego" finds, or rather refinds the attributes of the inner representations of good part-objects, thus establishing the symbolic relation between inside and outside ("it is evident that a precondition for the setting up of reality-testing is that objects shall have been lost which once brought real satisfaction").[28]

The name-language of Eden pre-supposed the boundaries and guaranteed a perfect symbolic complicity between inside and outside, and hence the stability of its reality judgment. The inversion of the order of judgments in the story of Genesis is significant in terms of the reality-effect of the parental Word, while foregrounding the role of "good enough" object relations in the real-ization of the subject: the priority of the ontological predication in the biblical story ensured the immanence of the creation and its independence of subjective conditioning of pleasure or unpleasure. God was no narcissistic parent, the Scriptures suggest, who bequeathed to his created "image" the fantastic unreality of his projected needs and desires. It was precisely the objective, apparently arbitrary nature of His *free* willed Word—a mark of parental self-denial in tune with the child's individuation needs—that guaranteed the credibility of his "text" against the subversive effect of compulsive overdetermination. It was the priority of the Symbolic reality principle in the creation that enabled that mature/separated super-parent to grant Adam a world whose reality could be literally "taken for granted." But in order to make sure that Adam would take it at all, the world had to be good, too, and pleasant . . .

The real-ization of the world—that is, its creation as well as its cognition—was, then, a matter of a Symbolic affirmation of reality in both senses of the term, the attributive or evaluative and the exsitential or ontological. Benjamin's Adamite name-language, the ideal actualization of the Symbolic order, re-cognized this symbolic affirmation by translating it into sound. The transgression of the prohibition of the tree of judgment was a negation of God's affirmative judgment, whereby Adam expelled himself from the Edenic order of the real: the punishment for that breach of the Symbolic trust was that breach itself, that is, the loss of ontological trust.

By Edenic standards, "man's first disobedience"[29] was the crime and punishment of the foreclosure of the Name of the Father, that is, of His law (reality) and of the Adamite name language that connected "man" to reality. The transgression faced Adam with the *nameless* knowledge of the pre-predicative ambiguity that preceded the naming of the separated "firmament" and the "earth"—or, alternatively, of the primal ambiguity of the object (/abject) of primal repression—which the Word had sublimated in name and law. But that prohibitive law itself testified to the fact that, even in Eden, repression had its limitations: the forbidden tree was a *symbol of negation* in the specific Freudian sense of the term, that is, a substitute for failed repression which yields "cognizance of what is repressed"[30] by articulating a negative judgment of it ("this is not my mother" suggesting, in psychoanalysis, that it is too; "thou shalt not . . . lest . . ." cognizing Eden's underlying evil). The tree intimated "the only evil [nevertheless] *known* to the paradisiac state" (Benjamin),[31] namely, negative ambiguity and the judgment on which it was founded, and thereby relativized the Edenic reality judgment. Indeed, already at that early stage it appeared that Symbolic law, when it lacks the grace of concealing itself, subverts name. Its self-reflexive representation in the Edenic "symbol of negation" was, or invited, a "lifting of [the] repression" (Freud)[32] upon which name was founded, or, in Kristeva's words, the "denial of [its secondary and retroactive] negation"[33] by the human sign. "Negation," Freud writes, is an "intellectual function [that] is separated from the affective process,"[34] thus reenacting, to some extent, the split which it purports to resolve. This is certainly true of law, with its implicit negative judgment, whose necessity may be accounted for by the fact there are no smooth separations, or natural sublimations, or super-parents . . . And so, because God could not help a little Self reflexivity, a hole gaped in the mimetic fabric of His text, through which an ambiguous silence revealed itself to the intrigued spectator. And once Adam had pulled that loose thread, the text began to unravel, as the split established itself between word and thing, dissolving the happy synesthesia of name. In its stead, the noise of "*empty . . . prattle*" filled the place (Benjamin):[35] the disharmonious sound of the "fallen," dissociated human language in its vain attempt to hush the gaping nameless silence.

Vain, indeed, and "in the deepest [and saddest double] sense" of the word, where megalomania acknowledges its underlying impotence. Based on the knowledge of good and evil, in "man's" fallen language "name steps outside itself" to "communicate *something* (other than itself)": a categorical judgment. In this it is, says Benjamin, the "uncreated imitation of [God's] creative word," which presumes (or is desperatetly compelled?) to repredicate God's now less accessible creation. But whereas name affirms what is, the human word signifies what is not, because categorical knowledge is abstract "knowledge from outside" from which the concrete essence of things escapes, leaving behind their frustrated, vainly prattling empty signifiers. For Benjamin, the very question of good and evil was mere prattle: "The tree of knowledge did not stand in the garden of God in order to dispense information on good and evil"—that question had already been settled by the creative Word, "but as an emblem of judgment over the questioner" who ventured to reopen it. Adam's verdict was to swallow that judgment together with the apple and never to be able to get it out of his (language) system again: "This judging word [which] expels the first human beings from paradise . . . punishes—and expects—its own awakening as the only, the deepest guilt" or negative self-judgment, that backside of megalomania whereby it predicates its own "emptiness," or tries to empty itself out to abide by the stern purism of abjection. "The sterner purity of the judging word arose" "since the eternal purity of names was violated,"[36] and pleasure gave way to that which is, according to Freud, "beyond" it:[37] "Affirmation" (which is what name does), says Freud, "as a substitute for [symbiotic] uniting—belongs to Eros"; the opposite "polarity of judgment," that of "negation" (and "the general wish to negate"), "as the successor of expulsion [=abjection]—belongs to the instinct of destruction"[38] and its domestic representative, the condemning super-ego that is the severe paternal successor of the abject.

Assuming the guilt of the predestined primal sin/punishment, Benjamin, the sad thinker, comforts us with a suggestion of the possibility of redemption through poetry: "the language of poetry is partly, if not solely, founded on the name language of man" and therefore has the potential of redeeming the "empty" metaphoricity of the human word (as if to illustrate the prospect of filling Thomas's "palavers of birds," he points out "the kinship between song and the language of birds"!).[39] Thomas, the poet who sets out to perform this task, is at the same time drawn back by his obsession with the primal predicament: his nostalgia for the lost Eden is countered by rage at the unjust persecution embodied in the Edenic (f)law: the devil of ambiguity incarnated in the old symbol of negation, which ambiguated the creator(s) and His/their creation, His/their human image, and his own creation—the poem.

Incarnate Ambiguity

Where? In the world or in the poem? Or both? The question remains unresolved in "Incarnate Devil," which is an ambiguous poem about ambiguity, the origin of evil—in God's or "man's" ambiguous word? A conflict between nostalgia and rage concerning the speaker's ambiguously mythologized origin suspends its conclusion with a positive thesis, and so the poem remains a reenactment of (whose?) primal ambiguity, that is, of a failure of judgment that suspends Symbolic predication.

The poem yields two readings, in the light of two interpretations which it suggests of the biblical story of the creation and the fall. By one reading, the poem negates the biblical notion of the "good" creation and its violation by the human fall, on the basis of an interpretation of the Edenic "symbol of negation" as evidence for the predestination of the fall: *both* "forked out" halves of the apple had the "shapes of sin," which left no choice between good and evil as far as its diabolical temptation was concerned. Evil was literally (iconographically) incarnated in that "*bearded*" and "*forked*" (-tongued) diabolical creation, from which follows the Blakian idea that the "world [fell] in the very act of creation" (Moynihan).[40] Thus, "In shaping-time the *circle*," the globe or "the cycle of life" (Moynihan),[41] was serpent-"*stung awake*." Indeed, the *divine* "judging word" could not but "expect its [diabolical] awakening" of the *human* "guilt" which it came to incarnate as soon as it was uttered. This idea is repeated, by this reading, in each one of the stanzas of the bitterly heretical poem, in variations which serve to settle accounts with the guilt-based authority of the Christian doctrine of the "primal sin." Thus, in the second stanza, a split, Manichean deity ("*the garden gods*") "[t]wined good and evil" in Eden as well as in "man," whose dual moral mortal nature follows from the psycho-somatic split that divides the sinful shape of his lunar being (the moon reverberates back to the "apple" and the cyclical-spinning "circle"): half "*handmade*" of *clay* ("the dust of the ground" moistured by the "*cloud*," or "the mist of the earth [that] watered the whole face of the ground" in Genesis 2:6,7), and half *spirit* (the moon "rose *windily*" as "a living soul" when "God . . . breathed into his nostrils the breath of life," [Genesis 2:7]), and consequently "*half holy*" and half not—"[*b*]*lack* as the *beast* and *paler* than the *cross*." This crops down, of course, the sting of the redemptive tale of the pale corpse (yes, "sting," for where would Eros be without יצר הרע, the "evil impulse"?), a tale that is as fabulous as the destinations of its successors on the Day of Judgment: the "*cloven myth*" of heaven and hell is as old as the immanently fallen world, for already "in our Eden" we "knew" *both* the "secret guardian" with his "sacred [baptismal] waters" and his "pale" morning light, *and* his nocturnal, "horn[ed]" and "cloven"-hooved counterpart, the beastly incarnation of the fall, which actually takes place between the third and fourth lines of the last stanza. The ambiguous inseparability of good and evil is dramatized in the oxymoronic "*midnight of the sun.*" Indeed (to echo an echo of Blake), "In the beginning . . . Heaven and Hell mixed as they spun" (Thomas).[42]

William Moynihan accounts for Thomas's "heretical" myth of the creation and his need to repeatedly express, in his early poems, his sense of "the inherent conflict in the creation." "The point of view for Thomas's treatment of creation," he writes, "is like that of Adam when he first perceived death. *He is too close to the horror of the revelation to think of how 'green' was the beginning,*"[43] that is (I interpret), to be able to idealize a beginning the horror of which had not been repressed properly, and therefore needed to be mastered by compulsive repetition (the domestic fights between Heaven and Hell are the most prevalent theme in Thomas's poetry). Moynihan explains that, once faced with it, "[Thomas's] purpose [was] to show the *truth* of the created world, to reveal the crocodile"[44]—the co-relative of the snake and other reptilian incarnations of death and abjection in his poetry. He reads this ambition clearly in Thomas's "I, In My Intricate Image":[45] "I, in a wind on fire, from green Adam's cradle / No man more magical, *clawed out the crocodile.*" What this "magical" gesture suggests to me, though, is not so much the desire for truth as the obsessive desire to claw it *out*, that is, to *purge* "Adam's cradle" of the creepy truth of abjection that blighted its greenness. The motivation for Thomas's obsessive repetition of the original "fall" here, as in many other poems, is to purge Genesis of its incarnate devil, so as to establish its famous Edenic integrity in retrospect. This corrective motivation manifests itself in "Incarnate Devil" by what appears to be, by an alternative reading yielded by the ambiguous poem, its *variational* pattern of repetition, within what would be a transformative act of faith which rescues its speaker from the deathly grip of the *same*, compulsive, self-aborting "Fall."

By this "faithful" reading of the poem, each stanza presents a different interpretation of the scriptural Genesis and fall, within a rhetorical "exegetic debate" that leads to a final reaffirmation of the Christian biblical version. The last, affirmative interpretation is a symbolic "translation" (in Benjamin's sense) of the biblical Eden into a personal, subjective experience of "*our* Eden," which corresponds to the notion of prelapsarian knowledge. The debate, which advances a deconstructive ("negative theological") argument through a procedure of triple negation (the first is of the biblical version), is a self-conscious attempt to purge the *speaker's* professed "primal ambiguity," that is, to transcend, as in "Poem on his Birthday," the "*serpent* cloud" of his fallen knowledge. This transformative attempt is symbolically represented by the interweaving of the three-chaptered Christian narrative of the creation, the Fall and notably the cathartic Redemption of the "primal sin" and punishment (the redemptive, integrative device of projecting the ambivalence on a narrative sequence is the same as in "Poem on his Birthday"). The evocation of the latter chapter, that of the crucifixion, foregrounds the mechanism of abjection as the origin of the primordial "evil without cause" (André Green on "primary masochism"),[46] which may be read as a latent concern of the biblical myth of the fallen Genesis, as well as of the "sterner purity of judgment" at work in the obsessive eliminatory procedure of the poem's "negative theological" performance ("out, damned crocodile! Out, I say!").[47]

But although its "exegetic" rhetoric addresses the question of the cause of "the evil without cause," the question itself is quite irrelevant to the poem's predominant concern. Thomas's real concern in this, as in all the other poems where he makes symbolic use of religious material, is first and foremost pragmatic: to ward off the nameless "truth" by naming and thereby transforming it—into, say, a "crocodile." Accordingly, the namer and creator of that specific reptile "in [his] intricate image" defines his poetic profession as "*Cadaver's masker*"! An effective mask, in this context, is one which transforms the ambiguous face of death by integrating it.

The ambiguity in "Incarnate Devil" lies, ultimately, in the tension between masking and unmasking the cadaver which it reproduces, that is, between sameness and difference in the correlatively compulsive or transformative repetiton of abjection. To see the extent to which that ambiguity and its underlying predicament are resolved, I will now pursue the second, "faith-full" reading of the poem as an attempt to achieve that resolution through a self-conscious, affirmative act of integrative symbolization. Then I will fall again, to reenact the poem's "stern[er] purity of judgment" and pronounce its guilt and verdict of faithless solipsism, and then . . . (no, the pendulum doesn't come to a stop, to be sure!).

A Theological Debate

Each of the three versions of Genesis in "Incarnate Devil" offers a different answer to the question of the relation between good and evil in the Beginning and thereby determines the speaker's position of faith or heresy, and the other way round: by acknowledging its source in a specific faithful or heretical authority and mode of knowledge, it qualifies (and relativizes) its statement. Thus, the first stanza is the version of the "*talking snake*"—a possessed speaker who voices a Miltonic devil's or an indignant Faust's view of the creation, as well as the abject's inherent inability to contain the ambivalence that triggers the debate. Faithful to Derrida's "devil's logic" of the supplement,[48] this blasphemous interpretation of the scriptural story inverts the power hierarchy of good and evil in the shaping-time. By the disjunctive logic of a dissociated psyche, it suggests, the evil design of the "forbidden fruit" could not have been God's, who supposedly created the world "good" (in His homogeneous image), but the talking snake's, whose iconographic trademark is imprinted on his creation. Cast in the shape of his "forked"-tongue, the talking devil's deceptive, "*sin*[full] ("empty," that is) word fore-casted both the primal sin and its consequences: the forking "*out*" of the Edenic unity and the agonies of separation and death. Those are suggested by the "*bearded apple*," whose facial and pubic hair, together with other goatly relics of the devil *in-carne*—the abject's dismembered body to be collected in stanza 3—pre-cursed the fatal misdeeds of the "*horn*[ed]"and horny devil. And by the same abject, disjunctive logic, it follows that not only the tree, but the whole garden was created by the devil, in his image: "In shaping-time the *circle*"—the snake curled around—"stung" himself to delineate his material *in*-carnation with his own body, and stung "*his* garden" "awake" to its "*shape* of sin."

And what did God do when the world was being caught up in that vicious "circle"? God was just "a *fiddling* warden" in the Devil's garden, who "played down pardon from the heaven's hill." Somewhat cynical of Him, given the circumstances of predestined eternal damnation, in revenge for which the indignant speaker plays him down to second fiddler in the creation, thus inverting the power hierarchy in the shaping-time. But the inversion is not symmetrical, precisely because of its cause: God is not reduced to an antithetical spark of goodness in the predominantly evil creation. He inherits not only the Devil's minor status in what was previously his garden, but also his qualifying features, which turns him into the latter's accomplice: like his biblical counterpart, God *fiddled about* idly, and was as much of a rogue. On his *fiddle* he played the sweet music of *pardon* that would seduce the dupes predestined to eternal damnation "*down* heaven's hill" to believe in him—a pardoner selling indulgences to the victims of false guilt. The mad rage underlying this charge of divine cynicism reverberates in the association of mad Nero, who fiddled while Rome was burning.

The fact that it was Nero who burnt Rome fits into the analogy, for the Devil and his fiddling accomplice figure in the stanza as two facets of the same psychic syndrome: if God here is the weak, unincorporated paternal function which therefore operates as a guilt-laying super-ego (a castrated and castrating narcissistic parent who binds his child to him by guilt), the Devil is the archaic "negative" of that divine archetype, namely, the maternal abject. The Devil's creative-abortive word is autoerotic (it comes into shape by the snake's stinging its own tail) and, by distinction from the paternal, metaphorical creative Word, it is metonymic and physically unseparated from its "talking" subject, who shapes it with his own, literally containing symbiotic body.

Once having subverted the Christian scriptural authority, the speaker reverts to the secular authority of the "*wisemen*," who anthropomorphize the problem of evil and ambiguity. Plural and anonymous, the Manichean deity in the second stanza is a rhetorical mythological configuration of the epistemological origin of ambiguity and of reality itself in a split subjectivity.[49] A solipsistic view of the creation as coinciding with the advent of consciousness emerges from the image of the Janus-faced man-moon. The man-moon rises from behind the cloud of unconsciousness to cognize and thereby *guide* the seas, that is, to symbolize the separation of the waters that made the difference whereby he "rose *windily*" out of his material inertness in the "[*un*]guided seas," to whose future guiding he had naturally been a "*stranger*" in that "handmade" phase. The role of the "garden gods" in this business is no more than to represent the constitutive principle of difference and duality embodied in their created image, the "pale" and "black" (or cloud-concealed) man-moon, by whose projective light—and its absence—the world is constantly re-created. It is the subjective rhythm of the waxing and waning moon that guides the seas, the wisemen suggest, and not the fixed, preestablished order of the Other *One*. The foreclosure of the latter's paternal name is literal here: the metaphorical "garden *g*ods" have usurped God's authority as well as His capital.

The dialectic lunar law that governs the sea also governs the maternal depths where the "twined" terms of the primal ambiguity are not yet separated and hierarchized under the aegis of the One. A second, subjectified version of Genesis is an "orphic" regression to that projective source of the "conflict in the creation," for the purpose of admitting and containing that conflict and thereby transforming its source into a *solar* One. This transformation brings about the final restoration of the usurped paternal Word in the sun-lit "mornings of the earth" in stanza 3. Its process, dramatized in stanza 2, consists in the moon-man's coming to acknowledge the actual, solar source of his projective light, which he appropriates in retrospect through the sacrificial gesture of rising "windily" and sublimatively to the stanza's final "cross." We have here, then, the same "eucharistic" process of integration as in "Poem on his Birthday." What distinguishes its depiction here, though, is the archetypal sun-moon trope, which illuminates, much in line with Yeats's symbolic cosmology,[50] the dialectic of subjectivity and objectivity, as well as the role of narcissistic projection in fixating the primal "fall" of the subject's genesis.

The Christian-orphic man-moon returns to the pre-predicative twi-lit zone of the lunar-maternal in order to undo the (Other's!) "primal sin" against which he implicitly protested, but which he also committed, in the previous stanza, by . . . committing it *again*, but with an apparent difference: he drowns the prosecutor and his accusation, together with the persecuted accused, so as to break the viscious circle of predestination and obtain a choice between good and evil that will enable him to judge for himself and *for* himself. The withdrawal of the narcissistic projection of good and evil into its subjective source is an act of separation between the inside and outside realities, which works backwards, to untangle the inner con-fusion between their more archaic correlatives—the good and bad terms of the pleasure-judgment. The symbolic polarization of these terms in the dualistic world of the Manichean deity yields the choice to hierarchize them, which the speaker undertakes in the next stanza, where he reaffirms "*our* [good old] Eden" in the solar Light of the Other's (scriptural) Word, which now fills his nocturnal firmament: "*All heaven* in a midnight of the sun." The Symbolic lighting of the firmament—the one that gaped between the separated "seas"—is the sublimation of the separation by the integrative law of the *undrowned* One, who now returns to shine through the sublimated, "sacred" version of the maternal sea-waters.

Derrida, no doubt, fiddles in this reshaping time, in the performance of the third con-version of the scriptural original—but with a difference: this final version of the Genesis story is the symmetrical inversion of the first (inversion, in stanza 1), whose author and chief protagonist is now the "fiddle[r] in the shaping-time" of the restored "sacred" garden of the "secret guardian." But in line with the subjectivist perspective opened in the previous stanza, the source of this *in*-version differs from that of the deconstructed original. Now, it is the speaker's personal experience ("[*w*]*e* . . . knew"), whose object is equally personal: it is "*our* Eden"—a lived, historical rather than a collective mythological Eden. (The source and the object of the Edenic knowledge qualify its *mode*, which is what the subjective Eden is all about, once the question of origins has shifted from the ontological to the epistemological level. Thus, whereas the notably "fallen" knowledge in the previous stanzas is mediated, verbal knowledge, transmitted by the Scriptures, the "talking snake" and the "wisemen" telling, here it is an intimate, unmediated knowledge, and it is therefore "proper" knowledge: adequate because personal, and hence designated as such by the proper verb ("[w]e *knew*"). Its unmediated object is the Nameless, "*secret* guardian"—the unnamed "God" who, stripped off of his "empty" "fallen" signifier with its heavy traditional capital, is presented (rather than re-presented) in "translation" into the name-"language of things": "We . . . knew the secret guardian/ *In* sacred waters . . . And *in* the mighty mornings of the earth." This Edenic, mystical knowledge is contrasted with the degenerated mythical knowledge, whose evil mode, much more than its specific contents, as it now turns out, the deconstructive poem has been seeking to demystify. Thus, evil and its incarnation, the "Devil" and his "Hell in a horn of sulphur," are a mere "cloven *myth*," whose horned and foot-cloven iconographic configuration reflects its own dissociation (cleavage) from reality.

The primordial Evil, the devil of ambiguity, originates, then, in the fallen human word that creates it, or in other words: the knowledge of evil is evil knowledge which, like the "serpent cloud" in "Poem on his Birthday," eclipses reality and its predicated univalence. The eclipsing "serpent" ("talking snake") and "cloud" are distributed here between the first two stanzas in that order, perhaps to qualify their respective "fallen" versions. A more direct evocation of an eclipse occurs in the third stanza, in "All Heaven in a *midnight of the sun*." Here the agent is appropriately the moon from the previous stanza, which diminishes to a yellow ("*sulphur*[ous]") crescent's "*horn*" to give way to the revelation of the sun. A parallel, and related self-sacrificial gesture is performed by the "cloud," a metonymical metaphor for the dark side of the "half holy" moon which it at once conceals and represents. The cloud condenses from one stanza to another in order to finally rain down the baptismal waters gathered in the cathartically clarified "morning" of the third stanza. These sacrifices on the part of the Christened moon yield the new testament between the antagonistic elements in the poem, testified by the prismatic radiance of the "midnight . . . sun"—a covenant between oppositions in an oxymoronic rainbow.

The last stanza effects the most radical turn in the poem's deconstructive sequence of triple negation, by shifting from the representational to the performative level. The idea of Edenic, experiential knowledge negates both the mythical knowledge transmitted by religious or "blasphemous" language as evoked and exemplified in the first stanza, and the predicative (categorical, or again, "cloven") knowledge of the kind that is transmitted by the "wisemen" in the second stanza. The latter kind of knowledge, the poem seems to suggest, cleaves our consciousness and tilts us between the "*horns*" of stupid theological dilemmas (*OED*: horn: "each of the alternatives of a dilemma [in scholastic Latin: Argumentum Cornutum"]).

It is precisely this kind of dilemmas that, so it turns out, the poem tries to transcend. By subverting the very terms of its own argument, the poem seeks to purify itself of the eclipsing "serpent cloud" of its own fallen prattle. For its performative task—like that of Benjamin's tree—is not to transmit information (mythical or rational) on the historical (aetiological) origin of evil (ambiguity), but to transform its *actual* source, and thus to *actualize* the integrative experience of the "Edenic" knowledge. In this performative light, the poem fulfills the original function of the tree of knowledge as a sublimative—i.e., affirmative—*symbol* of negation and judgment, and hence as "an emblem of [*affirmative*] judgment" over its signifying subject.[51] This affirmation constitutes the poem as a personal "translation" (in Benjamin's sense) of the scriptural story or "word," which is in itself a translation of the "Word" in the chain of the intertextual transformations that purify it.[52] The process of translation can be read symbolically into the renaming of the mythical "God" and His rationalized incarnation in the "categorical" "gods," who are un-named in order to return in the more discrete, indeterminate metaphor of "the secret guardian." The latter's connotative suggestiveness (rather than reductive categorical/denotative determination) is an invocative gesture which seeks to restore the immanence of the nostalgic "language of things," whose mode of signification is represented as the Edenic knowledge of its signified "*In* sacred waters . . . / And *in* the mighty mornings of the earth."

Sacrifice and Retribution

Such immanence shone in the mornings of the earth, perhaps, but it is not restored by the poem, which admits its own failure, as it turns out—as it turns itself inside-out, again, in the final stanza, to invoke the experience which it designates. By a deictic gesture of a signifier which, acknowledging its empty metaphoricity, resorts to its materiality for metonymical signification, the poem points its Edenic signified *out*—of its "fallen" linguistic boundaries. These boundaries are designated as such in the last, subversive line (indeed, the sting is in the tail), where the serpent returns to close the vicious circle of the poem which it incarnates and to sting it "awake" to its forked and circular "shape of sin." "A serpent fiddled in the shaping-time"—which is also the crumbling-time of the poem's motivating attempt to suppress that "beast" by a sublime metaphor. But this is not surprising, being perfectly in line with the Shaper's predetermined plan, which God pronounced in the serpent's curse: "[Man] shall bruise thy head, and thou shalt bruise his heel" (Genesis 3:15).

The return of the abject's symbol to negate its negation by the Edenic metaphor collapses the poem to the tautology of negative ambiguity which it has been seeking to escape, thus foregrounding its structure as one of repetition *without transformation*. Indeed, the subversion is inevitable, just as it was in the first place (the original, biblical Eden, that is), because "our Eden" with its blissful unity is the projection of a disjunctive, rather than an integrative imagination. It is the polarized term of the poem's *unresolved* conflict, which the third stanza does no more than displace onto a new series of dialectic oppositions. These oppositions, which will be discussed soon, illustrate the unbridgeable gap or "bar" between the divine and the human words and their respectively corresponding prelapsarian and fallen modes of knowledge, "shaping-time[s]," and orders of signification. Indeed, the categorical difference between the Word and the word is the negativity designated by the poem's deconstructive theological argument, by the elimination of the "fallen" mythical and categorical modes of knowledge. For the latter mode is synonymous with linguistic knowledge as such in this self-defeating poem, which does not believe in Benjamin's redemptive option of reconstituting the reconciliatory prelapsarian name language, nor does it suggest its existence in the first place: "our Eden," by distinction from Benjamin's, was pre- and translinguistic, and therefore irrevocably lost. We "*knew*" the "*secret*" Word before its destructive linguistic shaping-time—or inconsequntial reshaping *in time*—the poem's shaping-time self-reflected six falling lines ahead—in the era of categorical knowledge which the "wisemen" *tell* and the snake *talks* and the serpent *fiddles*. Presymbolic—indeed, symbiotic—the experience of the nameless takes place "In sacred [embryonic] waters that no frost [can] harden" into a distinct shape, and "*in*" the containing space of a warm and comfortable atmosphere generated by the generalized atmospheric metaphor of the "mornings of [mother?] earth." The im-manence of the Word is contrasted by human ex-pression of forked-*out* signs and shapes, or "shapes of sound," as Thomas put it in a synesthetic attempt to heal the split ("Poetic Manifesto").[53] And inside out: the signified that falls from within the poem is to be looked for out of its solipsistic "circle," the prison house of the subjective mind forked out of the Edenic real.

Under these sorry circumstances, the poem can do no more than abject itself by laying bare its own limits (both pragmatic and spatial), so as to declare its Symbolic inadequacy (its metaphorical emptiness—again, both spatially and functionally), and make metonymical use of its abject "body" as a material index to the world outside. Consistent with the poem's eliminatory procedure, this gesture signifies the poem's attempt to purge itself of itself, to claw out Adam together with the crocodile—which leaves "Adam's cradle" uninhabited. This sterile purism of the self-judging word is symbolized by the crucifixion of the moon-man, whose sacrifice brings no redemptive transformation, no integrative "new testament." This is so due to the zealous *totality* of the sacrifice (a mark of its disjunctive ambivalent logic), or the totalitarian nature of its receiver, namely, the abject's lethal super-ego. Thus, the "*half holy*" moon-man must wane altogether to give way to the *all-"sacred,"* "*Al[l] . . . mighty*" sun ("*all* heaven . . . of the [*mighty* morning] sun"), from whose affirmed territory he is excluded as wholly "beast" in the de-realized mythological form of the "horn[ed]" and foot-"cloven" scape-*goat*. Run out of blood, this desublimated abject goes "paler than the cross" and dies to the all-impaling sun—which is why he cannot even imagine the garden they had planted over his dead body, nor can his dejected creator (the poet), to judge by the pallor of his depiction of it: the secret guardian remains that way, effectively hidden "in [his] sacred waters" and his "mighty mornings" which, though sacred and mighty, are as opaque and stale as any dead archetypal metaphor that is not redeemed by a creative dialogue with its source. Any god would refuse to shine through such metaphor, which, after all that deconstructive havoc, returns to its source in some unassimilated cliché. There is nothing particularly personal in this Eden of "our[s]," and it is precisely this failure (or desperate renunciation?) of translation that marks the non-transformative consequence of the "sacrifice."

RAGE, RAGE AGAINST THE DYING OF THE LIGHT; NOW
Say nay,
Sir no say,
Death to the yes[54]

Some resurrection does occur, however, on the performative level of the stanza, by virtue of a more effective trope, which displays Thomas's characteristic way of extricating himself from the holy "mantraps"[55] he lays for himself by way of reenacting his paralyzing predicament. The redeemer is the abject's unsublimated persona—the outraged survivor of the "cross" who, like the poet "On His Birthday" under similar conditions, rages himself out of the sacred waters that have almost liquidated him,[56] but without being christened: faithful to his "beast[ly]" nature, the stubborn moon rises "windily" from the dead Edenic metaphor in energetic "rage against the dying of [his] light,"[57] in the explosive form of a sulphurous-yellow crescent's horn. "*Hell in a horn of sulphur*" heralds the manifest reincarnation of the abject poet in the last line and makes some difference in the return of that same, unsublimated abjection. Finding himself dissolving in the sanctified but no less lethal paternal version of his bearded mother's garden, the man-moon-beast must assert his subjectivity *against* that all-devouring Other. For the "secret," unnamed Other who inhabits it admits no other into his dead-silent, amorphous territory. Totalitarian in his namelessness, that super-father gives no sign of life, no language whereby his son may incorporate his holy omnipotence—which threatens to annihilate him: the moon fades out into his solar light, is condensed into his sacred *waters*, returns to the dust of the "*earth*" out of which he was "handmade," etc. Thus dissolved back into his elements (fire, water, earth), it is no wonder that the man-moon should rage to save itself by drawing on its last resource, the animating element of air, and an antithetical, *subterranean* fire: indeed, it rises "*windily*" again, to blow its "*H*ell[ish] . . . *h*orn of sul*ph*ur" (onomatopoeic for the apocalyptic occasion), which disturbs the muting sacred silence of Eden—or the false note of its dissociated metaphor. In a vulcanic *semiotic* eruption of "*sulphur*[ous]" rage, the "brassy orator," as its speaker referred to his own "intricate image" elsewhere,[58] reanimates his scapegoat's "*horn*[ed]" corpse in defiance of their shared condemnation (put to the horn: proclaimed a rebel, outlawed [*OED*]), and restores it to its natural element of the living (maternal) flesh (sulphur: one of the supposed ultimate elements of all material substances, [*OED*]). This *semiotic* outburst, which subverts the sublimative *symbolic* content of the stanza even before the manifest return of the serpent, gives affective vent to the primal conflict between Spirit and Matter, Heaven and Hell, signifier and signified and what not, which is much more effective, it seems to me, than any serpentine theological argument. It sets "all heaven" in an apocalyptic war between the elements and inverts their symbolic order: the creative, animating Spirit (air and fire) is assumed by the overreaching Devil ("horn" and "sulphur"), while God dwells in the clay ("earth" and "waters") of which the moon-man's body is said to have been "handmade." Thus the Nameless is once again deprived of His copy-rights—by the one who names, or talks, or even blows his horn in perfect cacophony with a serpent's fiddle, to animate the dumbshow of Nature.

Once again, but a little differently, from the point of view of the speaking subject, who now, in the poem's shaping-time, emerges into presence as a provisional, "fully" signified integral position vis-à-vis the provisional alterity of a raged against other. Provisional as any lunar transformation, but still a transformation: it is true that the new moon, like the speaker which it incarnates, is as diabolically rebellious as it was when it first rose to defy the divine or scriptural judgment. Now, however, it is no longer possessed by its diabolical rage, but assumes it and symbolizes it, to the effect of possessing it as *his* rage, as *his* position—not the Devil's nor of the "garden gods's," the Scriptures', or "the wisemen's". The speaking subject is now the performing "we" and his knowledge is "our[s]." The man-moon now contains the abject's anger in his crescent's "horn," and displays his formal and ideological identification with the self-reflexive "talking snake," as well as with the latter's evolving reincarnation in the textual performance. Indeed, when the "circle" returns to complete its shape two lines ahead, it will reflect the shape of the newly risen full moon. The event is anticipated by the penultimate line, where the full moon in the making eclipses or "midnight[s]" the "all heaven[ly] . . . sun," and thereby asserts its antithetical subjectivity.

In (or Ex-? or) Con-clusion: Moebius's Antithetical Subjectivity

The mode of "antithetical subjectivity" yielded by the sun/moon opposition, which calls to mind Yeats's similar, if less radical and less aggressive notion of it,[59] obviously diverges from the integrative conception of the object-relating subject postulated in this book. It corresponds, in the light of this conception—as in Yeats's lunar model, for that matter—to a negative "phase" in the dialectic process of the subject's advent, whose productivity is suspended in "Incarnate Devil," and in other poems by Thomas which fail to bridge (that is, symbolize) the difference between their underlying opposition (although it must be noted that once effectively symbolized, as it is in the section of the poem analyzed above, this failure is no longer a failure). The "antithetical subjectivity" that emerges from "Incarnate Devil" corresponds to the provisional identity of the archaic not-yet-subject, which is generated—or rather sketched or forked *out*—by way of exclusion, expulsion, abjection of the not-yet-other (the bad=outside discriminated from the good=inside by the pleasure-judgment that establishes, according to Freud, the pre-subject's archaic boundaries).[60] An assertive reenactment of the separation, this "identity" *is* the negativity which constitues it: I am *not* the other. The subject's *positive* identification depends on the integrative symbolization of that negativity by introjecting, to use Yeats's terminology again, his "primary" source in the Other (namely, the phase of self-identification with the Other, as opposed to the "antithetical phase" of self-authentication).[61] In metaphorical topological terms, one could say that the two phases constitute the form and substance, or outline and content, or inside and outside, of an integrated subject (a subject who has integrated the other). While Yeats succeeds in integrating the "primary" (solar, objective) and the "antithetical" (lunar, subjective) by symbolizing their difference within a comprehensive cyclical model, Thomas reenacts that difference within a disjunctive pattern that negates its antithetical terms, or at least short-circuits their respective life spans. Thus, the lunar beast and his incarnating discourse are saved from de-forming in melancholic Narcissus's sacred waters and in the liquidating silence of an aborted metaphor by an *outrageous* (expelled rage) negation of the Other—whose eclipsing is also their own negation. For if, as the second reading of the poem suggests it to manifest, the pre-subject's (provisional) "antithetical" boundaries are not filled by introjected "solar" content, these boudnaries are bound to collapse. The empty form they delineate crumbles into its own emptiness, into its own narcissistic wound—or into the sheer materiality of the signifier which, failing to metaphorize its unbearable content, or signified, comes to em-body, or "incarnate" it *semiotically*, in the sinful shape of a vicious "circle": an abject body whose psychic meaning lies somewhere outside, in the inaccessible realm of the nameless Other.

The snake/moon's attempt to create itself and its garden/poem ex-nihilo, without the affirmative pre-dication of the Other, is doomed to fail, because it is only by the intervention of that third party that the tautological dialectic can be broken, the condition of the eternal repetition of abjection be transformed. The sacrificial way to the Other in "Incarnate Devil" is short-circuited because its compulsive border-liner (in the literal, not the diagnostic sense) is ambivalent about separating. He would rather die than separate, says the moon as he dives back into the cloud of Narcissus's sacred waters—and *almost* means it: "To preserve himself from severance, he is ready for more" (Kristeva);[62] he is ready to risk the whole of his being—until he reaches the critical point where he must extricate himself in order to survive (not *be*)—antithetically. The "being" of that surviver is his sheer movement, or the fluid boundaries which he constantly demarcates, transgresses, and displaces to signify his identifying split (Green);[63] a primal ambiguity ("good" and "evil") repeatedly displaced onto various oppositional pairs: past/present, fluidity/shape, up/down ("played down"/"rose"), etc., and, in particular, *in/out*.

The topological dialectic in the poem concretizes the archaic oral dynamics of the border-liner's ambivalence underlying the non-transformative, repetitive movement of "Incarnate Devil." The analysis of this dialectic in the light of Kristeva's account of the problematics of poetic symbolization in terms of abjection[64] may help clarify the abortive consequences of the poem's de-constructive, compulsively dissociative attempt at self-signification. The inside/outside dialectic marks all of the poem's levels of signification, namely, the rhetorical structure of its argument, its pattern of imagery and its lexis. The sequence of inversions advancing the poem's "theological argument" consists of shifting container/contained relations (between God and the Devil in each other's respective gardens) which enacts the conflict between the transgressive desire to be contained in the maternal body and the need to out-line oneself against its voracious inside—by incorporating it (that is, by devouring the unintrojected and therefore devouring mother).[65] The incestuous desire for containment is manifested in the obsessive repetition (eleven times) of the word "*in*," by which the autoerotic snake-poem invites itself to the fatal paricidal literalization of the prohibitive symbol of negation: concentric like a pregnant *babushka*, the first stanza talks its dissolving subject into the watery/sulphurous hollow of the apple's seductive shape of *s-in*, embedded in "the *central* plains" of the bearded mother's fair and foul garden.[66] But, each time the horror of the maternal is about to be confronted, an *ex*pulsion/*ex*trication and defensive splitting takes its antithetical shape. The ambiguous center is turned *inside-out*: the apple is *forked out* (as the postlapsarian world "down . . . heaven's hill" and outside the "central plains of Asia" comes into view), the *cross*ed-out moon rises from the cloud to display its dual nature (in that world in need of redemption), and then from its sacred sublimation in an onomatopoeically *ex*haled vulcanic sacrilege. These inversions concretize the intrapsychic "centrifugal"/"centripetal" dialectic, as Kristeva describes it,[67] of the ambivalent abject who, polyplike, "introverts" and "extroverts" between equally failing—because ambiguous—sites of being or becoming. The terms of this dialectic are the narcissistically wounded, "impossible [,] inside," where the sought-for maternal containment displays its fanged emptiness (or "brambled void," as in "Poem on his Birthday"), and a "powerless outside," which, subjected to a weak Symbolic order (unassimilated paternal function), fails to redeem that de-realizing narcissism by providing stable objects for identification. In consequence of this failure, the outside world and its objects and signs are "in-significant, 'empty', 'devitalized', 'puppet-like' "[68]—unreal. The only reality, in this case, is the border-lining movement between these poles, the reenactment of abjection in the indigestive convulsions of one who tries to swallow too much, without discriminating, and then to vomit—himself out . . . It is, in other words, the reality of the self-defeating attempt to perform the border-lining pleasure-judgment that preconditions reality judgment and effective predication, by which the ambivalent would-be—or rather would-*not*-be—subject double-binds himself in the spell of his constitutive Moebius ring.

The dialectic of primary ambivalence is condensed not only in the metaphorical, round and split shapes of sin (the Urberus-snake, the garden, the apple, the moon, the poem), but also in the relationships between them, which ambiguate them also semantically—in a way that actualizes the transitive potential of the ambiguous "in-carnation" (*x* incarnates the spirit of *y* in its flesh, *y* is in the flesh of *x*). Like the relation between creative words and their speakers, and between subjects who devour their devouring mothers who devour them *en abyme*, the relationships between the concentric snake-garden-apple as well as that between the poem and the moon is at once metaphorical and reversibly synechdochical. Thus, the sexually ambiguous "bearded apple" is at once the containing maternal body and the circle's cradled baby, who looks just like his round and forked-tongued Mummy (and the Devil they *both* icon, whose metaphorical function credits him, of course, with certain *paternal* rights—but over whom?). The same applies to the relation between the speaking moon and the circular-serpentine poem, which "incarnates" the lunar subjectivity which it at once embodies and represents—by dint of the same filial resemblance to the horned and horney "beast" (the sexual element is suggested, in relation to the moon, by the connotation of solar-Jupiter's phallic "horn of plenty," demonized in "hell in a horn of sulphur"). Finally, an equal relation of mutual ambiguation marks the poem and the world (the speaking subject's imaginary object) which, once un-translated to its nameless, visceral origins, flees the inside of the poem's "empty form." The longed-for *reality* (effect) of the continental "*plains* of *Asia*" is eclipsed by the contrary, vertical, and vertiginous fascination with the oceanic, subterranean geography of the maternal body—which is *semiotically* out-lined by the poem's final gesture of emptying itself out, as it approaches the deadening closure of its shape: for the abject, like any speaking subject, lives (and dies and lives, etc.,) in the perpetual motion of setting and crossing the boundaries of his Moebius ring.

To Conclude (really this time)

By the stern purity of its negative judgment, the poem is an empty form because (it stings itself to the sense that) it signifies no other but itself—and the emptiness of its subject's narcissistic wound and its devouring maternal correlative. But this emptiness, if one looks closely enough into it, as the poem does, is inhabited by the fascinating horror of the psycho-somatically split subject's unintegrated body and its maternal correlative—which the poem fails to incorporate "symbolically" and is therefore "empty" and at the same time so obsessed by the redemptive idea of in-carnation. That (psycho-somatic) dissociative predicament and the "incarnation" as an artistic solution is suggestively manifested by the poet's characterization of himself as well as his poetry in terms of "animal" or "flesh" and "ghost," "blood and bubble,"[69] and by his corresponding professed thirst for "the blood of words."[70] Indeed, the abject's redemption of his sense of disembodiment or "ghostliness" is (thus Kristeva) in the erotization of the unassimilated content of his empty form: "urine ("bedwetting" [Thomas][71]), blood, sperm, ('seed'), excrement then show up . . . to reassure a subject that is lacking its . . . ('proper') 'self.'" (By taking the place of the other, eroticized abjection "spares [him] the risk of castration.")[72] The redeeming erotization of the empty poetic signifier is, precisely, the direct, *semiotic*, sematization of its materiality: the body of the "beast" and its discharge: the sacrificial blood of the aborted moon and the raging sulphur of the bowels of the earth—a "harebrained staging of an abortion, of a self-giving birth ever miscarried, endlessly to be renewed. . ."[73]

CHAPTER FOUR

Under the Sign of Loss, a Recuperation

THE DOUBLE DETERMINATION OF REPETITION

SIGNS OF LOSS, SYMBOLS OF NEGATION

What "Incarnate Devil" is "empty" of, ultimately, is the *nostalgic affect* which propels and animates the poetic text as a sign of loss. Poetic texts, like Benjamin's "translations," are set in motion by nostalgia for a lost Edenic Word—or its subjective correlative: a nostalgic plenitude that would heal the split and give being. But whereas some texts express this nostalgic desire by fulfilling it (or filling themselves with it), others deny it, out of a melancholic despair, or angry refusal, of the recuperative function of language and the imagination. The latter is the case of "Incarnate Devil," whose "sulphureous," energetic negation of the mythical as well as "our" (personal) "Eden" in the context of its expressed mistrust of its symbolic efficiency, betrays the "emptiness" of its obsessive deconstructive acrobatics to be a melancholic denial of its underlying nostalgic affect. It is a "revolt," as Freud characterizes Melancholia,[1] against the reality of loss by denying its object; a refusal, expressed by a symbol of affective negation, to mourn the lost object and thereby replace it by reality and its signs—of loss.

This chapter is about nostalgia and its pivotal function in the creative process as an elaboration of narcissistic loss. By distinguishing it from melancholia, I will explore the role of nostalgia in the temporal dimension of signification, that is, in the recuperative process of metaphorization which constitutes the "history" of the speaking subject and his substantiating sense of "being in time." As distinct responses to the archaic loss, nostalgia and melancholia relate differently to time. Both involve a repetition of the loss, but whereas the first dotes upon its object, the latter obsesses about its loss. While nostalgia bridges the rupture of loss by "remembering" the lost object in a recuperative, idealizing image of plenitude which it projects *upon* time, melancholia negates image and memory in its fixation on the subject's immemorial material prehistory. "Archeologically" speaking, nostalgia and melancholia relate, therefore, to psychic realities that pertain to *once upon a time* and *once below a time* on the axis projected by the liminal event of the subject's separation into being—of being, that is, under the *sign* of loss. Both repeating the loss and its sign, nostalgic and melancholic texts alike touch, as it were, the threshold of time, but their respective "border-linings" differ. The nostalgic text eroticizes loss and thereby sublimates its object (re-presenting its sign or foregrounding it against the background of loss), while melancholic texts banalize it, to the effect of negating the object (anaesthetizing its want, and wanting). In short, nostalgic texts involve a transformative repetition (as in the "orphic" boundary crossing in "Poem on his Birthday") which spans a history between the beginning and its representation, while melancholic texts indulge the negativity of loss through an obsessive-tautological repetition ("Incarnate Devil"), which suspends history on its threshold.

In this introductory section, I will distinguish between nostalgia and melancholia in the light of Freud and a few references from Thomas's melancholic poems, and engage the phenomenology of nostalgia at work in creative signification. These issues will be further developed in the second section, through a juxtaposition of Walter Benjamin's nostalgic "history" of signification ("translation") with Thomas's melancholic approach as it emerges from relevant aspects of "Incarnate Devil," and through a concluding discussion of a nostalgic manifesto which he presents in another poem in relation to the concerns of that haunted poem. The second and major section will be dedicated to two of Thomas's distinctly nostalgic childhood poems, "Fern Hill" and "Poem in October."[2] These poems project a nostalgic poetics that locates the phenomenology of nostalgia in the psychobiographical history of their subject, and foregrounds the creative manipulations that generate the sense of "being in time" in the "transitional" *chronotopoi* of childhood's projective fantasies and poetic texts alike. The analysis will draw on Winnicott's notions of the origin of creativity and, predominantly, on Bachelard's phenomenological approach to the relation between poetry and childhood in *The Poetics of Reverie*, and particularly in his chapter on "Reverie towards Childhood."[3]

Nostalgia and Melancholia

The role of nostalgia as the origin of desire and signification is suggested by Freud in "Inhibitions, Symptoms and Anxiety,"[4] where he refers to the infant's way of coping with its mother's absences. At this stage, the child "cannot as yet distinguish between temporary absence and permanent loss," and what saves him from despair in the face of his mother's absence is the psychic inscription of "repeated situations of satisfaction" in "an object created out of the mother"—a "mnemic image"[5] which he invests with an "intense cathexis which might be described as a '*longing*' one."[6] The inscription of this object is facilitated by the hope for the mother's return, which she encourages "by playing the familiar game of hiding her face from [the infant] with her hands and then, to its joy, uncovering it again"[7]—a game which the child will develop into the more sophisticated *fort-da* game ("Beyond the Pleasure Principle").[8] This latter game (of making objects disappear in order to find them again), which reenacts the loss in order to master it, subjects the compulsion to repeat to the service of the pleasure principle which, provided that there is enough real maternal encouragement to sustain and consolidate its psychic inscription and the hope for recuperation embodied in it, will in turn prove to serve the reality principle, that is, the transition to sign and object relations. The transition begins to take place already at this stage, thanks to the partial wish-fulfilling function of the imaginary object, which enables the child to tolerate deferred satisfaction by sustaining a desire that feeds, for a while, on its own representation. The *partial* recuperation availed by the nostalgic representation opens the *future* for its eternally deferred completion, in representations that will draw on its affective residue, namely, the basic trust and hope ensured by the integration of the maternal function.

The cognitive dynamics at work in nostalgic recuperation here as well as in poetic representation, as I understand it, is the optical illusion of the *trace*, that is, the cathected "mnemic image" which embodies the sense (or sensation) of the object. The mnemic trace confuses between presence and absence (object and representation, wish and fulfillment), but in fact draws its signifying power from the tension between them, which is, precisely, the tension of "longing" that constitutes the sign as a representation of both. This effect, whose phenomenology has been discussed in relation to defamiliarization, is the transformative effect of integration: the *inherently nostalgic* poetic sign is a condensation of *fort* and *da* which subjects the negativity of the first to the transformation that yields the second.

Nostalgic longing idealizes the lost object by projecting the negativity of the loss that ambiguates it onto the dimension of time (the time of mourning and aspiration). This is how the Edenic unity comes to be "re-membered" as such, that is, as a re-membered split. When trauma reactivates the splitting conflict, then "Eden" is dis-membered again, retroactively, to be replaced by the fantasy of abortion. The dis-membering of the fantasy of the original integrity is *melancholic forgetfulness*, which represses what happened between the first and "my second [traumatic] death," or dismisses its reality. Thus, writes Thomas, "I *dreamed* my genesis and died *again*," upon the breaking of Lacan's mirror, when death "muzzled" through the "hole / In the stitched wound" ("I Dreamed My Genesis").[9] Melancholia is a belated, traumatic reaction of denial to the tantalizing insufficiency of a plenitude that *was*—not enough. In the face of traumatic danger, says Freud, "longing turns into anxiety" which, I interpret, forgets the "mnemic image" of the lost object and thus reenacts its own archaic antecedent, the "primal anxiety of birth" that knew no object ("Inhibitions"):[10] "at birth no object existed and so *no object could be missed*."[11] The narcissistically deprived subject would rather have been born an orphan than have had a mother to long for in vain and face the danger of losing his own, dependent existence. "I dreamed my genesis and died," says the poet to de-realize the loss—and die together with his affect (and his object)—of his *own* accord.

This affective suicide, which yields to the compulsive wish which Freud attributes to any organism,[12] is repeated and somewhat illuminated in Thomas's ". . . Refusal to Mourn the Death, by Fire, of A Child in London"[13] (during the Blitz), whose subject suggestively asserts: "*After the first death, there is no other.*" The poem may be read, with David Holbrook, as "a manic denial of the reality of death"[14] which echoes (faintly?) the magic incantation in "And Death Shall Have No Dominion."[15] But the obverse side of this denial, as Holbrook shows the poem to manifest, is the denial of *life* by the affectively dissociated poet who, suffering from "an inability to mourn"[16] his *own* "first dead," can mourn "no other['s]." This inability is, ultimately, a defensive refusal. After the first death there *shall* be no other— or "other" to die on me again. Let there be only the first death, my death, says the desperately angry Narcissus facing the perturbed face of the water that can no longer reflect his image, and joins Orpheus in the pursuit of his object in the Dionysian deeps of oblivion. For as Freud explains in "Mourning and Melancholia,"[17] melancholia is a denial of the reality of loss by unconscious identification with its ambiguous object, which the subject thereby at once preserves and kills. This cannibalistic procedure turns back on its subject, whose object ends up eating him from inside. An inner object of "anticathexis" rather than conscious affective investment, it sucks up his emotional energies away from reality into the narcissistic "wound"[18] that it is (the site of "ego-loss" created by identification with "object-loss"[19]), to the effect of "emptying" him out.[20] By this evacuation, or depletion, the subject is de-subjectified, and becomes, as it were, the *object* of his dissociated affect. The unconscious introverted affect functions as an inner otherness that absorbs him, rather than him being the subject of an other-bound affect. As such, the melancholic subject may be sucked outside-in to the point of ultimate condensation: "the seed-at-zero" (Thomas),[21] or, alternatively, the "black hole" where all conflicts and differences are resolved.

Nostalgia opens the way toward subjectivity by cognizing the affect in an imaginary representation of it (the object of nostalgia is a *state*, not an object), which will be realized in sign- or object-relations. I have pointed out this *transitional*, binding function of nostalgia at work in "Poem on his Birthday," where the cathartic boundary crossing idealizes the "first death" in a vision of a future "Heaven" which, in turn, opens the way to its projection onto the present, external reality. The fantasy of "Heaven that never was" procures *something to miss*, whose loss in the end of the vision propels the desire to attain its substitute in the world. This momentum is missing in "Incarnate Devil," where, for want of an object to mourn, miss, and desire, the "orphic" boundary crossings become almost mechanical, thus banalizing the loss they represent and undermining the real-ization of a substitutive "world" (-representation). The subject that emerges from that poem is a proficient *fort-da* player, but one who knows it is only a game, because the ball is only a ball, "*not* my mother."[22]

The Double Determination of Repetition

"Incarnate Devil" sees itself collapse into tautology because, in its search for origins, it transgresses the boundary between meaning and matter once signified by the forbidden tree. By this transgression, it denies its *Symbolic origin*—and future, which make the *différance* that sustains its actuality as an act of repetition in time. For in the beginning there *must* be a "word"—a *sense* of plenitude that transposes matter into meaning and constitutes the origin and telos of desire and signification; an affect which transforms the impossible material / somatic object into a psychic possibility, and thereby constitutes at once the prompter and the product of the alchemy of nostalgia that turns lack into desire, want into wanting, the absence of what is no more nor yet into the presence of sense. By denying its Symbolic origin, the poem confronts itself with the negativity of meaningless matter which it (complains it) cannot signify but only reenact: God's *mute* waters and the Devil's dismembered body, unsublimated by an animating word, remain an abject corpse, an impossible object, an inaccessible referent—an "untranslatable" matter which the self-reflexive poem reincarnates. In other words, the negation of affect confronts the poem with the impossible, that is, with its self-inflicted impossibility—as a translation without an original.

By negating his symbolic origin, the speaker of "Incarnate Devil" denies himself a history, for in the beginning there must be, practically speaking, a "Word" in the "full" sense of the word: a re-presentation which is at once the originating signifier and the signified original (object) of the chain of translations that spin, time and again, the nostalgic history of the speaking subject. This is why Benjamin, who, it seems, was no less obsessed with origins than Thomas and presumably for the same melancholic reasons, left the apple alone when he set out to write his "history" of language. Familiar as any with its taste, he nevertheless stopped short, in his distinctly nostalgic works, before the boundary between meaning and matter: as Stéphane Moses points out, "it is only in appearance" that his early theological essays "deal with the [pre-historical, extra-Symbolic] origin of language; in reality they speak about the *language of the origin*."[23] The prepositional ambiguity of the underlined phrase suggests the alchemy of nostalgia at work in Benjamin's "history" (as I translate it) as a metahistory of all signification: the "language of the origin" is at once the essence of the original which subsequent translations seek to recapture, and an *achronic* property,[24] that is, an inherent functional "principle" of the language of translation which originates its signified by way of retrospective/projective idealization. Therefore, "if the question [of origin] is that of a genesis, of a beginning," Moses explains, "its concern is not a historical point of departure, but an ontological foundation that is projected back, in the manner of a myth, onto an immemorial past."[25] Indeed, Benjamin's Edenic language is a transformation of the immemorial "pre-historical" past into a mythical memory which provides a fictive point of departure for the history of language, as well as the utopian telos of its constitutive chain of recuperative translations, including Benjamin's own, which tells that history of origins. The motivating principle of this history (and its "history") is, then, a wishful remembrance (nostalgia) which follows "*the double determination of repetition*" (Moses)[26] of an idealized beginning that never was, as such: backwards towards a past that is in effect a future-bound projection. And one can say that, in the phenomenological sense, it is between the end terms of this double movement that every signifier (text, "translation") which activates it, spans its history—as a correlative of its performative actuality. But one can say this only provided that one avoids, in this "meta-history," the negativistic trap of the melancholic devil, who deems its origin to be a *mere* myth. For the "ontological foundation" of myths is not purely fictitious; and nostalgia, idealizing as it is, is based on the loss of—or dissociation from—something *real*, whose "achronic essence," though elusive and untranslatable, persists to animate translation in a "*nuclear*" form (Benjamin).[27] The grain of truth in the nostalgic myth is, then, nostalgia itself, or, as Benjamin formulates it, the "*intention*" of the text as "translation" that embodies its object—its "*intended effect*" in the nuclear form of a "seed of pure language."[28] And it is the task of the translator, as well as the poet, to judge by their respective words, to try and "ripen" this [mustard]-"*seed*" of beginnings into a [sun-] *flower.*[29]

Or a rose: the "loud" "crimson sun" which "roars at the prayer's end" in Thomas's "Vision and Prayer" rises through the "briared hands" that "hoist" the "fatherless," "the unborn and the undesirers [!]" to "the shrine of the world's [original] *wound*" idealized into "the blood drop's *garden*," which, in "There Was a Saviour,"[30] is "the drooping [. . . home] / That did not nurse our bones," but is a *future* origin, the eternal exile's as yet "*unentered* house." And here, as we "Ride through the doors of our unentered house," T. S. Eliot's "Footfalls echo in [our] memory / Down the passage which we did *not* take / Towards the door we never opened / Into the *rose-garden.*"[31] The words of this fine expert on nostalgia "echo / Thus, in [my] mind":[32] a mixture of memory and desire, nostalgia takes us back and forth into "our first world" (where the projected roses have "the look of flowers that are looked at"),[33] which beckons to us from the future of its re-pre-sentation: a presentation (making present), in the differential space of the re-petition of an infinitely deferred antecedence that yields, time and again, the actual "sentation" of the nostalgic affect. The condensation of the double determination of repetition in that "sentation" (sense as sensation) reproduces the "achronic" remedy to the *spatial* problem of intrapsychic "exile" (dissociation), as we see in the vaginal image of the opening of the rose in "There Was a Saviour," as well as in "the bud of the world," on another, more explicitly sexual and object-relating bush: "*Exiled in us* we arouse the soft, / Unclenched, armless, silk and rough love that breaks all rocks."[34]

❧

By negating his symbolic origin, the *speaker* of "Incarnate Devil" denies himself a history, because the beginning according to the Devil of melancholia is not a beginning, but a prehistory without a future: "to-morrow['s]" "cavernous" "blind cage"[35] self-reflected by a suicidal all-eyed Chronos (the hyperconscious poem), who chases his own tail to "[re]-bolt the dark" that precedes and supersedes time and sight. Indeed, for all its eyes, the devil of melancholia is blind and caged—in the prehistorical cave of his carefully forgotten object, or, more precisely, the cave of forgetfulness, where he hides the affect that would signify it away from the eyes of time and men. This resolves the paradox incarnated by its archetypal form (of self-negation), which is really no paradox at all, but incarnate blindness. For the denial of the nostalgic affect is no less of a "misrecognition" ("méconnaissance," Lacan) of the archaic loss than the nostalgic re-presentation of its object, and is, in effect, a more radical one, because whereas nostalgia, by re-presenting its object by way of its substitution, in a way also acknowledges and represents its loss, melancholia, by denying its object (a representation), denies the reality of its loss, which it reenacts instead of representing. Eden never was, for those who fail to remember it, an activity which requires some amorous imagination without which, however, there is also nothing to forget, not even the impossibility of Eden that propels the history of our remembering and forgetting.

Thomas acknowledges the sense that not remembering is murder, indeed, a dis-membering, which he depicts as such in "To-Day, This Insect."[36] The poem is an illuminating commentary on "Incarnate Devil," perhaps an intended one, given the fact that Thomas chose to place it in the following page of his *Collected Poems*.[37] In this strange process poem, the devil's tale is literalized, indeed concretized in an act of murder and dissection which foregrounds the aggressive aspect of narcissism that destroys image and identity, and even the very category of the human. The dissected body in the poem is that of "this insect"—some real worm or other "crocodile before the chrysalis" which, as Moynihan suggests, had the bad luck of straying across the sheet on which Thomas was writing.[38] This insect serves as a scapegoat as well as a source of inspiration for the poet's fable on the "plague of fables" (dissociated texts) and their contaminating origin in the murderous/suicidal forgetting of "Eden." The insect symbolizes both the subject and the object of the autoerotic melancholic ordeal, which is foregrounded by the syntax of the synchronic report and interpretation of its murder in the first stanza. "This insect, and the world I breathe" are gradually "outel-bowed" to death by the poet's actual pen and the "symbols" which it jots down. "To-day, *this* insect, [. . . this *instance*?] and the world *I breathe* / [into life . . . during the] [t]ime . . ./ I take to nudge the sentence,/. . . *have I* [already] *divided* sense, / [and, by the same gesture, have] *Slapped* down the guillotine, [of my pen on the by now breathless] blood-red double / Of head and tail [,which I have thereby] made witness to *this / Murder of Eden and the green genesis.*" Then the victim and witness of the aborted genesis becomes the aggressor: "The insect certain is the plague of fables." "This story's monster" is both the baby with its "caul"—choked "[b]lind in the coil" of that "*serpent* caul"?—and the serpent itself who, coiled up "head [to] tail" like the "circle" and like the other, pyromaniac "fiddler" (Nero), "scrams round the *blazing outline*" of the garden by "measur[ing] his own length on [its] wall" and thus creating it—as a distorting, incredible tale (a "children's piece / Uncredited") which turns Eden into burning Jericho ("blows Jericho on Eden"). In the course of the telling/killing, the serpent itself dies, as it "*scrams* round" its object ("scram: to be *paralyzed*; to be benumbed . . . Also transf. of a *wheel*" [*OED*]). But in this poem the sacrifice does bear its cathartic fruits, perhaps because "the blood of words" is so literal . . . and aggression is returned from the ego back to an external, sacrificial insect: the "serpent caul" of the scapegoat is also the sacrificial baby's saintly halo ("when a portion of [the caul] is found on a child's head [it is] a good omen . . ." [*OED*])—which belongs with the poet's matching "*cross* of tales" and "*tree* of stories," and so "[t]he insect fable is the certain promise." The promise is the "tale-tell lover['s] . . . end" "behind the fabulous curtain" of "the fibs of vision" and fiction, where the cross of tales conjures the "ageless voice" from "[*b*]*efore the fall from love*" into the monster's story. The moral of that story is: don't believe a crocodile when he tells you that he was "winged" "before the chrysalis"—a chronological confusion in the history of the butter-"flying heartbone" which can only make sense by the circular temporality of a "*blind*" "*serpent . . . / in* [its] *coil*."

THE PRINCEDOM OF THE APPLE TOWNS

The Truth of an Illusion

Thomas's works about childhood and adolesence thematize the dynamics of nostalgia in the creative process in its "historical" context. They acknowledge their nature as recuperative elaborations of the loss of childhood's narcissistic state of contained, creative well-being, as well as of the archaic unity for which infantile narcissism compensates. As it emerges from the double perspective of the child and the adult in these works, the intimate "parented" world projected by the child's omnipotent imagination is in itself nostalgic. Displacing the space of an original integrity (Winnicott's early "maternal environment,"[39] Jung's *nostalgic/*potential "primordial unity,"[40] *not* the melancholic object of Freud's repetition compulsion), the "transitional space" of childhood, and specifically of the "solitary reverie" which, according to Bachelard, helps the (maladjustive) child to "inhabit the world,"[41] is a kind of a second mirror (in Lacan's sense) which heals the rupture of the first and represses the anxiety of its consequent sense of powerlessness. This is reflected in the metaphorical structure of Thomas's poems, "Fern Hill" and "Poem in October," and of his short story, "A Prospect of the Sea," which spin their respective narratives—of journeys through memory—through a series of variations of a genesis fantasy. By acknowledging their serial nostalgia, these works at once re-create and contextualize themselves as links in the chain of mirrors, or series of losses and nostalgic recuperations which constitutes their subject's (mnemonic-metaphorical) history.

This "historical" insight is deepened in Thomas's depiction of the crisis of adolescence (which is discussed in more detail in chapter 5, in the analysis of "A Prospect of the Sea"), where its experience emerges, in conformity with Freud's retroactive notion of melancholia as set off by narcissistic loss, as a traumatic repetition of the archaic separation. The loss of childhood's narcissistic relational mode, or the breaking of its recuperative "mirror," involves, for Thomas's adolescent persona, an intense experience of the preoedipal conflicts and anxieties underlying the returning repressed sexuality. "A Prospect of the Sea" literally anatomizes that crucial event in Thomas's history, and elucidates its implications for his life and poetic career. Tracing its details "from history to the thigh,"[42] the story shows how the ambiguous "prospect" of that latter site, which "returns" to accompany an adolescent sexual fantasy, triggered by the appearance of a dangerous country girl, confronts the autobiographical protagonist with the liminal intersection between psychotic regression to the melancholic sea "below time" and its poetic sublimation to a nostalgic "once upon a time . . . ," the site of its metaphorical "Prospect." Significantly, the end of the story, where the autobiographical narrator emerges, after the death of the girl, as an old man recollecting his life experiences in an organized metaphorical pattern, provokes the conjecture that the way of sublimation allows, for him, an integration of the conflicts activated in puberty not in adult love, but only in nostalgic story-telling. This conjecture aligns with the sense shared by many, that the crisis of adolescence which constitutes the point of departure for Thomas's adolescence and childhood poems is in effect the fixational point of departure for his notably narcissistic work as a whole. Indeed, his work, as I have been suggesting all along, displays an attempt to ward off the always lurking melancholia of a disenchanted adolescent, who cannot renounce the narcissistic mode of relating to the world, and yet suffers the painful consciousness of the insubstantiality of fantasy and of a consequent libidinal depletion. His poetry is an attempt to restore the intensity of experience by re-substantiating fantasy; to reproduce a lost vitality which, for him, is irrevocable other than within the bounds of what resembles its natural, infantile-narcissistic habitat, that is, the intimate, because omnipotently controlled, projective space of the text.

But the syndrome, so evident in Thomas's writing, of the eternal youth in exile from some nostalgic princedom, marks, I believe, an aspect of the creative process in general, even if in a manner less desparately acute and often hardly traceable. What I wish to dwell on (or in) in this chapter, however, is not the suffering narcissism of dethroned princes, but their lost and recaptured princedom itself, where, under the aegis of the benevolent "irreality function" (Bachelard),[43] creativity procures for itself its originating maternal habitat. That site is the protoypical site of the *benign* narcissism which, as a positive relational disposition, fosters creativity as subjectivity *in potentia*. Within the "autistic" bounds of the Imaginary, the specular world lends itself to a *real* internal relatedness and a *real* potency which constitute, as such, a nucleus of subjectivity that is *beyond* narcissism. Its productive habitat is in what is felt to be its subject's *uninflated* experience of his manipulative relation to the world—a relation of dialogical (playful) intimacy and spontaneous trust (and even gratitude for the world's graciouly generous submission to one's projective manipulations, as in "Fern Hill") which, *within* its controlling, narcissistic limits, affirms rather than negates the world's otherness. The reality of "potential subjectivity" is testified by the sense of integrity and hence also the communicative power of poetic expression which are the mark of Thomas's childhood poems. Indeed, the engaging directness and the rich simplicity of expression in these poems are the effects of a creative force that is grounded in a subjectifying reality which transcends its originating idiosyncratic habitat. In these poems one is with Thomas, not inside him (for a change). Instead of being employed in the effort of putting him (and oneself) together, as one is in the process of sorting out his difficult, conflict-tormented poems, one receives the gift of an easy, out-going communication. These poems (my favorites, as you may have guessed) let the *reader* "be"—in their generously shared "transitional space," whose sharability derives, to a considerable extent, from the positive intimate relations that established the imaginary space of their nostalgic object. Here lies, I feel, the truth of the Romantic illusion of "intersubjectivity," whose significance is often wrongly dismissed by its deprecating qualification as "the pathetic fallacy."[44] For Thomas, Winnicott, and Bachelard, the prototypical habitat of the productive, benign narcissism is the creative experience of reality in childhood's containing "potential space" or "solitary reverie" (respectively), where the world, assuming the projection of a positive maternal image, adjusts itself to one's needs for placement and playing by the simple virtue of the "magic omnipotence" of these needs. For Winnicott, that virtue is indeed a virtue, and an effective one in terms of its "transitional" function, if it is fostered by the reassuring (immediate-mnemic) presence of the "good enough mother" who made it possible in the first place.[45] The mother (or a substitute), being in tune with the separating child's adjustment needs, provides a "holding" environment for the child's imaginative negotiation with reality. When the security of her presence is missing, the imaginative space bears the anxious strain of "holding" or mothering itself, and its autonomy is the dissociative mark of fantasy or daydream (and, in the extreme, of psychotic hallucination). Bachelard's "reverie," as well as the imaginative spaces of Thomas's childhood poems, are somewhere in between these options. Though the child's experience in "Poem in October" is that of "[f]orgotten mornings when he walked with his mother," "Fern Hill," which relates its subject's childhood experience from within and in more detail, presents an *autarchic* "transitional space," in which the world, and mainly—interestingly enough—time, is subjected to the child's mothering needs. And though the notion of time and loss is present in that autonomous fantasy world, its feeling is by no means one of anxiety or manic strain. In this respect, its experience corresponds to Bachelard's notion of *self*-mothered, peaceful reverie (reverie of repose),[46] in which the maternal function is autonomous (and constitutional: for Bachelard it is the Jungian "anima"). By distinction from the nocturnal or day-dream, Bachelard's "reverie" is a conflict-free "feminine" mode of imaginative being, which, like fantasy, is sustained as such *despite* a possible context of narcissistic deprivation. Such a context is indeed implied by his association of childhood "reverie" with the mythologem of the "divine child," whom Dylan, the sea-son of Welsh mythology, impersonates in many respects.[47] This mythologem, says Bachelard (paraphrasing Kerényi),[48] "expresses . . . 'the solitary state of the essentially orphaned child but who, in spite of everything, is at home in the original world and loved by the gods.' "[49] Abandoned in his cradle and carried away from the society of men (or, alternatively, aborted), he "[adheres] to the *original cosmos*" where "the world takes care" of him. "The child god is [thus the] son of the world."[50] But Bachelard is not interested in the suffering during and due to "badly spent childhoods," nor in the question of their pathology, which he "leave[s] to psychoanalysis" (to cure).[51] His concern is, rather, with the phenomenology of the "*Other-Childhood*"[52] experienced in the "happy solitudes" of self-mothered reverie, which is the specific object of his, as well as my, proposed "poetico-analysis."[53] By confining itself to a discussion of the nostalgic experience as it were from within, such an approach focuses on the immanent psychological value of its object—"the truth of illusions"[54] which exceeds the defensive or adjustive functions of transitional spaces—as well as childhood itself. Bachelard qualifies it by his suggestive statement that "reverie [is] not simply a reverie of escape. It [is] a reverie of *flight*";[55] a flight *to*, not (only) from, being. "Reverie gave us freedom," he says, and when "we idealize the worlds in which we were solitary children" in order to "reach the memories of our [liberating] solitudes,"[56] we regain that very freedom—the freedom, at least, to recreate our origins, as I am about to do now with Bachelard, Thomas, and a great deal of nostalgia.

Reverie on Bachelard's *Poetics of Reverie* Towards Childhood

The nostalgic recreation of childhood is, for Bachelard and Thomas alike, the poet's way of connecting with the source of his creativity. What the poet of "Fern Hill" and "Poem in October" as well as Bachelard in reverie on poetic reverie are after, is some kind of *nostalgic integrity* where their creativity lies—at peace with the maternal. From a Freudian perspective, that "peace with the maternal" is bound up with the *guiltless* incest which marks the "maternal" containment in the undifferentiated spaces of narcissistic fantasies, which accommodate the subject's imaginary integrity by repressing the "oedipal" conflict that divides him. In this light, the "peace" is in effect with both parental functions, and as such it may also be seen, from the perspectives of Winnicott and Bachelard after Jung, as the integration of the feminine and the masculine elements of the personality. This integration, which I will discuss in this section, is experienced as being in time, that is, contained in (or through) motion within an imaginary world in the temporal course of its creation. Combining the maternal-spatial conditions for "being" and the paternal-temporal ones for creative becoming through "doing" (Winnicott),[57] the projected world of childhood's reverie/"transitional space" thus realizes the (nostalgic fantasy of) subjective integrity which it represents. The synthesis of the different perspectives will be substantiated in the course of the rest of this chapter.

For the poet, this nostalgic creative integrity is "the truth of [the] joy" of the "long dead child" which he restores as his "sung" "heart's truth" in his birthday–"Poem in October," and in the "morning song" of the child of Fernhill reverberated in "Fern Hill." For the phenomenologist of "poetic reverie" it is the (same) "permanent "nucleus of childhood" within us"[58] (another seed, yes), which is the nostalgic object and engrained essence of "poetic reverie" as well as of "childhood reverie." "What draws us towards the reveries of childhood," says Bachelard, "is a sort of *nostalgia of nostalgia*," a "redoubled nostalgia,"[59] whose nuclear object, in distinction from the suicidal "object" of melancholia, is an "*antecedence of being*" that bears the *futurity* of a subject "in-potentia."[60] The futurity embodied in the "pure memory" of that antecedence is the abstract sense of "possibilities" generated by the "that double force of the mind which remembers and the soul which feasts upon its own *faithfulness*."[61] It is generated, in other words, by the double determination of "the union of imagination and memory" at play in the alchemy of nostalgia.[62] "Hypnotized by the faraway," the "mnemonics of the imagination," as Bachelard defines the reverie in and toward childhood, feeds on its own creative re-sources—by re-creating its sources. Reverie "looks to go *back up* ["upstream"] to the springs (*sources*) of being," thus re-cognizing its subject in his "endlessly striving to be born" by remembering and creating his nostalgic origins: "poets look for this antecedence of being; therefore it exists"[63]—and vice versa! (nostalgia is not Cartesian). The nostalgic "origin" of "reverie" of and toward childhood is, then, the beginning in the proper, generative sense of coming into "being in time," which sets in motion the chain of nostalgic significations.

The meaning of the notion of "being in time" is elucidated by Bachelard, who underlines, precisely, "the *detemporalization* of the states of great reverie."[64] In these states, as he views them, the feminine (or the maternal) encroaches upon the temporal as well as spatial differences that define subjective being. For the purpose of a phenomenologial discussion that is faithful to the "feminine" feeling texture of reverie, he postulates a specifically pertinent "*penumbral ontology*"[65] which softens the blinding, paternal-sun-lit, subject/object and being/non-being categories. The nostalgic enchantment of reverie ("hypnotized by the faraway") places its subject in a state of "sub-being" ("*moins-être*") in a temporal "limbo" in which he "is trying itself out as being."[66] Now is not the imaginative "trying out," on the part of the inhabitant of that "limbo," to connect to some imaginary nostalgic "self," the very being in time of our "subject in process"/"on trial" ("*en procès*": Kristeva[67])? But this may be no more than a semantic argument. What does seem significant to me is precisely the *complicity* that emerges from Bachelard's discourse (as well as from Thomas's texts), between the spatial-feminine and the temporal at play in childhood "reverie" and its poetic reproduction. It is precisely in the temporal "tension of childhood reveries"[68] that the nostalgia takes its "feminine" place of softened boundaries—the space which embodies its constitutive "nucleus."

"Being," for Winnicott (I remind), is associated with the female aspect of the personality (a maternal environment internalized), which is experienced in states of "low instinctual tension," and which provides the "ground" for the "male doing" of effective creativity. The latter he distinguishes "not so much by the originality as . . . by the individual's sense of the *reality* of the experience,"[69] which is generated by the harmonious balance between "doing" and "being." This seems to apply to the experience of childhood "reverie," where the child inhabits the world while creating it as if it were already there, granted from outside (by virtue of magic omnipotence), thus enjoying the joint-parental grace of "being in time" (but without knowing that one is nostalgic). That "grace," as I have suggested in the previous chapter, is also generated by effectively mimetic poetry, but there the nostalgic tension is felt, because the limitations of the adult's imagination are reflected in the conflict-ridden effort of the poetic "doing" to establish "being" by coming to terms with the less graceful maternal. Thus "being" is felt—vaguely or in dis-gracing blatancy—to be the synthetic product of the dialectic "doing" that it is, which accounts for the nostalgic hauntedness of the poetic text. The perceptual "trick" underlying this simultaneity (by causal inversion) is the seeming annihilation of *différance* (deferral and difference) by the seemingly immediate gratification of the desire projected onto the yielding spatial environment—only seemingly, though, as it is that very *différance* which ensures the imaginative or *metaphorical* investment. This spatialization of time is the "detemporalization" which marks the states of reverie and poetry alike and, for that matter, any state of intense imaginative investment.

"Time allows" this manipulation (of it) "by the [particular] mercy of his means" during childhood (in "Fern Hill"), when "time let[s one both] play (=do) and be" at the same time. Or in other words, time submits itself to the child's particular means during the latency period, in which a "low instinctual tension" (Winnicott) permits him to "be" in a world which he plays into parenting him—by transferring to it the mother's "mirroring" function (Winnicott).[70] In the projective "maternal" space of the world's empathic gaze (even the paternal sun, in "Fern Hill," has that feminine look in its eye), one is whole. Incorporating the joint parental functions—of creative perception (playful "doing") and its projected percept ("being" and its space)—the wholeness yielded by the mirror is a self-created, self-sufficient *androgynous integrity* which manifests the (wishful-filled) peace with the maternal. To put it differently, when prince Oedipus is asleep to the differences that make his mother conflictual—that will fork out his apple-shaped world (created in his green and golden image) into "Adam and maiden" ("Fern Hill")—time lets him play himself into being at once "*green*" and "*golden*": a futured potential and its dying realization, desire and its realization, the beginning and the end that generates a new beginning, child and mother, Oedipus's wishes all satisfied, safely . . . This happy state of affairs is enjoyed by the mythological, *sui generis* "primordial child," the archetype of creativity as synthetic origination and "the one and only true *filius ante patrem* whose life, seen in retrospect, first produced the checkered history of his origins" (Kerényi).[71] Psychoanalyzed by Jung, that would-be Rex is the "hermaphrodite" "symbol of the creative union of opposites"[72] anticipating the consummation of the individuation process in the integration of the female and male aspects of the personality, which constitutes the "entelechy" of a primordial, potential unity.[73] Such "entelechy" takes place in Bachelard's reverie as a synthetic origin of consciousness which, like Benjamin's "translation" in relation to his "seed" of "pure language," embodies its "nucleus" of "pure memory" as at once its nostalgic object (contained memory) and its animating essence (realizing quality). Thus, "reverie," according to Bachelard's essentially Jungian reverie, is an origin in the dual, androgynous sense of "germ" (masculine-filial/paternal sprouting/founding) and "ground" (feminine-maternal). Or in other (Thomas's and my) words, it is a creative potential in a "mustardseed," a metaphorical impulse engrained in nostalgia, the "heart's truth"-full wish come true—or wishful truth come wished . . . ? Phenomenologically, *inside* poetic reverie, they are one and the same thing.

Thomas's Childhood Reveries

Both "Poem in October" and "Fern Hill" acknowledge their "redoubled" nostalgic movements "upstream" toward their source, which determine their temporal as well as metaphorical structures. As in "Poem on his Birthday," the narrative movement in both poems follows the rising of the meta-metaphorical sun, which embodies the nostalgic destination of both the reminiscing poet and the recalled child, or more precisely, of their respective "morning song[s]." This destination, the primordial *chronotopos* of their nostalgic creative integrity, is attained along the way ("[a]ll the sun *long*," in "Fern Hill") in a series of analogous metaphorical spaces which are projected in the symbolic light of the sun, and which *thereby* give it its meaning as the metaphor of all metaphors.[74] These spaces are the sites of childhood's projective world and its imitations in the poetic images, which recreate that world in the nostalgic *chronotopos* of the poem.

While presenting the same elements involved in the creative and perceptual mechanisms at work in nostalgic reverie in and toward childhood, the two poems differ in focus. "Poem in October" concentrates mainly on thematizing the recuperative movement of "poetic reverie" toward childhood (and back), whereas "Fern Hill" is concerned more with the phenomenology of childhood's reverie and its creative strategies, which it shows to be its analogous origin. The poet "In October" sets out on a journey from the "rainy autumn"-al morning of his thirtieth birthday back through the years, in order to connect with the origin of his creativity in childhood's ever-shining "summer noon"-sun. The latter being made to shine in his nostalgically inspired poem, ensures its triumph over the birthday-melancholic prospect of death and loss in the rainy "town below," which is "*leaved* with October blood," that is, with the torn pages of the calendar and the poet's counted bygone birthdays (his thirty "year[s] to heaven," each beginning in October 27. The leaves assume the same symbolic function in a similar nostalgic context in "A Winter's Tale,"[75] where "the long ago she bird," the muse, "rises" back from "the long ago land" in the "*Calligraphy of the old / Leaves*").

The poet of "Fern Hill" begins his journey through memory where the "October" poet ends his, that is, "*now*," in which I am "*as I was* young," and yet not quite. "As," by its dual sense of *like* and *when*, designates the nostalgic tension between recuperation and the longing that triggers and sustains its desirous occurrence. This tension is sustained throughout the narrative journey by the simultaneity of the child's and the adult poet's respective—internal and reflexive—points of view. The double perspective conveys, however, not only the difference, but also the essential similarity between the child's perception and the poet's, whose metaphorical strategies for representing the world of childhood seem to imitate the child's projective strategies for creating it in the first place. It is by the grace of such imitation, too, that "Fern Hill" restores childhood's Fernhill, while laying bare its constitutive origin in the metaphorical play of projection and identification.

"Over the Past Table I Repeat this Present Grace" ("Because the Pleasure-bird whistles")[76]

FERN HILL

Now as I was young and easy under the apple boughs
About the lilting house and happy as the grass was green,
The night above the dingle starry,
Time let me hail and climb
Golden in the heydays of his eyes,
And honoured among wagons I was prince of the apple towns
And once below a time I lordly had the trees and leaves
Trail with daisies and barley
Down the rivers of the windfall light.

And as I was green and carefree, famous among the barns
About the happy yard and singing as the farm was home,
In the sun that is young once only,
Time let me play and be
Golden in the mercy of his means,
And green and golden I was huntsman and herdsman, the calves
Sang to my horn, the foxes on the hills barked clear and cold,
And the sabbath rang slowly
In the pebbles of the holy streams.

All the sun long it was running, it was lovely, the hay
Fields high as the house, the tunes from the chimneys, it was air
And playing, lovely and watery
And fire green as grass.
And nightly under the simple stars
As I rode to sleep the owls were bearing the farm away,
All the moon long I heard, blessed among stables, the nightjars
Flying with the ricks, and the horses
Flashing into the dark.

And then to awake, and the farm, like a wanderer white
With the dew, come back, the cock on his shoulder: it was all

Shining, it was Adam and maiden,
The sky gathered again
And the sun grew round that very day.
So it must have been after the birth of the simple light
In the first, spinning place, the spellbound horses walking warm
Out of the whinnying green stable
On to the fields of praise.

And honoured among foxes and pheasants by the gay house
Under the new made clouds and happy as the heart was long,
In the sun born over and over,
I ran my heedless ways,
My wishes raced through the house high hay
And nothing I cared, at my sky blue trades, that time allows
In all his tuneful turning so few and such morning songs
Before the children green and golden
Follow him out of grace,

Nothing I cared, in the lamb white days, that time would take me
Up to the swallow thronged loft by the shadow of my hand,
In the moon that is always rising,
Nor that riding to sleep
I should hear him fly with the high fields
And wake to the farm forever fled from the childless land.
Oh as I was young and easy in the mercy of his means,
Time held me green and dying
Though I sang in my chains like the sea.

The course of the nostalgic reminiscence in the performative "now" of "Fern Hill" moves under the signs of the apple and the sun, whose metaphorical transformations mark the time of the poem's recounted narrative. That narrative moves from the rise of childhood's "green and golden" "prince[dom] of the apple towns" "[i]n the sun that is young once only," through the space/course of the Sun-day ("the sabbath") that symbolizes its leisurely *chronotopos*, toward the ripening of the green apple-prince who becomes "golden" in the analogous sun "[grown] round" like the apple that drove "Adam and maiden" "out of [childhood's] grace." The fall of the "golden apple," the "orb of the regalia" (and an imitation of the British one [*OED*]), is anticipated from the beginning by the temporal nature of its space, which is also the condition for its foundation: the Sun-day begins "once *below* a *time*" that is also represented by the night sky "*above* the dingle starry," the site of its genesis. The "sabbath" that "*rang* slowly" is the acoustic space of a bell which "*dingle[s]*" to announce its flow "[d]own the rivers of the windfall light," through its "holy streams" toward the night of its end. That night (in stanza 3) anticipates the acceleration of the movement of the sun and its less holy days toward the night in which the poem is written (in stanza 6): after the Sunday, which stretches over the first three stanzas, "the sun [is] born over and over" to advance the narrative all the way forward to "now," where, in its reflection "in the moon that is always rising," the golden apple is being reflected (upon) in "the shadow of [the poet's writing] hand."

The poet's reflections on childhood are concerned mainly with time, and particularly with the changes in its experience in the course of his recorded life until "now." From his "*golden*," mature perspective, time means loss and depletion, and therefore the course of life from its very beginning is one continuous fall. From the "lamb *white*" innocent perspective of the "*green*" child, by contrast, time is not a sequence of losses and regrets, but a benevolent time of promises and possibilities, and of anticipation towards their "*golden*" realization ("when I grow up"). The double perspective of the child and the poet is made explicit at the end of the poem, where "golden," which represents the child's growing in expectation toward ripening, is displaced by "dying": "Oh as I was young and easy in the mercy of [*hiding*] his means, / Time held me green and dying / Though I sang in my chains like the sea." The child's "lamb white" innocence is, then, his ignorance of the fact that golden is dying. But this innocence is the effect of an ingenious manipulation whereby he transforms time's destructive nature and subjects it to the service of his recuperative, symbolic purposes—a manipulation which the poet will imitate in order to regain that very innocence. Indeed, the latter's poetic performance manifests such regained innocence, despite its disillusioned conclusion: the recuperation of childhood in the poetic reverie toward it is a testimony for the mercy of time's means—or for those of the poet who, forever green and dying, continues to sing in his chains.

The double temporal perspective is reflected in the ambiguity of the images in stanzas 1–3, and particularly in two kinesthetic metaphors in the opening stanza, which also concretize—indeed analyze—the way in which the child subjects time to his playful means of creating for himself a place to be *in* it. "*Time let me hail and climb / Golden in the heydays of his eyes*" is about the child climbing the sun's (eye-) beams—which represent the temporal course of his climbing or growth—toward their projective source, which will "grow round" in the course of the (hey-) *days* to reflect the *heyday* of his youth. The image is, then, a metaphorical synopsis of the narrative of the boy's progression towards "that very [hey-] day" on which the "horses" of his desire will step out of the "green stable" into the golden "fields of praise" and further "out of [childhood's] grace." But the sunbeams are also "*eye-beams*,"[77] that is, a metaphor for the projective gaze which constitutes the desired sun as a mirror of its source—in the child's eyes. The child will come to know this once he reaches the desired site in stanza 4, to attain the insight that will bring about his fall in the following stanza (5). Looking into his own eyes, he will realize that the futured object of his desire is no other than a *nostalgic* fantasy of his genesis, which returns from the repressed to reveal the metaphoricity of the golden fields which it sustains: "*So it must have been after the birth of the simple light / In the first, spinning place.*" But the object of the child's nostalgic desire is restored already *on the way* toward its attainment, *within* the projective/desiring gaze: the boy climbs "in" the golden heydays toward which he is heading, and he is already made "golden" just by looking at them—or looking forward to being in them. The "heydays" is thus a condensation of time and space that reflects the simultaneity of wish and fulfillment in the projective gaze. By displacing the temporal difference that sustains desire onto the spatial field of its wish-fulfilling projection, the gaze turns Fernhill into a "golden" princedom: the golden "*hey*-days" anticipate not only the "hay" of the future "high fields" "of praise" (stanzas 6 and 4)—"the hay / Fields high as the house" (stanza 3)—but also the hay of the "barns" and the "green stables"—the "house high hay" (stanza 4) in the "farm [that] was home" (stanza 2). Thus, the princedom of the apple towns is a mirror of the futured mirror of the nostalgic gaze which sustains them both. The golden hay/eye-beams are the light-time which make the metonymical difference that sustains the metaphor of Fernhill. The negative temporal aspect of this difference is perceived by the poet, for the hay is also a dry stalk (the "*ricks*" with which the nightjars fly when they bear away the farm in the end of stanza 3); in contrast with the green grass, it stands for the course of time down which the boy is falling.

The child's faith in time (and ultimately in himself) is the source of his creativity, which consists, I recapitulate, in projecting his future-bound desire onto the space of the present environment of Fernhill. In this way, he manipulates time into letting him be both green and golden—but without dying—in a *live metaphor* which condenses desire and its deferred (and "lethal") satisfaction within its present, projective space. Or in other words, by projecting the promises of the future onto his present environment, the child at once fulfills his golden wishes and defers his dying. The simultaneous productivity of the metaphorical gaze, or act (of climbing and sunbathing) is concretized more vividly in the following configuration of its time in "*the rivers of the windfall light.*" Now, from the poet's perspective, the image represents time's destructive movement: "windfall" connotes the premature fall of the green and dying apple, who "trail[s] down" (rather than climbs) together with its sustaining environment ("the trees and leaves") down the rivers of *time*—which is what they will eventually turn out to be, when they recur as the "holy *streams*" which carry the time-toll of the ringing "*sabbath.*" Their eventual accumulated momentum will mark the Sunday's "running" (out) to its end in the night of the third stanza, which bears the farm away temporarily, to foreshadow the nocturnal reality of "the farm *forever* fled from the childless land" in the last stanza. From the child's perspective, however, the "windfall light" is the grace of "unexpected good fortune or legacy" (*OED*) bestowed upon him by the "holy," luminous rivers of time, who answers his wishes without delay, by the magic virtue of his omnipotent imaginative means. Indeed, the good fortune that befalls the child is no less than the royal legacy of the paternal sun, who bequeathes (lends, really) his omnipotent rule to the heir *apparent* in a bright coronation ceremony: trailing down the rivers of sun-light, the "trees and leaves . . . daisies and barley" wreath ("*trail*") the oedipal crown for the "prince of the apple towns" who, in the following stanza, will become the "golden" ruler of Fernhill. The coronation has been anticipated by his climbing up the solar eye-beams toward the attainment of their projective source at *the radial center of the orbit*—which the paternal orb has only been waiting to bequeath to the darling apple of his eye.

The heir-apparent manipulates the majestic parent's means in the second stanza in order to make the farm his "lordly" "home." Thus, with the help of the poet who imitates him, the boy usurps him of his "green" and "golden" metaphors and uses them for designing the costumes for the imaginative games he stage-sets for generating himself as anything he likes—in the space of a yielding time: "And green and golden I was huntsman and herdsman" by the mere gesture of blowing his omnipotent horn, to which the calves and the foxes sang and barked without delay. The dialogue between the boy and the animals who answer or *echo* his wishful horn creates the princedom as an acoustic space which is the analogue of the projective-reflective space of the mirror. This space for "being," or the need of it, is projected onto the maternal figure of time in its configuration as a tree and a bell, which also represent the child's temporal "doing": "once *below* a time," "*under*" time's sheltering "apple boughs" (which the boy "climb[s]"), there is a vibrant "dingle" or a "*lilting* house," whose acoustic space is expanded in the following stanzas by the "clear and cold" bell-like barking of the foxes, "the *tunes* from the chimneys," etc., to amplify the child's "*hey*!"-*hailed* "morning *song*." Thus, as in "Poem on his Birthday," time is as it were spatialized by being filled with inhabitable sound, a dynamics which identifies its moving rivers with their goal, the sea in the poem's final, enigmatic line: "I sang in my chains like the sea."

The cock in stanza 4 announces the day on which the boy must look time straight in its round eye and renounce the oedipal bliss of its inheritance. That in-sight brings about his fall, because once the gaze reaches its end (in the two senses of the word), the mirror which it has sustained breaks, and the boy finds himself looking through it into its projective source and sees its underlying reality of loss and longing. At this point (or right after it), the child's and the poet's perspectives unite, and the narrative movement turns out to be a dramatization of "redoubled nostalgia" toward their shared "antecedence of being." The climbing/falling that has led to it turns out to have represented not only their different perspectives, but also the double determination of the child's nostalgia—toward recapturing the past in the future. The object of the child's and the poet's redoubled nostalgia is their common creative origin in time, the Edenic earth "*after* the birth of the first . . . light" *in the apple of the eye*. It is, in other words, the origin of their creativity in the (maternal) mirror and the (paternal) gaze projected by the child's chronotopical live metaphor as well as its poetic representation in (the bisexual parental metaphor of) a redemptive time. Both generative functions—of feminine "being" and masculine "doing"—and their simultaneous, mutual causality are configured in the metaphor of origins: the "spinning place" of origination is a place originated by motion (of the gaze in time) to accommodate and originate its originator, the spinner of metaphors.

The phenomenology of these creative dynamics is further clarified in the poet's reflections on his relation to time in childhood after the depiction of its loss: "And nothing I cared, at my sky blue trades, that time allows / In all his *tuneful turning* so few and such morning songs / Before the children green and golden / Follow him out of grace." Nothing he cared because time maternally tuned into his childish needs for a space to play and be—by tuning up with his "morning song," that is, by the sun's (or the earth's) "turning" (or "spinning") *slowly* ("the sabbath rang slowly") to suit his rhythm of "being." The experience of "being" as it is evoked in the poem is, then, a matter of *being in tune with time*, that is, of a harmonious balance between "doing"/"playing" and "being." Falling out of this grace is falling out of tune with time, which is anticipated by the gradual acceleration of the narrative movement already during the "long" Sunday which occupies the first half of the poem. It is in the second stanza that the spatial "dingle," the acoustic correlative of the sun's fixed eye, becomes the signifier of the latter's motion, which accelerates as the initially "*slowly*" dingle shifts to "*running*" "all the sun long," as if measuring its dial course (the course of its "day") toward its setting. After that moment, the acceleration is explicitly associated with the anticipated loss: the night birds bear the farm away "*flying*," and the horses are "*flashing* into the dark"—in the ("dew"-) wet dreams that will become tomorrow's conscious fantasies. In stanza 4, the horses of desire walk "spellbound" in the sun, and though the boy no longer rides them, as he did when his sexual wishes were still confined to the realm of the unconscious night, their movement is still tuned or bound by the spell of the tune that sustains the nostalgic-metaphorical tension between "the fields of praise" and "the first, spinning place." In effect, they may be envisioned as *creating* the spell of this desire-binding (specular-metaphorical) "spinning place" by their tuneful *merry-go-round*, which accumulates momentum in stanza 5 by the boy's *running* (his "heedless ways") and his "wishes" [horse-] *racing* to keep up with "the sun [that is] born *over and over*," until the centrifugal force of the accelerated turning/spinning throws them "out of grace" and the spell breaks.

But if the aspiring sun-bound movement of the first half of the poem turns out to be also a movement down-stream, the fall from its metaphorical climax, or collapsed climactic metaphor, turns out to be also an ascent back "*up*" (or "upstream," as Bachelard puts it) to the source of both movements in the nostalgic poet's expressive "Oh." The return of the poem back to "now" (the initial position of which is now occupied by "Oh") is an upwards movement towards its *lofty* "spinning place": "*the swallow thronged loft by the shadow of my* [writing] *hand*" to which time "takes" the poet is a reproduction of the hay-loft (barn) of childhood's "heydays"—the "high house hay," as well as the "dingl[ing]" belltower where *swallows* "*throng*" (crowd) to build their "lilting house," and the top of the tree whose boughs "*shadow*" the cosy "dingle" in the starry night. It is also "the whinnying green stable" ("stable in general" or "the apartment over a stable, usually appropriated to hay and straw" [*OED*]), where the racehorses live before they step out to fulfill their "wishes" in the golden "fields of praise," and where the "lamb white" is reborn ("blessed among the stables") under the stars and the dingle of the Annunciation, in the "*throngs*" of the creation of the poet's "morning song." And higher still, it is also the sky (obs. [*OED*]) of the night *before* "the birth of the simple light," which *re-turns* from the beginning of the poem to complete its spun circle and re-generate the round sun and its nostalgic antecedent, the first place to be spun "over and over" by the swallows' tuneful wheeling upwards, to design their intricate patterns in the sky.

"Parables of Sun Light" (Words in the Air about Time and the Weather)

POEM IN OCTOBER

It was my thirtieth year to heaven
Woke to my hearing from harbour and neighbour wood
And the mussel pooled and the heron
Priested shore
The morning beckon
With water praying and call of seagull and rook
And the knock of sailing boats on the net webbed wall
Myself to set foot
That second
In the still sleeping town and set forth.

My birthday began with the water-
Birds and the birds of the winged trees flying my name
Above the farms and the white horses
And I rose
In rainy autumn
And walked abroad in a shower of all my days.
High tide and the heron dived when I took the road
Over the border
And the gates
Of the town closed as the town awoke.

A springful of larks in a rolling
Cloud and the roadside bushes brimming with whistling
Blackbirds and the sun of October
Summery
On the hill's shoulder,

Here were fond climates and sweet singers suddenly
Come in the morning where I wandered and listened
To the rain wringing
Wind blow cold
In the wood faraway under me.

Pale rain over the dwindling harbour
And over the sea wet church the size of a snail
With its horns through mist and the castle
Brown as owls
But all the gardens
Of spring and summer were blooming in the tall tales
Beyond the border and under the lark full cloud.
There could I marvel
My birthday
Away but the weather turned around.

It turned away from the blithe country
And down the other air and the blue altered sky
Streamed again a wonder of summer
With apples
Pears and red currants
And I saw in the turning so clearly a child's
Forgotten mornings when he walked with his mother
Through the parables
Of sun light
And the legends of the green chapels.

And the twice told fields of infancy
That his tears burned my cheeks and his heart moved in mine.
These were the woods the river and sea
Where a boy
In the listening
Summertime of the dead whispered the truth of his joy
To the trees and the stones and the fish in the tide.
And the mystery
Sang alive
Still in the water and singingbirds.

And there could I marvel my birthday
Away but the weather turned around. And the true
Joy of the long dead child sang burning
In the sun.
It was my thirtieth
Year to heaven stood there then in the summer noon
Though the town below lay leaved with October blood.
O may my heart's truth
Still be sung
On this high hill in a year's turning.

"Poem in October" celebrates its birthday-poet's "thirtieth year *to* heaven" by moving backward to its childhood antecedent: "hypnotized by the far-away" echo of the song of "the long[ed for] dead child" at the bottom of his memory, which is reverberated by the "morning beckon[ing]" him toward its source, the poet climbs "back up" through past weathers and seasons, to find and reverberate it "On *this* high hill," from which he looks forward to its future repetition: "O may my heart's truth / Still be sung / On this high hill in a year's turning." The poet reaches that depth/height through a process of identification with the child, in the course of which he gradually appropriates the latter's creative perception. He first assumes his receptive "heart" and vision, and finally his creative "voice," whereby he re-creates the world of childhood's reverie in the space of his self-reflexive poem. Thus, the poet's journey is in effect a mimetic process, which leads to self-identification by way of reestablishing the ground or originating environment for the identifying expression of a nostalgic, creative self.

The narrative movement of the poem draws on a metaphorical correlation between changes of weather and mood, or to use Thomas's words, between "A process in the weather of the world" and "A process in the weather of the heart . . . [and] A weather in the flesh and bone."[78] The weather-scapes through which the poet moves are "atmospherical" *chronotopoi* in his mnemonic journey, which bear at once the relative sense of time (the time of reminiscence and the recalled times) and the feeling quality or "atmosphere" of their spaces. The identificatory process is advancd by three transformations in the landscapes of the poet's symbolic journey from "the town below" up to the summit of the country-hill. These transformations are marked by geographical "border[s]" and coinciding "turning[s]" of October's fickle weather, which concretize the transitions between four mental landscapes in the speaker's mnemonic journey and their qualifying perceptual modes and colouring moods. The movement from one perceptual mode to another is advanced by a causality which is analogous to that of poetic signification (creative reception or "reading"), namely, that of sound which opens an indeterminate connotative space, on whose *semiotically* charged "ground" (charged, that is, with sensory and affective associations) the denotated sight of a coherent "world" is crystalized. The governing mood in each landscape is associated with a particular season which magnifies or totalizes the momentary weather scene, so that their full "geographical" sequence constitutes the mnemonic narrative as a journey through the zodiac of the "year's turning."

In stanzas 1–2 the poet *hears* the echo of the child's as yet unidentified voice in the "*rainy autumn*" "morning beckon[ing]" (the "water praying" and the "call of seagull" will turn out, in stanza 6, to be the reverberation of the "mystery" of the child's whispers "[sung] alive / Still in the water and the singingbirds"). The episodical autumn rain anticipates the permanent rain of a winter mood, pouring down a melancholic-birthday prospect "in a shower of all [his] days." This mood is modified, however, as soon as the poet takes the road "*over the border*" of the town to stanza 3, where "a *spring*-full of larks" heralds "the sun of October / *Summery* / On the hill's shoulder." The change in the actual weather perceived in the actual movement out of the town and uphill anticipates the change of the season-scape in stanza 4, where "all the gardens / Of *spring* and *summer*" will bloom in the landscape of the memory of childhood's "tall tales."

The "*tall tales*," like "the *legends* of the *green* chapels" in stanza 5, represent the child's creative perception of his projective "gardens." The poet's metaphorical-mnemonic journey toward them is, therefore, an unfolding of "the *twice told* fields of infancy," that is, a poetic reverie toward childhood's reverie. The nostalgic signified and telos of this "redoubled" reverie is signified by the metaphor of the sun, the same "spinning place" whose annual ("the year's") "turning" turns the weathers and the seasons—or their metaphors—through which the sequence of both the speaker's "sung" poem and the child's "whispered" "other air" (= tune) (stanzas 6, 5) are metonymically (that is, vocally) spun. The child's original (re-) creation of the solar universe is imaged in the fifth stanza, where he is seen to "[walk] with his mother / Through the *parables* / *Of sun light*." By the way of his walk, he creates the fabulous season-scapes of a childhood projected in the light of the metaphorical sun. The poet, who follows his footsteps towards the sun (of the "summer noon" in stanza 6), imitates the child's walk through the meteor-ological "parables" that constitute his "history," by performing his own *historio-graphic* tour through the metaphorical zodiac. His nostalgic re-creation of his history sublimates "the shower of all his days," which as it were change their direction in the process of their sun-bound metaphorization.

The perceptual change that opens the mnemonic chain occurs already "*here*," in stanza 3, where the feeling-quality of the foreshadowed (or fore-lighted), but as yet unrecognized "spring and summer" is "suddenly" recognized as the generalized, subjective sensation of "*fond climates*." This sudden vague recognition is the effect of an as yet unidentified involuntary memory triggered by way of association (of the actual springfully-clouded-summery-sunny weather with the corresponding mnemonic seasons), whose characteristic feature of making "the past . . . encroach upon the present" (Proust)[79] is suggestd by the ambiguous deictic "here" (significantly juxtaposed with "there" in other places in the poem). The invocatory dynamics of this mnemonic-metaphorical experience is concretized by the recurrence of the echo of the "returning" child's still unidentified voice, which is once again reverberated by the birds ("sweet singers") and the water and/or the wind: the "fond climates . . . suddenly / Come in the morning where I . . . listened / To the rain wringing [or ringing in the] / Wind" across the enjambment (which momentarily gives the rain the syntactic status of a "ringing" subject). The "fond" sensation is the resonance-effect of the invocatory "sound" of the returning memory, which constitutes the *inner climate* of the nostalgic reverie into which the poet is sliding here by way of *semiotic* enchantment. This inner climate is the "ground" for the reception of the concrete images of childhood's "tall tales," toward the subject of which the poet moves (unaware) by following the sun up "the hill's shoulder" toward its sonorous zenith at the end of the poem (that familiar audio-visual site, the "tuneful" "loud sun" of "Fern Hill" and "Poem on his Birthday," will acommodate the child's "burning" song of "joy"). For the time being, however, the poet only begins to enjoy the sense of being "here," in relation to the past, whose presence grows to be so dominant in stanza 4 that the rainy town below shrinks to "the size of a snail" and fades away in the "mist," to give way to the visual concretization of the "fond climates."

But the "gardens / Of spring and summer" "blooming . . ./ Beyond the border" reach their fruition only after "the weather turn[s] around" again, and the "border" is crossed to stanza 5, where the reminiscing poet "turn[s] away" from the actual "blithe country," the site of his reverie toward childhood, *into* the "*other air*" of childhood's reverie. That "other air" (= air), whose "fond" atmospherical texture has enticed the poet to seek its original environment, is the textual atmosphere of the inherently metaphorical "other childhood" (Bachelard), that oral-aural *chronotopos* of "*whispered*" "parables / Of sun–*light*." In order "to breathe a new air," an air which, says Proust, "is *new precisely because we have breathed it in the past*," "the returning memory" which ventilates it must be such that "throw[s] no bridge, [that] form[s] no connecting link between itself and the present minute," so that the memory should "[remain] in the context of its own place and date [and keep] its distance, its isolation in the hollow of a valley or [alternatively] upon the highest peak of a mountain summit."[80] What has prevented the poet from breathing that new/old air earlier, prior to the emergence of a breeze of it to give another turn to the weathercock, was the perception of the "gardens" as "*tales*" of the past, defined as such from the external perspective of their present reminiscing. Juxtaposed with the dim prospect of the rainy town below, they too were therefore "under the lark full cloud" of the consciousness of the present; in the filtered light of that cloud, their mediated vision was situated "beyond the border" of self-conscious reminiscence. By "turn[ing] away" from the actual landscape, however, the poet comes to actually *inhabit* the metaphorical space of the "other childhood" (Bachelard). He crosses the border into it by identifying with the child's mode of perception, which has made possible the creation of the "fond" seasons in the first place, and which now enables him to perform "again" the "wonder of summer." That wonder consists in transforming the "*pale rain*" into "apples / Pears and *red* currants" that "[*stream*] down" "the *blue* altered sky" (the "red currants" are a truly fruitful sublimation of the red currents of October blood, whose dead leaves give way, by the year's turning, to the "blooming" and the fruition of the "tall" tree-tales in "the gardens of spring" and summer). Coming closer to the subject of the voice by yielding to his invitation to (re-create) his place, the poet can now identify him. Zooming in (and inwards), "I *saw* . . . so clearly a child's / Forgotten mornings." What he sees so clearly is not the child, but the world as it is seen through his *eyes*, which explains how "his tears burned *my* cheeks" in stanza 6, and how the gardens, formerly fenced off by the distancing border of the tall tales, become "*these*" (immediately perceived) woods and river and sea which sing "*alive*" the "mystery" of the now identified boy's whispers. But the pilgrim's progress does not reach its consummation yet, for the "mystery [sung] . . ./ *Still*" is still "the truth of *his* joy," which pertains to the "summertime of the *dead*." It will take another turning around of the weather for the "Joy of the long dead child" to become "*my* heart's truth," and for "still" to shed its (secondary) connotation of *stillness* and confirm, in its recurrence and its rhyming with "*this* high hill," that of *continuity*—between the past and the present in the one long, uninterrupted future-bound note of the poet who has found his voice.[81]

The poet's "recuperation" of his voice is the consummation of an integrative process of self-identification: by assimilating the nostalgic affect represented by the child's metaphorical voice, the poet becomes the subject of its articulation. This subjectivizing recuperative process is a signifying process whose four-staged dynamics are essentially similar to the textual process of poetic language—a similarity noted by the great expert on the nostalgic *Remembrance*, who speaks of *reading, listening* [to] and *deciphering* the "magical scrawl" of the "hierogliphic" "traces" of *Things Past*.[82] The "reading process" transcribed in the poem, as I have suggested, is a sequence in which the resonance of foregrounded sound creates a *semiotic*-connotative space or "climate," which represents the voiced affective "truth" and colors the denotative (*symbolic*) articulation of the concrete impressions that constitute its sustaining "landscape." These three "phases" are, in effect, the simultaneous components of the fourth, identificatory moment, that is, the rearticulation of the textual "voice" that constitutes the reader as the subject of the text. The rearticulated "truth" in mnemonic as well as poetic "reading" is, to use Proust's language, the "necessary truth" inscribed in the "hieroglyphs." But this "truth," as well as the "pure *joy*" which accompanies its return, is "a new truth," generated by the "effort" we make "to hear and transcribe" the ideas that come back to us "like *tunes*" which, in fact, "we have never heard . . . before."[83]

Bachelard's parable of sunlight closely converges with Thomas's. "The pure memory has no date," he says, "It has a *season*. The season is the fundamental *mark* of memories. What sun or what wind was there that memorable day?" and I would add (idiosyncratically, and in affinity with Thomas): what was the color and texture of the air like? "[Those are] the question[s] which [give] the right tension of reminiscence,"[84] because their "atmospherical" terms refer to the most suggestive—at once intimate and evasive—sensation of the mnemonic/imaginary space, or, as Thomas words it, to its "colour of saying."[85] The poet of "Fern Hill" remembers the spacious time that let him "play and *be*": "it was *air* and playing." "*The other air*" of "Poem in October" is that of an ever blue sky—a clear October moment totalized into an eternal summer. "All the summers of our childhood bear witness to 'the eternal summer,'" says Bachelard to illustrate the phenomena of childhood's "total seasons,"[86] and explains: it is eternal "because [it is] faithful to the colours of the *first time*"—the "*once-upon-a-time*"—and for all subsequent seasons, which bear the original color trace of its mnemonic gestalt (we saw this color trace being refreshed in the transformation of the "*pale* rain" into the "*blue* altered" sky and the streaming *red* currants or currents in the "*green* legends"). "The seasons of memory" are the "indelible *signs*"—or "parables"—of our once intense experiences of being/becoming in intimate, creative relation to the world: "With each season there resounds in us one of the dynamisms of our entry into the World . . . the world with its original colours." The "pure memory" of this dynamism transcends its specific context or climate: "it is the very memory of our belonging to the world, to a world commanded by the dominating sun" in its "full," "*anthropocosmic*"[87] (that is, properly symbolic) sense.

The world commanded by the Symbolic (cohesive anthropo-cosmic) sun accommodates childhood's "existentialism of the *fabulous*":[88] Childhood is a world of "*fables*," Bachelard tells us, told in "the language of *enchantment*" (the fabulous) which engages its subject in the here and now of its articulation, thus enabling him to "live" (in, rather than recount) his fables. Drawing on the same language of enchantment, poetic reverie toward childhhood has the same initiatory effect of enabling one to "*enter into* the fabulous times."[89] The "phenomenlogical meaning" "proper" to childhhood's "fables" is "pure . . . meaning since it is under the sign of *wonder*," that is, of the spell-(that is, desire-) binding futurity of the new and the fabulous and its present subjectifying signification—which poetic language reproduces: "By the poet's grace we have become the pure and simple subject of the verb '*to marvel*.'"[90] Now this is a fairly accurate description of what happens to the poet "In October" in his reverie toward childhood, who "could *marvel* / [his] birthday away" in two different sites in the poem's fabulous course—but does so significantly elsewhere: each time he proposes to settle for a "marvel"—once on perceiving the "tall tales / Beyond the border" in stanza 4 and once on hearing the "mystery [sing] alive" in stanza 6—his plans are jeopardized by a change in the weather. The "marvelling" does take place finally, but only in the unexpected moment of the change, whose spatio-temporal liminality *defamiliarizes* and thereby renders marvelous the landscape. The "wonder of summer" "*stream*[s] *down*" the simultaneous course of two "*turns*," atmospherical and geographical: "the weather turned around. // It turned away from the blithe country" (to cross "the border" into the gardens). The simultaneity is designated by the "streaming" syntactic structure of the phrase, in which "down" qualifies the movement of both the *turning* weather and the *streaming* "wonder," both of which bring about the simultaneous "return" of their original subject: "And I saw *in the turning* . . . a [child]" who, in and through his analogous walk, has spun the "parables of sunlight," which are now being reinscribed by the poet: the "*apples*," for instance, may be the child's "legends of the *green* ch*apels*," which stream down with the rest of the fruits of the looming (=solar) Horn of Plenty.

The sense of wonder which facilitates the entrance "into" the space of the fable of the fabulous times—that is, the mimetic effect of that fable—is the magic effect of the boundary crossing which marks metaphor as an act in time. We have seen this effect in "Poem on his Birthday" and in "Fern Hill," where the metaphorical spinnings/turnings blur the spatio-temporal boundaries between the signifier of desire and its differred signified by creating a space which sustains their simultaneity. In this dynamics, the turning performs the magic of turning (the signifier) *into* (its signified). It effects, that is, the metamorphosis of the literalization of the figurative which enables one to enter into metaphor—*in the turning*. The phenomenology of this optical illusion is more closely foregrounded in the poem, in the play of the corresponding images of borders and turns, which lays bare the temporal-active dimension of boundary *crossing* underlying the spatial illusion (of blurred boundaries). The poet's active participation in the signification of the "tall tales" in the transition between stanza 4 and 5 is contrasted with the static metaphorical representation in the tall tales, where the only verbs are "were" and "*could* marvel" (but did not), and whose meaning is closed off—indeed fenced-off—by the "border" between the tale and its telling. The fruition of the blooming gardens is wondrous because in the course of its syntactical streaming and turning—rhythmed by recurrent *and*s and red currants and other kinesthetic tropes—one can actually see the sky "alter[ing]" and the fruits streaming/growing down/up the sky/trees in the course of their telling. One can see, in other words, how the "tall tales," those unlikely stories, *actually* turn into the trees which they represent, and how their stock expression comes alive—to be dwelt on, and in, by the invited imagination.

The turning of the weather in stanza 7 marks the same shift from passive reception to active participation in the metaphorical process, which is reflected in the poet's transition from listening to the "mystery / [sung] alive" to singing it himself. His entrance into the fable is suggested by the change of the deictic "*there*," where he could, but didn't marvel, to "*this* high hill," where his "heart's truth" is sung "*in* [the] year's *turning*." The dynamic metaphorical act in this stanza bridges (or blurs) the geographical "border" or perceptual difference between the autumnal "town below" and the summery hill, manipulating its liminal experience so as to turn the temporal threat of "October blood" into a self-realizing faith in time's generative turning. And it is precisely the tension of the perceptual coincidence of summer and autumn that generates the seasonal turning which reconciles their opposition. This is what metaphor is all about: the superimposition of opposites (or elements pertaining to incompatible semantic fields, or times) which generates a new, paradoxical entity: a golden entity born out of the superimposition of "green" and "dying," which draws on the dynamic tension between similarity and difference, presence and absence, the literal and the figurative, and which can only be conceived in the dynamic terms of a quick *movement* of the gaze from one perceptual field/time to another.

The most illustrative example I know for this marvelous optical trick is the ambiguous meaning of the arche-metaphor of the sun in the morning ritual of the African Elgon tribe. According to Jung's account of it in his autobiography,[91] every morning at dawn, the tribe's people go out, spit into their hands and turn them up toward the rising sun. The rising sun, so Jung was told, is God, to which the tribe's people commend their spat spirits or creative breaths (their "magic power")—or rather *lend* them to it—for the sun is God *only at the moment of its rising* (as is the moon, in the equivalent moment), which reflects the genesis of consciousness in a symbol created by the magic of the creative breath.[92]

The creative breath, often mixed with spittle, comes out of the mouths of fat-cheeked little cherubs on geographic maps (where they represent winds), including Thomas's "The Map of Love,"[93] a short story in which, as Annis Pratt suggests,[94] they also represent the mythological "weathers." In Indian mythology (the relevant sources of which, according to Pratt, Thomas acknowledged reading), the "weathers" or "Maruts" "toss the clouds across the surging sea" (as they also do in the Thomas story), to represent "the primordial forces of the universe before all other gods were born." In Thomas's "A Prospect of the Sea," (as Pratt notes), the weathers are placed above the heavens,[95] which suggests (I interpret) their primacy in the authorial-geneological hierarchy of the world's "book of days" (which the poet-protagonist carries on his shoulder "like *Atlas*"—to tighten the geographical-meteorological link). In "Poem in October" they turn around the weathercock to advance the poet's journey "to heaven," and thereby also create it—as the dynamic site of his re-birth (-day). But whereas the "weather"s in the poem as it were appropriate the birthday-poet's creative force (by their metonymical representation of him), their Indian collegues identify with him "occasionally, [by] assum[ing] again the form of newborn babes.'"[96]

Something to Miss: Peace with the Maternal

The sugary cherubs might be an appropriate figure with which to conclude this nostalgic chapter, but to conclude here would be to stop just when nostalgia is about to reach its most heavenly hill, which would be a shame.

"Poem in October" draws a clear symbolic connection between the experience of benign narcissism in childhood and its poetic reproduction, and a nostalgic (and incestuous) birth fantasy, whose "Edenic" quality is associated with a benevolent image of the "remembered" maternal. In this the poem differs distinctly from "Poem on his Birthday," where the analogous birthday-journey toward the sun, the integrative Symbolic origin in whose light the poet's productive habitat is signified into being, involves killing and forgetting ("dis-membering") the bad mother in a reenactment of the aborted genesis fantasy that maintains her as such. In the "October" poem, the boy's positive relationship with his projective environment is based on, and seems to grow out of an original peace with the "re-membered" benevolent mother. That peace, which is established by the remembering poet, is the basis for the integrity which marks the child's disposition of trustful openness in relation to the world—an openness which also marks the poet's relation to himself (to the child in him), to the represented environment of his journey, and ultimately also to his interlocutor, the reader.

Stanza 6 depicts the birth of the child in the memory of the poet, who recognizes his habitat in the present environment ("*These* were the woods the river and sea / Where a boy / . . . whispered"), as well as in the past, through his intersubjective relationship with his environment.

Here,

> Where a boy
> In the listening
> Summertime of the dead whispered the truth of his joy
> To the trees and the stones and the fish in the tide,

a dialogical communion or "dual-union" (Deri)[97] takes place between the child and mother-nature, whose "anthropo-cosmic" message is the "*mystery*" of a subjectivity that sings itself "alive" (itself, as there is no object between the verb and its complement). The dialogical relation, with its implication of some degree of separateness, is dramatized by the enjambment between "listening" and "summertime," which makes the boy at once the listener—"*a boy / In the listening*"—and the whisperer to the summery environment.

The initial, receptive "listening" disposition is significant, because it illustrates the child's trustful sense of a world that is already there, to welcome his birth-giving speech actively, intentionally: nature speaks, it does not merely reverberate, which enables the *poet* to hear, by a similar listening to nature's animated and animating voice, the mystery sung alive "Still *in the waters and the singingbirds.*" The "mystery" which that birth-site reverberates, the "truth" of the child's "joy," is the poet's self-fulfilling birthday-prayer ("to heaven"), which is voiced/echoed by the same water and birds in the first stanza. Here the poet, like the "boy in the listening," "[w]oke to [his] *hearing*" the "*water* praying" and the *seagulls* "call[ing]" on the "*heron* / Priested shore." His birthday begins, then, with the realization of his prayer to be born into a welcoming world, which he then realizes actively, by yielding to nature's "morning beckon" and the seagulls' "call" to "set forth" on his journey out of his womb-town. The birds and the water are, as we have seen in "Poem on His Birthday," recurrent configurations of the archaic maternal in Thomas's poetry. In the second stanza, they star in the nostalgic genesis fantasy which motivates the poet's birthday-prayer and journey:

My birthday began with the *water-*
Birds and the birds of the winged trees *flying my name.*

Here—in contrast to the aborted genesis fantasy of the melancholic poet "On his Birthday," who is baptized to death and speared by the beaks of phobic mother–birds which prattle ("palaver") away the Symbolic potentia of his "mustardseed" being—a successful birth takes place: the unambiguously life-giving water-birds ensure the psycho-somatic integrity of their offspring, who springs off from the symbiotic-*semiotic water* and up over the enjambment, to be Symbolically identified by the birds who fly his *name* (and thus deliver him as a separate being). "And [consequently] I *rose* /. . . and walked abroad" into the future ("the shower of all my days"), through the yielding gates of the mother-town, which opened "*abroad*" to deliver the "sailing boats" that have knocked on the "wet webbed wall" of the womb. The maternal image here is one of an unimpinging mother who lets her child be, that is, separate: "High tide and the heron dived [to make way] when I took the road / Over the border." This is why the poet need not kill or tame the maternal: unlike the survivor of "His Birthday," who must domesticate the maternal sea/horse and ride it so as not to drown, the "October" poet can trust the tide to recede. This trust is bound up with his trust in the reassuring regularity of mother-nature's movements and changes. Indeed, changes do not exasperate him because he knows that the weather-cock on the hill'd shoulder will always turn to return the sun, by the rules, set by the poem, of nature's *fort-da* game.

Unlike the melancholic poet "On his Birthday," who must erect his tongue strenuously and sing loud so as not to hear the deadly silence of the castrating underwater or make sense of the lethally nonsensical "palavers of birds," the "October" poet can afford to be "in the listening." "Poem in October" is a poem about listening, both inwardly and outwardly, and its subject's poetic "doing" is grounded in that listening, which gives its represented world as well as its subject a communicable reality or "being." In contrast to "Poem on his Birthday," whose manic tone betrays the poet's mistrust of the world and of his own capacity to recreate (in order to inhabit) it, here the world and the poet's creative "self" *are*—by dint of his (nostalgic) faith in them, or faithful nostalgia for them. The integrity which generates this sense is reflected in the relation between the metaphor of the sun and of the journey toward it and its signified, the maternal water-birds. While the subject of "Poem on his Birthday" is born into the paternal order of the metaphorical sun *despite* the lethal sea and spearing/prattling birds, by way of a paranoic, dissociative sublimation of the maternal which they signify, here there is a harmony between the paternal and the maternal, as the turning sun and the waterbirds alike embody *both* functions: the water-birds also "name," and the sun is also a place (in "Incarnate Devil" they are also homologous, but there they collaborate in the diabolical ordeal of the sacrificial abjection). It is that harmony which redeems the incest in the poet's birth-fantasy—an incest that is sublimated by the notion of the "*mystery*" which sings the "*truth* of his *joy*" in the baptismal Communion, as well as by the (child's and the poet's) "parables / Of sun light," which signify love, not murder, of the baptized body and the maternal. The symbolic act which "names" (and calls) the child is not a paternal "doing" that excludes the maternal—the "being" of/in the body—but such which, being at peace with the maternal, combines both body and name to the effect of restoring, or re-membering its creative origin in a nostalgic "original integrity."

The reality of this integrity is manifested in the easy style of the poem: unlike the hypercondensed, quasi-material ("too full") verbal construction which the "Birthday" poet posits as if to hold on to as to a fetish, against his existential (maternal) anxiety, in "Poem in October" there is more air, so to speak (again . . .). The poet can let go, and be content with *symbolizing* his lost object instead of clinging to its fetishistic, material equivalent. He can do this because, thanks to his listening disposition, there is someone out there who listens; a reader in whose attention he trusts enough so as not to need to squeeze a response out of him or her by confronting them with the desperate opacity of a discourse of whose private meaning he is reluctant to let go. There is something to say when there is someone to say it to, and there is someone when one listens out—and in, to connect to the wish that someone be. Sometimes that wish must be re-called, by seagulls or praying waters, out of the deeps of oblivion, to re-member the son of a two-headed sea-gorgon as a child who "walked with his *mothe* / Through the parables / Of sun light." There is some-*one* speaking.

CHAPTER FIVE

The Lover, the Poet, and the Lunatic

OEDIPUS AND THE PROBLEM OF BOUNDARIES

In conformity with the oscillating pattern which has been establishing itself in this discourse in response to the double pull of its subject matter, this chapter will deal, once again, with the reality of loss under the recuperative sign. After attempting to show in chapter 4, as in chapter 2, how the poetic act heals its underlying split, I will now return to mourn here, as in chapter 3, the vicissitudes of the conflictual rupture which haunts the reality of the split subject and his symbolizations as these are dramatized in two of Thomas's surrealistic stories in poetic prose. The analysis will focus on the problematics of boundaries—ultimately the boundaries of subjectivity and signification—as the major symptom of this predicament. "A Prospect of the Sea" and "The Mouse and the Woman" provide an illuminating insight into this issue by exploring the boundary between poetry and psychosis within the context of a manifestly oedipal symbolic crisis. As it is drawn in and by the two stories, that boundary is the point in which *semiotic* enchantment stops being bound to symbolization and begins to "possess" its subject, who thereby loses his identity as such. It is placed, in other (Lacanian) words, where the maternal Imaginary exceeds the paternal, Symbolic limits of representations that contain its underlying conflicts, to the effect of "flooding" their subject and submerging him in chaotic delirium. By consequence of such incestuous transgression, which short-circuits the metaphorical distance and the "misrecognition" that sustains integrative, imaginary, and symbolic representations, the protagonists of Thomas's stories find themselves face to face with the prospect of the (Lacanian) Real, that is, with the Impossibility of "being" or the raw reality of "castration" in psychic disintegration.[1]

The symbolic crises depicted in both stories consist in the conflictual return of the sexualized maternal, which confronts the protagonists with the choice between yielding to its melancholic seduction to psychotic regression and resisting it. The first option involves the transgressive blurring of the paternal boundaries between fantasy and reality, text and context, signifier and signified, etc., while the second is to be effected by confining the "maternal" enchantment to the boundaries of poetic symbolization. The consequences of the choice determine, in each story, the destiny of the protagonist's interdependent sanity and poetic creativity. "A Prospect of the Sea" depicts the crisis of adolescence which constituted the point of departure for its autobiographical subject's poetic career. Activated by the "traumatic" return of his repressed sexuality,[2] the adolescent protagonist's oedipal conflicts shatter the benign maternal space of childhood which has so far sustained his integrity, and subvert the imaginative omnipotence which he has enjoyed within childhood's peaceful reverie. The boy tries to reconcile his conflictual inner reality by way of restoring his castrated imaginative omnipotence through daydreaming and innocent storytelling, but his fantasies get out of hand, turning into hallucinations which subject him to the power of the conflicted, sexualized maternal. And so he loses himself to the enchantment of a symbolic "mermaid" who steps out of an innocent children's story to "love him until he die[s]" (6) by drowning in the archaic prospect of the sea of the unconscious from which she came, and which she also represents. After an orphic dip in that tidal site of psychotic con-fusion, when the flood of chaotic hallucinations abates a little, the conflict which they represent crystalizes into a clear choice. The adolescent chooses to resist the melancholic temptation to regress back *into* the prospect of the maternal sea and, taking a nostalgic distance from it, sets out to symbolize it instead, in "A Prospect of the Sea." The autobiographical narrator of the self-reflexive story appears in its end, in the figure of an "old man building a boat" in the horizon (12). Assuming Thomas's Noah persona,[3] the old narrator builds his ark to ward off the "flood" of "to–morrow's anger"—at the death-tainted reality of sex and time—and confines its maternal agent and her imaginary representations back to the textual space of its "three *storied* decks" (12).

"The Mouse and the Woman" dramatizes the reverse movement in an account of a psychotic crisis which puts an end to its subject's poetic career.

The crisis is brought about by the poet-protagonist's attempt to substantialize his symbolic creation by employing his writing as an exercise in black magic. He is seduced to it by a devil of a woman ("a woman of the devil" [65]) who, in the innocent disguise of the Edenic Eve, urges him to give her a "flesh and blood" reality and then make love to her. Her "transubstantiation" is effected by a symbolic black mass in which the sacraments of the eucharist and of marriage are performed. These rituals lead to the poet's "possession" by the imaginary creature of his creation, who oversteps her textual boundaries to deprive him of his creative power as well as of his sanity.

The different consequences of the symbolic crises depicted in the two stories are determined by the protagonists' inherently different dispositions toward them, which in effect predetermine their respective "choices" between yielding to and resisting the melancholic/psychotic seduction of the maternal. While the poet-protagonist of "The Mouse and the Woman" destroys his symbolizations out of an irresistible attraction to the real thing, which confronts him with its impossibility, the adolescent in "A Prospect of the Sea" keeps trying to patch up the fissures which unbound desire creates in his representations. He constantly tries to ward off the haunting negativity underlying them by new imaginary representations, which help him to assimilate the change he undergoes as he is compelled to face the consciousness of his sexuality and of death. Indeed, these representations keep slipping out of his control, but it is precisely the sequential motion of their perpetual displacement that facilitates his gradual transformation toward maturity and adult creativity.

Both stories draw the oedipal link between the problematics of textual and sexual boundaries and their respective transgressions. This link is reflected in the symbolic configuration of the maternal in the feminine figures in the stories. The women represent at once the conflictual oedipal *object* of the returning unconscious fantasies and the unconscious itself, that is, both the representational *content* and the *space* of the fantasy, whose return involves a transgressive blurring of the boundaries between inside and outside. They also represent the unconscious performative agent of this regressive transgression, that is, the repetition compulsion which "seduces" the protagonist to it. Thus, in both stories, a seductive and bewildering *femme fatale* step out of some text to seduce the protagonist to guilty sex in a delirious landscape which bears her projection: the sea in particular, but also the woods and the hill which the raving protagonist inhabits are, in both stories, also "anatomical" landscapes of the female body, and thus at once metonymical and metaphorical of Woman. The metonymical, compulsive agent of the projection, the seductive regressive drive, is configured in the diabolical, witchlike aspect of the woman who, in that fatal capacity, is incarnate Death or its Angel: "I'll run you to the sea" (10), says the sea-blue eyed Venus to the boy in "A Prospect of the Sea," and, "that was the best joke of all" (69), she sneers at the poet in "The Mouse and the Woman," upon revealing herself to have been the Devil in disguise.

The landscapes of the sea, the wood, and the hill are also the maternal settings of "Poem in October," but unlike their benign equivalents in the childhood poem—those welcoming, harmonious spaces of reverie at peace with the maternal—their form here is ambivalent. Here, they are also (respectively) the sites of drowning, being lost and bitten by snakelike twigs and thorns, and the abode of rats and mice. These chaotic, paranoic spaces represent the "castrating" aspect of the ambiguous (sexualized) maternal, whose return as such makes the difference between childhood's guiltlessly incestuous imaginary and the delirious imaginary which transgresses the paternal Symbolic boundaries accentuated in adolescence. These boundaries are implied in the very notion of "maternal castration," which is a retroacted projection of the Oedipus on the ambiguous archaic object. The term condenses the sequence of Oedipus's "crime and punishment": at once symbiotic *fusion* and splitting *abjection*, it is, in the extreme of psychotic con-fusion and di-fusion, a transgression that is its own punishment. This is reflected in both stories, in which the incestuous transgression of the symbolic boundaries confronts the protagonist with the same impotence that he wishes to ward off by his omnipotent delirious projection. Foreclosed, the paternal law implements its persecutory punitive function by haunting the raving protagonist from the outside in paranoic projections of guilty sex (castrating incest), whose actual consequences are the unsettling ontological confusion which characterizes the experience of "the uncanny." In contrast to its *integrative* specular counterpart, the "penumbral ontology" of reverie, the blurring of the boundaries between fantasy and reality in the psychotic "uncanny" is a fragmenting, de-realizing experience of negative ambiguity that is caused by the inevitable but inapplicable consciousness of ontological boundaries. The boundaries are there, in principle, but *only* in principle; in practice they are unstable and fluid, signifying the impossibility of both the maternal and its substitutions in reality. Like the tree of knowledge in the garden of "Incarnate Devil," they contaminate the maternal space of the imaginary with their censuring presence, sticking out as tokens of error and guilt which generate confusion and paranoia and spoil all the wishful possible fun.

In particular, they spoil the prospect of imaginative omnipotence by introducing a corrosive reflexive consciousness into the fantasy. Such a differential consciousness, however, is also present, and in effect constitutes the "penumbral ontology" of childhood's integrative reverie (and its poetic or aesthetic recuperations, for that matter). But what sustains the sense of the reality of the infantile imaginary is precisely its subject's capacity to contain the ontological paradox that constitutes its heterogeneous "transitional space," a paradox that makes it a metaphorical space *par excellence* and as such, a manifestation of peace with the maternal. The perception of reverie maintains the reflexive *as-if* consciousness of play which, to use Bachelard's terminology, sustains its self-conscious "*cogito*,"[4] while, at the same time, suspending the disbelief in the reality of its projections. The imaginary projection in reverie obeys the metaphorical law, so well illustrated by the African worship of the rising sun which I mentioned earlier, according to which the signifier is *and* is not its wishful signified. This paradox makes childhood's "live metaphor" both alive and a metaphor, whose literalization is integrative because it is confined to the boundaries of symbolic play. In psychotic fantasy, by contrast, the game is too serious: designed to heal the unbearable split by making the metaphor real, it collapses it, while radicalizing the split of its subject's "*cogito*" between the "either" and the "or" of the disjunctive "uncanny." Paradoxically enough, though sustained by conformity to the Symbolic order, sanity and symbolization are paradoxical, not logical.[5]

"A PROSPECT OF THE SEA"

Exposition 1: A Three-Storied Story and Its Double Determination

The double determination of repetition was designated by the tree of knowledge as a *choice* between two interpretations. Its ambiguous symbol could be read either as a prohibition, which implied affirmation of the Symbolic order of the world as a point of departure for the nostalgic history of its representations, or an invitation to a transgression, which opened the regressive way toward the timeless and nameless destination of melancholia. These "negative" and "positive" oedipal readings must have been the good and evil between which Adam couldn't choose, of course, until after the inevitable breaking of the Edenic mirror—or the awakening from "the blinding country of youth," when "*good and bad*," as Thomas anticipated to his son Llewelyn, turn out to be "*two ways / Of moving about your death*."[6] The bad way (evaluated as such from the point of view of the negative oedipal perspective which posits these categories) is death by maternal castration, and the good way is its suspension by submission to paternal castration. These unattractive alternatives present themselves as such to the apple-prince upon his forking fall, when the integrative simultaneity of the double determination of repetition is polarized. Upon the splitting symbolic crisis of adolescence as it is manifested in Thomas's work, and notably in "A Prospect of the Sea," the complicity between futured *symbolic* re-*pre*-sentation and *semiotic* regression which maintains childhood's playfully magical "parables" is disrupted by reality, and so the reign of the pleasure principle is subverted. With the emergence of the differential reality of sex and (destructive) time, the harmonious "blind country of youth" gives way to an insight into its underlying rupture, which confronts its subject with the choice between the two ways of going about it. The "good" choice taken in and manifested by "A Prospect of the Sea," once taken, turns out to be considerably good after all, as the nostalgic alchemy at work in its (symbolic) performance restores the simultaneity of the double determination of repetition within a new magical parable. That parable depicts the process of its creation within a symbolic *Bildungs*-narrative which, concentrating on the critical moment of adolescence, traces its subject's psycho-symbolic development toward becoming a poet. The autobiographical narrator's "history" is structured by an exposition, a complication, and a resolution, which dramatize his three-phased movement from the symbolic continuity in childhood's integrative "fables," through the dissociative psycho-symbolic rupture of adolescence, to its ultimate healing in creative maturity, when the old poet emerges to recount the self-reflected story of his life. These phases, which trace the oedipal history of the dramatized narrator from latency through the oedipal crisis to its resolution in the integration of the Symbolic function, also reflect the dialectic of de-symbolization and re-symbolization that constitutes his, as well as his author's, symbolic performance.

As the optical connotations of its title suggest, "A Prospect of the Sea" is a story about perception, whose metaphorical object—the sea—changes according to the perspective from which it is viewed. The changes of perspective occur in the course of the protagonist's autobiographical cruise through a variational series of nautical vistas or "sea-prospects," which structure the narrative symbolically and advance its dramatic course. Providing the symbolic setting for three phases in his "history," these archetypal mental prospects illustrate the protagonist's changing perspectives vis-à-vis their latent content, namely, the primal, endopsychic fantasy of the ambiguous maternal beginning and the oedipal drama that it condenses—and which the narrative "history" unfolds. Thus, childhood's peace with the maternal is dramatized in the boy's being cradled in his reverie among the waves of the corn swaying to a wind from the sea. The sea's positive maternal aspect is foregrounded by the association of the Egyptian corn goddess (of fertility), which is further suggested later on in the figure of the country girl who comes from Egypt (7). The destructive aspect of the maternal is repressed by an innocent children's story about a "drowned princess" who, as such, saves the boy from the danger of being in her situation. Things become complicated, however, when this situation is reversed, upon the return of the maternal from the sea of the unconscious to drown the adolescent in its conflictual hallucinatory prospect. The conflicts activated by her return will find their ultimate resolution back on the water's surface, when Noah, the nostalgic "old man" in the story's "*horizon*" (12) facing his prospective death, will build his ark against its nautical prospect and its archaic representation. The journey of the "three-storied" ark is realized by the narrative performance that it symbolizes, which spans the historical "detour" (in the Freudian sense) of its captain from the first to the last sea. The detour is channeled by the narrative stream of consciousness, which flows between its end terms in a wavelike movement of flashbacks and anticipations, propelled by the metonymical association between metaphors: the sea-prospects as it were grow out of one another by the surrealistic technique of the literalization of metaphor which "de-fossilizes" the nautical archetype to the effect of liberating its performative symbolic potential, an effect which reflects the compulsive realization of the psychological fate inscribed in the latent endopsychic fantasy.

The surrealistic technique of the literalization of metaphor concretizes the dynamics of *semiotic* enchantment and its poetic and psychotic potentials explored in the poem. Involving the transgression of the metaphor's *symbolic* boundaries, this dynamic is, on the one hand, what animates the representation and makes narrative and psychic transformation possible, while bearing, on the other hand, the potential of the loss of symbolic and psychic control, as happens to the protagonist when his magical fables get out of hand. But in its romantic *Bildungs* context, the adolescent protagonist's psychotic crisis constitutes, as I have suggested, the transformative phase in the orphic journey that will lead him to the possession of the poet's harp, while elucidating, at the same time, the psycho-symbolic dynamics involved in its poetic representation. The boy's sexual initiation through his hallucinatory encounter with the country girl is a symbolic unfolding of a psychic initiation or deepening of consciousness or, as Annis Pratt suggests, of "the Jungian motif of rebirth through a plunge into the waters of intercourse or into the depth of the unconscious."[7] Indeed, as its optical connotations also suggest, "A Prospect of the Sea" is about *insight*—to the endopsychic fantasy at the bottom of the sea-prospects, as well as *foresight* to the psychic fate embodied in it. In other words, the story is about the realization, in both senses of the word, of the Freudian reality of instincts and their vicissitudes or "destinies,"[8] which the protagonist intuits and the autobiographical narrative unfolds: Eros and Thanatos in the pre-oedipal, bivalent sea, and their predestined dialectical reenactment in the oedipal detour that divides the waters into the first and the last seas.

The story is also, as Pratt says, a story "about the search for a source of all story,"[9] which the narrative lays bare by the performance of its symbolic transgressions and "detour," and this in conformity with Jakobson's formula for poetic language.[10] Both aspects of the narrative "history"—representation and performance—are symbolically related by the protagonist's sea-voyage along a double track of "vertical" diving and "horizontal" surf riding (or ark sailing). The threefold recurrence of this double track determines—maps, times—the nautical *chronotopos* of the protagonist's triple mental prospect within the narrative's "three-storied" mise-en-abyme structure outlined below. The horizontal tracks are paved by the metonymical unfolding of the protagonist's history in the metaphorical sea-prospects/journeys, which provide different degrees of insight into its psychological meaning according to their place in the diegetic scale. The vertical tracks are paved by the protagonist's deepening introspection, gained by his diving down the paradigmatic axis of the sea metaphor, across the symbolic/diegetic boundaries of its variations toward their ultimate, *sub*-marine endopsychic signified. Thus, the exposition and the resolution provide the extradiegetic, realistic frame narrative of the protagonist's horizontal journey from the first sea of his cradled childhood to his boat-steering maturity. Crossing that axis, the adolescent dives into his intra-diegetic, intro-spective sexual fantasy (about, or inspired by, the encounter with the girl), whose metaphorical, horizontal unfolding reflects the realistic history within which it is embedded and anticipates its end. Occurring during the real course of one summer morning (we learn, toward the end of it, that it was still "that morning," [10]), it takes its symbolic place between "his first terror . . . like a sun returning from the sea that sank it" (6) and "the afternoon [that] was dying . . . drifting westward . . . down the tide of the sun on to the grey and chanting shore where the birds from Noah's ark glide by with bushes in their mouths" (7–8). Crossing that horizontal East-West track at the moment of sunset, "as the day began to die," the boy plunges into another dream within the dream which, dramatizing the sexual-textual dialectics of Eros and Thanatos, anticipates the rest of the story and its resolution. The vertical dream journey goes "*from history to the thigh*" (8), that is, to the origin of that history in the signifying body and its parental origins—the maternal "*cave*" in "the *thigh* in the dark" and its paternal sublimation in "*the loving room of the world*" "*roofed and floored with the live pages of the book of days*" (9)—and back up again, through the diegetic scale, to its creative destination in Noah's ark. The simultaneous ascending/descending movement toward the biological and the symbolic origins reflects the "historical" sequences within which it is embedded, in its projection on the axis leading from the East to "the first and West print between the dark and the green Eden" in the East ("under Asia") of "the [turning] earth that rolled on to its music in the beginning evening" (8–9). The beginning takes place in the evening to anticipate, one might suppose, the old man's regeneration in the decline of his days. It takes place, I recapitulate, by the projection of the vertical paradigm of its metaphorical sea-prospects onto the horizontal narrative syntagma, which realizes the metonymical destiny that these metaphors condense—by way of transgressing their metaphorical boundaries. Indeed, it is by following Jakobson's formula that the beginning "once below a time" is temporalized as a historical beginning, that is, as the "once *upon* a time" that opens the future destiny of the drives toward their end which, sublimated, becomes a regenerative origin. In the following close analysis of this narrative destiny, I will concentrate on the dynamics of *semiotic* enchantment and its determinant role in its oedipal course.

Exposition 2: The Voice and the Echo

The opening paragraph of the story provides a synoptic exposition of its entire sequence and shows how the literalization of a sea metaphor actually leads the protagonist from childhood to adolescence. The associative sequence in this passage manifests the transformation in the boy's relation to the maternal through the gradual change in his perception and mode of inhabiting his space. This change consists in an increasing predominance of active "doing" over passive "being" within a symbolic activity that is marked by a growing degree of sophistication, which manifests a growing need to patch up the psychic breach opened by the re-ambiguation of the "returning" sexualized maternal. Thus, a stimulative chain of associations set off by a *sensation*, followed by a *day-dream* and a *game*, finally leads to the *story* that tells of the problematics of the pre-oedipal ambivalence, which the adolescent will eventually *reenact*. At first the boy is passively cradled in the maternal space of his childhood *reverie* under "the *unbrokenly* blue sky" (3), and is as yet unconscious of its being about to be broken by the ominous flock of "blackbirds . . . in a cloud" (5) which foreshadow the "flood" that will upset and divide his homogeneous perceptual field. Immersed in the *semiotic* space of his sensations, he feels the "*hot*" weather while staring into the "*blue* sky falling over [in 'unbroken' continuity with] the edge of the corn" which he "*heard*" "sway from side to side above him" in the wind which, "after the *warm* rain before noon, *smelt* of rabbits and cattle" (3). This containment in the mammal-smelling, swaying-wet-warm-blue sensation generates a *daydream* which translates its oceanic space into a clear image of the sea, and its passive experience into an active one that anticipates the sexualization of the maternal mind-scape: "Now he was riding on the sea, swimming through the golden corn waves, gliding along the heavens like a bird" to build "a nest in the sixth of the seven trees that waved their hands from a bright, green hill," where he will eventually meet the country girl. In the "active" scene of the daydream, the boy realizes his imaginary omnipotence. Assuming whatever identity he fancies ("now he was . . . gliding along the heavens like a bird," "now he was a boy with tousled hair" [3]), he appropriates the containing space by acting on it, delineating it by his movement through it, and activating it (making the trees wave to him). But his omnipotence is not really his, for in effect he is subject to the power of the unconscious maternal agent, who is cunningly preparing its return from the repressed: the narrative way to the beckoning trees is smooth with *semiotic* devices which prefigure their seductive metaphorical signified and lead the boy to his crisis imperceptibly, by maintaining the sense of the continuity of his mothered "transitional" world. Thus, the verbs in the continuous form (*lying*, *swimming*, *gliding*, etc.) suggest uninterrupted iterative motion and join in the sonorous binding of rhyming words which as it were slide out of one another (*riding-golden-gliding-along*), warding off any suspicion of rupture. The boy yields to the seduction and, "rising lazily to his feet, wander[s] out of the corn['s]" cradle to enact the oedipal fantasy underlying his imaginary omnipotence in a *game* which he plays in the river by the hillside. He makes "a mock sea-wave" which foreshadows the disturbance of the smooth face of the "unbrokenly blue" mirror of his childhood sea upon the eventual tide of his sexuality, which is in turn anticipated by the fish that swims "in and out of the tower gates" of his fingers. The fish flashes back the subject of the "swimming through the . . . corn" in the daydream and conjures his desired object, who stars in the *story* which the game inspires: "He made up a story as the fish swam through the gates into . . . the moving bed" and into the story, where he plucks the hair of a drowned princess (3).

The story evokes the repressed contents which are about to complete their return by bursting the symbolic limits within which the boy has so far managed to confine them. Failing to ensure their psychic containment, the boy's symbolic "doing" will be substituted by compulsive action in a reality that does not know the *as-if* limits of the game, the story, and the metaphor. That the drowned, or repressed, princess returns from the sea of the unconscious to drown the boy in the chaos which her sexy appearance will set in his mind, is anticipated by the vertical movement of the boy's imagination in the space of his changing sea-prospect: after "riding *on* the sea," he breaks its surface by "swimming *through* the . . . waves" of his associations, till he finally reaches the bottom story of the "*drowned* princess," where the image of the maternal emerges in its original ambiguity:

> There was a drowned princess from a Christmas book, with her shoulders broken and her two red pigtails stretched like the strings of a fiddle over her broken throat; she was caught in a fisherman's net, and the fish plucked her hair. He forgot how the story ended, if ever there were an end to a story that had no beginning. Did the *princess* live again, rising like a *mermaid* from the net, or did a prince from another story tauten the tails of her hair and bend her shoulder-bone into a harp and pluck the dead, black tunes for ever in the courts of the royal country? (3–4).

The two options configure the returning maternal and the two ways of going about its ambiguous, dangerous, and animating charms which are, essentially, the ways of the *siren* and the *muse* and their metonymical correlatives, the *voice* and the *echo*. The first option involves letting the maternal "live again" by yielding to the melancholic voice of the siren, who seduces toward the lethal site underlying her *semiotic* representations, while the second option is to re-verberate her voice on a *symbolic* "harp," whose orphic "black tunes" (4) tell the nostalgic story of the drowning in and of the ambiguous mermaid in order to turn her into a good princess (the true princesses are the princesses which we have killed, to paraphrase Proust on nostalgic idealization).[11] These two options are, of course, the story's absent beginning and its as-if forgotten end, that is, the beginning which the boy must forget in order to make up the story that represents it, which *is* its performative end and the self-reflexive reverberation of its beginning: its protagonist, the drowned princess, is the siren turned into the muse so that her voice may animate the story that kills her and saves the fisherman. But the two options are also the beginning and the end of the "other story" which the metaphorical story of the princess anticipates as well as metonymically propels: the indeterminate ending is the double determination with which the adolescent will be confronted upon the return of the ambiguous maternal to complicate his life by making ambiguous not only his representations, as she does here, but also the ontological status of their performance. She will do this presently, by stepping out of the story and blurring its textual boundaries—until she is confined to yet "another story," outsteps its boundaries, etc., etc. The dialectical *fort-da* game of reviving the siren and killing her again will lead to her final liquidation at the story's end, so that her song may resound "forever" in a "three-storied" ark made of her wailing shoulder-bones (or, to be literal, of the "Eastern timber" which was once her seven beckoning trees [12]).

Complication: From History to the Thigh

The mermaid begins to gain power over the boy as soon as he forgets the end of her story. The indeterminacy of the story's forgotten conclusion ambiguates not only its content, but also its boundaries: its open-endedness leaves the siren an opening from which she can step out of the story, or alternatively, the boy must forget the end of the story (of his life) and its menacing significance—so that he may reenact it. Unconscious, he yields to the voice of his destiny, letting its *semiotic* enchantment take him beyond the boundaries of the innocent children's story which it has animated to the uncanny world of hallucinations that blur the boundaries between text and context and between fantasy and reality. This process of desymbolization (which, let us remember, also dynamizes the imaginary chain that deepens the protagonist's insight and enhances his ultimate maturation), appears innocent at first, such being the way of all effective seduction. Thus, following (and repressing) the insightful story and preceding its realization, a quasi-mystical experience of pre-verbal affirmation of the sleeping God's creation restores childhood's innocence and the sleep of both father and son to the Symbolic law which turns them into rivals: "there were *no words* for the sky and the sun and the summer country; the birds were *nice*, and the corn was *nice*" (4). But this affirmation is not really innocent; it is a foreclosure of the paternal law and its function as well as of the fallen knowledge of its conditions, which enables the boy to pursue his desire *despite* the notion of loss and death which the story of the princess has intimated. Indeed, that notion is reflected in the conscious nostalgic nature of the experience which, like its analogue in the "fields of praise" in "Fern Hill," reflects the lifting of repression underlying its intensity. The comparison in "[t]his was the best summer *since the first seasons of the world*" intimates the archaic loss and manifests the dawning consciousness of its repetition upon the present breaking of the "second mirror." What makes the "field" ("of praise") "nice" and the trees "innocent" *like* "after the birth of the simple light" is, precisely, the work of an almost willed repression of what has already begun its irrevocable return, so that desire may be realized without an inhibiting, guilty self-consciousness. The defensive repression of the loss is reflected in the emphatic negation of its signs: "There were *no* chimneys on the hills with *no name* in the distance"; "he could think of *no words* [—which implies that he had thought of them—] to say how wonderful the summer was." Similarly, "he *did not believe* in God, *but* God had made this summer" for the boy to appropriate in the absence of his (denied) authority. Thus, the apparently unmediated, primary experience of a pre-verbal Eden is actually the secondary effect of *un-naming*, which the boy performs in order to hold on to the instinctual innertness from which he has already begun to awaken. It serves to anaesthetize the conflict triggered by his awakening sexuality, so that he may pursue his desire without fear or guilt toward the hill in the "*nameless distance*" (4).

And so, he "crossed the nice field and climbed the hill" on which she stood, to pursue his vertical—sexual-textual—dive toward her "undrowned" garden (8) at his story's "abyme," where he will find (a revealing representation of) its lost beginning and end. But the origin and destination of his journey are suggested already at this point, by an allusion to the mythical woman who spins his destiny. In Celtic mythology, as Annis Pratt notes in her source study of Thomas's early stories, the hill is associated with "Banshee," the "White Woman," "whom Graves describes as '*the woman of the hill*' wailing in prophetic anticipation whenever anyone of royal blood is about to die."[12] In some legends, her hill is an island in the sea, "to which a number of sacred kings, including Arthur, sail at their deaths." But "the lady on the summit of the water"—that teat for which Orpheuses of both sexes risk their lives—is also Gwenhwyvri, the wife of the "ark lord" in the Welsh version of the story of Noah, which Dylan the "sea-son" will have his autobiographical narrator impersonate once he comes to marry, or reconcile himself to, the ambivalent female inscribed in his imagination.

The completion of the process of desymbolization occurs when "[t]he story of the princess died. That afternoon there was no drowning sea to pull her pigtails; the sea had flowed and vanished, leaving a hill, a cornfield, and a hidden house" (4). The story dies, of course, so that the girl may rise out of it "like Venus" and make love to the boy in the "undrowned" landscape—which she appropriates by way of hallucinatory projection—of the beginning as well as the end, as she insinuates by mentioning the metonymical "pyramid" of her mummified sister (7). The return of the maternal in its original, castrating ambiguity is foreshadowed by the configuration of the boy's fear of its consquences in the "*blackbirds* [which] flew out towards the sun" to fore-shadow its symbolic light (4). They did so by their ominous symbol as well as by their sound, whose *semiotic* effect, transgressing the *symbolic* boundaries of her story, summons into life the girl with the *br*own *l*egs and the *black* and *bro*k*e*n nail*s* that will eventually "snip off his tongue" (6), and with "*be*r*r*ies" stains around her mouth which will turn out to be blood. The blackbirds also herald the flying "*broom-rider*" who, with her metonymical raven and like a cuckoo bird which is "after nests," will steal the boy (from the nest he was building for himself in the "seventh tree" in the exposition) and "*r*un with [him] *r*attling insi*d*e her" to her "*d*en in a woo*d*" and her "hole in a tree" where his "uncle will never find [him]," etc., etc. (6–7). The performative *semiotic* effect of the sound repetition here makes palpable the boy's experience of his paranoid hallucination by way of strong onomatopoeia which concretizes his fear (*brrr* . . .) and by seeming to accelerate the pace of the chase so as to reflect his sense of losing control over the creature of his imagination, which threatens to swallow him.

The fantasy of the witch manifests the archetypal fear of the omnipotent mother who, giving life, can also take it when she will—unless her power be appropriated by her speaking offspring, that is, subjected to a symbolic articulation whereby he may generate himself, independent of her ambiguous favors. The intrapsychic power struggle between these options is determined, at this point, in favor of the one represented by the girl in her capacity as a witch, who realizes the boy's fear by exerting her enchantment to the *semiotic* effect of defamiliarizing his sense of reality and of his own identity. Her performance, or the conflictual dynamics of the psychic state which her emergence triggers, throws everything into confusion in a hectic rhythm which destabilizes all perceptions. In contrast with the slow motion and spaciousness of the initial childhood reverie, in which the child could take on any identity he chose, now everything "happened in half a second" (5), in a crazy series of optical distortions ("prospect": short for prospect glass . . . *telescope*, *microscope*, field-glass [*OED*]), which deprive him of any possibility of identifying himself in relation to reality: "He saw the many-coloured country shrink like a coat in the wash. Then a new wind sprang from the pennyworth of water at the river-drop's end, blowing the hill field to its full size . . . (5)" The boy tries to gain some control over things and reassert their boundaries as well as his own by framing and distancing them as "stories," but the stories become too real and burst their boundaries as hallucinations:

> Her mouth was an inch from his. . . . This is a story, he said to himself, about a boy . . . kissed by a broom-rider; she flew from a tree on to a hill . . . and when she had loved him until he died she carried him off inside her. . . . But the story, like all stories [and boys], was killed as she kissed him (6).

Although the literalization of the story places him momentarily back in reality—"now he was a boy in a girl's arms"—the daze of rapidly changing scenes and their status defamiliarizes him to himself: "*Who* had been frightened of a wind out of the light swelling the small country? . . . *Who* had been frightened of a sunburned girl . . . ?" (7). No answer. "What's your name, Amman?" No answer still: "The afternoon was dying; lazily, *namelessly* drifting." And when the girl volunteers to identify herself, the boy forgets her name as soon as she articulates it (9), which accounts for the hectic changes in *her* identity and for the reader's consequent doubt as to the reality of her existence at all outside the protagonist's private masturbatory fantasy.

The peak of this fantasy, the protagonist's submarine journey to Eden in the thigh (8–9), provides a concise and direct insight into the oedipal drama enacted in his process of desymbolization and, more generally, into the traumatic (adolescent) causality underlying the relation between sexuality and textuality in the history of his advent as a poet. It does so both by reflecting the story within which it is embedded and by its causal relation to it. The *timing* of the fantasy's projection elucidates the relation between the pubescent's dawning consciousness of the differential reality of sex and time and the pre-oedipal conflict which it de-fossilizes. The journey takes place when "the day [begins] to die" and the girl is about to leave the boy. She has already "stroked her clothes into place and patted back her hair," getting ready to disappear into the sea, from where she will ring her nipple-bell for him to follow her, the occurrence of which is anticipated by the sun's approaching the waterline. Thus, the future prospect of the sea revealed at this point signifies the double death of separation *and* symbiotic (melancholic) fusion, in the sea which is the place of loss and / *or* of being lost, as well as the temporal and Symbolic reality which determines these alternatives: it is also the prospective tide of "*to-morrow and to-morrow tower[ing]* over the *cracked sand castles*" (or mirror) which the boy dreads on finding himself "out of love." In order to avoid the prospect of that nautical *chronotopos* of loss, which combines the paternal and the maternal forms of castration, the boy dives into it so as to transcend it and inherit what underlies it, namely, the parental generative properties—in the procreative "thigh" and the creative Word (or alternatively, in the origin of subjective history in the signified and signifying body). He gains the omnipotent power of self-generation by an act of simultaneous blindness and insight—the paradoxical combination characteristic of poetry and psychosis alike (and not alike) as attempts to ward off death and castration. "When God was sleeping," he "*awoke* . . . into . . . [the] dream" which *forecloses* the reality of time and loss by a voyeuristic act of penetration, or *in-sight*, into the "garden" in the thigh and "the loving room of the world" "roofed and floored with the live pages of the book of days," thus usurping its lawful proprietor and author. Killing time, he moves beyond the *dead* pages of the book of days—the "time-cast shade[s]" and the fossiled traces ("print[s]," "signature") of the sea of time—back to the "pitch *space*" of the maternal Eden in the thigh, which he conquers by illuminating its pitch-darkness with his "*shaft of light*." That ambiguous object signifies, on the one hand, his sex ("spear," "lance" [*OED*]) and his symbolic faculty ("ray of light") and, on the other hand, the space in which it moves ("tunnel of blast furnace"), which he redeems from its deadening "darkness" by an act of re-symbolization that regenerates him and the dead world: sublimating the "turning knives" and the by now familiar phobic "flesh-white birds" in the prehistorical "*cave*" into the "summer *vision*" of "the *loving room* of the world" in "the *beginning* evening," the boy shifts the direction of his vertical journey from the westbound, de-symbolic dive to the "dark Eden," to the eastbound climb to the "green Eden" up the ladder of creation, to appropriate "the room three jumps above the final rung." By his voyeuristic in-sight to their maternal signified, he revives the pages of the book of days, thus inheriting its author and re-creating his history and the world, which he carries on his back "like Atlas" (8–9).

But as "the two *poles* [kiss] behind [the incestuous overreacher's] shoulders," he begins to "*lope*" down the "*slope*" of his megalomanic dream back down to the girl'*s lap*, slip-sliding on the *semiotic* soundtrack from the summit of his imagined creativity back to the actual source of the enchantment in "the hill in . . . the fields" which is all that that summit really is. "'Wake up', she said into his ear . . . and Eden shrank into the seventh shade" to clarify whose creative and destructive power has dominated and will continue to dominate here. Look in my eyes, says the witch, and the obedient boy sees that "her eyes . . . were sea blue . . . [and] made a round glass of the sun" (9).

After returning to snatch Eden away again, the country mermaid drives the boy mad with despair at the reality, which he can no longer control by fantasy, of her inevitable loss—*or* his. It is at this point that his conflict reaches its climax, manifesting itself in a chaotic confusion of conscious but unstable and therefore unassertable boundaries. Thus, antithetical symbols emerge to confuse him with antithetical messages:

> The hill in two searchlights: the back moon shone on seven trees, and the sun of a strange day moved above water in the spluttering foreground. The hill between an owl and a seagull: the boy heard two birds' voices as brown wings climbed through the branches and the white wings before him fluttered on the sea waves. 'Tu wit tu woo, do not adventure any more' (10).

But the choice between "to wit" and "to woo" the girl—between exerting prudent reason and yielding to madness—is impossible. The brown owl says "do not adventure any more," but "the gulls told . . . him to race on along the warm sand until the water hugged him to its waves," and the boy cannot judge because all the symbolic values are confused: the prohibitive tree owl is dark like the ominous raven and the blackbirds while the seductive seagull is white, the moon in charge of the feminine tide shines on the trees and the sun hovers on the waters (as it previously shone in the girl's mirroring eyes), and just when he feels glad of the girl being near him, thinking, as he has done several times before, that the "monstrous" and "frightening" princess was "broken," she runs him "to the edge of the sea" into which she disappears (10).

At this liminal point, the boy hears the siren's voice in "the noise of the sea breaking" on the shore amplified by "the whole world's voices" whose origin, "a white-faced sea of . . . the terrible mortal number of the waves," beckons him with "deliberate" "long . . . sea gestures" to the "one direction" of melancholic suicide (9–11). But the experience of limits shocks the boy into clarity and self-assertion, and so he runs for his life and "[t]he sea was lost behind the dunes" and the boundaries of another story—about the temptation to transgress them and follow the voice which it reverberates:

> There was a story once upon a time whispered in the *water voice*; it blew out the *echo* from the trees behind the beach . . . until the

> musical birds and beasts came jumping into sunshine. [But then a] raven flew by him, out of a window in the Flood to the blind wind tower shaking in to-morrow's anger like a scarecrow made out of weathers (11–12).

Once again the boy is on the waterline, in the conflict between the dark and the bright birds, at the crossroad between the vertical gesture of the echo ("*wind-tower*") and the horizontal axis of time which it sublimates, signified a little earlier as "the *horizontal rainfall*," which threatens to collapse it. But this time the ominous raven who foreshadows "to-morrow's anger" is stopped by a *scarecrow*, which is also a weathercock that facilitates the resolution of the conflict by pointing the directions clearly:

> 'Once upon a time', said the water voice.
> 'Do not adventure any more', said the echo.
> 'She is ringing a bell for you in the sea.' (12)

Resolution?

"'. . . *you shall never go back*,'" say "the owl and the echo" that reverberates all the way foreward to the story's "horizon," where a "dove with a green petal follow[s] in the raven's flight" and the "cloudy shapes" of the rest of the "mad, nameless animals," now named and tamed, step into the "*hewn* door" of the old man's ark (12). Sailing its three-storied charge to what end, "if ever there was an end to a story that had no beginning" (3)? For the end of the story is ambiguous—just like its beginning, and because of it: "Cool rain began to fall" (12). Is the siren rising again, or is it only the echo of her voice, reverberating "forever" the eternal beginning of the circular story? For such is the way of the echo: it roles backwards and forwards between its source and its end, ambiguating its double destinations by re-verberating its beginning toward an end that is the re-pre-sentation of the beginning, etc., etc. This is how the old man suspends the prospective end of his history—the prospect of the last sea—through the re-presentation of its archaic signified and propelling origin (in the first sea). By remembering the adolescent's desire he subjects it to his sublimatory purposes, turning it into the animating force of his "history."

The dialectic of memory and desire governs, as I have indicated in the beginning of the analysis, the wavelike structure of "A Prospect of the Sea" (the story is, indeed, about structuring the sea and making it sing in its chains like the boy in the sea of "Fern Hill"), as a flux of flashbacks and anticipations, of insights (to instinctual origins) and foresight (to the vicissitudes and the destinies of the instincts). The doubly determined narrative flow suspends the determination of the status of its end terms by ambiguating the narrative time and point of view: the anticipatory foresights suggest the possibility, which I have raised in passing earlier, that the final "resolution" is a future projection rather than the point of departure for the retrospective "history." This possibility seems likely in the light of the preoccupation, which dominates a great deal of Thomas's work, with his vocation as a poet. Many of his generally self-reflexive works, most of which were written early in his poetic career ("A Prospect of the Sea" was written in 1935, when he was twenty-one), project different versions of the "prophetic" (wishful) autobiography of an orphic (Christ-like, Noah-like) poet. To his biographer, Paul Ferris, the course of Thomas's life seems a "progress of an oddly mannered kind," because "[t]here is always a hint with [him] that he planned his life . . . that he set up his biographers in advance."[13] The significance of this planning, as it were, for me in the present context, is not the (fatal) aspect of self-dramatization involved (which Ferris emphasizes), but its underlying sharp introspective awareness, and the determination, on Thomas's part, to put it to practical consequence. Thomas felt that his life depended on his writing away the psychic traumatism activated in his adolescence, whose meaning and implications he clearly intuited and expressed. Beyond his thematic concerns, his dense, meticulously structured and overcharged language reflects the tension of a symbolic over-"doing" that is motivated by a need to constantly catch up with the bubbling up of some inner catastrophe and lock it up in words. Like his protagonist, he had to turn it into "stories" quickly, before it overflowed to drown him. And for this purpose he exercised penetrating and highly (and perhaps overly) articulate self-analysis, which he rationalized in the claim that "poety must drag further into the clean nakedness of light more even of the hidden causes than Freud could realize."[14]

But the obsessive self-analysis—the clawing out of the crocodile—and the compulsive over-structuration of the threatening internal materials do not always reflect integration. The first to feel this was Thomas himself, who, with all his effort "to take the *dead* flesh, and . . . build up a *living* flesh from it,"[15] was very worried about killing the living "flesh" with his dissecting, tightly-woven words; he was worried, that is, about the linguistic fossilization of his emotional experience, whose reality he found difficult to tolerate.[16] This is precisely what happens in "A Prospect of the Sea" to make it possible for the protagonist to become a poet: just as, as an adolescent, he needed to turn his affair with the girl into a story every time its imaginary reality became too much for him, so, at the somewhat sad end of the story, the girl must die so that the lonely old man can make his questionable peace with life—by renouncing it. In an ark made of the neatly compartmentalized "*cloudy shapes*" (12) (which echo the "time-cast shades" that are the fossilized pages of the "book of days"), he sails toward the death signified by watertight stories which replace life. Indeed, we are back to the same dissociative Lacanian predicament, the disjunctive choice between *either* Symbolic castration *or* its maternal counterpart; either literature or life—which is too "Real" to be possible. And when the siren, too badly abused to agree to become a muse, refuses to lend her voice to the harp (which is not so much the case with the performance of "A Prospect of the Sea" as with the worry which it expresses), Noah's peace with his destiny is bound to be disrupted at some stage by another flood, which is forecast in the story's closing sentence. The unintegrated body is bound to rebel and retrigger the dissociative dialectics between the *two* modes of its *derealization*, which are characteristic of the kind of humans who "[c]annot bear very much reality" (T. S. Eliot).[17] These are clearly dramatized in the way in which the adolescent protagonist handles the experience of his sexuality. The ordinary girl ("[s]he was no taller or stranger than the flowery girls on Sundays who picnicked in Whippet valley," [5]) turns into a fantastic witch because the boy cannot contain the *ordinary* ambivalence she arouses in him, and when that defensive paranoic strategy (the fantasies of castration are no more real than the idealizations of the maternal) becomes intolerable, the boy shifts to the opposite one, turning his experience into a story which fossilizes it, until it bursts the story's boundaries precisely because it fails to integrate it, etc. It is in view of this syndrome that I interpret "The Mouse and the Woman" as the continuation of "A Prospect of the Sea," which tells how the "rain began to fall" (12) again, to wreck the mature poet's watertight ark. It is, as I read it, the story of a poet whose words do not satisfy him as such, because they seem to kill what is alive or life-giving in him. And so that "thing" protests: "'Let me be born,' it had cried" (62) and the pressure which "it" puts on the words that fail to contain and express it is so great that they break, and so "it" loses its meaning, and the poet—his mind.

"THE MOUSE AND THE WOMAN"

"The Mouse and the Woman" is about a poet who tries to write the woman of his dreams into being and consequently goes mad. His degeneration from poetry to psychosis is depicted as a transgression of the symbolic limits of the magic function of language, whereby, it seems to me, his author vicariously checks the limitations of his own creative power. By taking the realization of his protagonist's desire for verbal mastery of reality to its pathological extreme, Thomas conveys here with the greatest lucidity the semiology of poetic enchantment and its narcissistic dynamics, as well as his own fear of, and fascination with, the possibility of madness. This ambivalent attitude is reflected both in the plot itself and in its linguistic casting, which projects an at once compassionate and critical attitude toward the subject of the events. The story traces the process of the protagonist's psychic disintegration so closely and meticulously as to suggest its author's enchantment with it as well as his need to control it. The same need is also suggested by the slightly, though half playfuly moralistic presentation of the process as a drama, or "morality play," of narcissistic inflation and consequent deflation. The defensive casting of this drama yields a revealing insight into Thomas's conflict-ridden preoccupation with the vicissistudes of his own narcissism, and into the essentially narcissistic aspect of creativity in general. This critical attitude, however, is effectively balanced by the poet's delighted and stylized approach to his ultimate concern, namely, the magic of poetic language, the ultimate triumph of which manifests itself in the poetic performance of "The Mouse and the Woman."

As in "A Prospect of the Sea," the dynamics of enchantment are explored in the story through a thematization of *voice*, the paradigmatic device and metaphor of *semiotic* signification. By dramatizing its material effect and psychological image, the story analyzes the mystique of voice which often motivates poetic creation and governs its dialectic dynamics—or, alternatively, ensnares its subject into madness. The narrative display of its pathological occurrence foregrounds the fallacy of the "true," intuitive or poetic "inner voice," as well as its originating source in the narcissistic desire for self-authentication and the power which it implies (the self-generating or self-signifying narcissist's omnipotence). As in "A Prospect of the Sea," a feminine voice which "presents" (as in *makes present*) the maternal object which it signifies is contrasted with the object's differential, symbolic "representation." The latter (symbolic) mode, which "A Prospect of the Sea" concretizes in the image of the reverberating echo, is configured here by reflexive *vision* (associated, naturally, with the solar metaphor of metaphors). Here, too, the voice conducts, or compels, a passive, receptive movement of *listening*, which is countered by the assertive movement of its mediated symbolic articulation. The interplay of these two, passive and active, modes, as we have seen in "Poem in October," may take the dialogical form that validates the fallacy of voice—in retrospect: the wishfully "attentive" utterance of the voice actually generates its wished-for subjective "source," that is, the original integrity or truth of the "dead child" which comes into being in the integrative course of the "dialogue" between the subjective *symbolic* position and the *semiotic* otherness which inspires it (while and by subverting its asserted boundaries). In the drama of "The Mouse and the Woman," however, the conflict underlying this dialectical tension is too intense to allow for an integrative dialogue, and manifests itself in the dissociative overpowering of what is consequently proved to be the fallacious mystique of voice: abandoning himself to its magic—to passive "being in the listening" to his wishful authenticity, the poet-protagonist finds himself enchanted away from reality and out of the symbolic control which sustains it, and, indeed, into the fatal knowledge of his origins. . .

❧

Oh, what a world of profit and delight,
Of power, of honour, of omnipotence,
Is promised to the studious artizan!
. . . . . .
. . . his dominion that exceeds in this
Stretcheth as far as doth the mind of man:
A sound magician is a demi-god.
. . . . . .
Hell hath no limits, nor is circumscribed
In one self place.

(*Doctor Faustus*)[18]

The protagonist's self-defeating transgressive enterprise is dramatized as a Faustian tragedy of overreaching, which "drag[s] into the light" the demonic aspect of the Janus-faced poetic daemon, namely, the death-driven repetition-compulsion underlying the creative and destructive manifestations of the "inspired" narcissistic predicament. Induced by the demon, the Faustian poet aspires to overcome his human limitations by a necromantic practice of the divine technique of the Word, and ends up being overwhelmed by them, driven by the unbearable deflation of his wishful omnipotence into sterility and madness. As in the Faustian drama, the overreacher's downfall is the consequence of a bad deal with the devil, to whom he sells his limited but real creative power for a short-term loan of a greater but imaginary one. Ensnared by the seductive manipulations of his poetic daemon—"that still small voice that speaks in the night" (72)—he becomes the object of demonic possession: "I have a devil, but I do not tell it what to do. It lifts my hand. I write. The words spring into life" (65) by the *poetic* blurring of the boundaries between signifier and signified, and then they die by the hyperbolic extension of that magic to the *psychotic* blurring of boundaries between sign and object, text and context, fantasy and reality. The tragic, hyperbolic, determinism of the fatal gesture of the possessed hand is anticipated—in conformity with the rule of the dramatic genre—metonymically: "There was an *oracle* in the lead of the pencil" (62).

The trangressive peformance of Marlowe's overreacher is a rebellious repetition of the primal sin, the aim of which is, in the final, oedipal analysis, the foreclosure of the law that predestines the "punishment" for it in order to enact it—but upon one's own choice. This assertion of mastery is the joint enterprise of Wrath and Pride, the major Deadly accomplices of the compulsive Devil of repetition, who claim the choice that has been denied to Man by a blasphemous reading of the story of Genesis (see "Incarnate Devil"): if death, or castration, or the fall from Eden are inevitable, let it at least be their victimized object's own doing, whereby he will at least gain his "antithetical subjectivity." Thus, Doctor Faustus explains his decision to specialize in "necromancy" by a parodic argument which refutes the paternal law that rationalizes death as the result of a moral choice by exposing its arbitrariness:

> *Exhaereditare filium non potest pater, nisi—*
> [a father cannot disinherit the son, unless—]
> Such is the subject of the institute
> And universal body of the law.
>
> . . . . . .
>
> . . . Divinity, adieu![19]

he concludes, and turns his back on the law of the Father, only to implement it by sentencing himself to eternal damnation in the maternal "dominion" that "hath no limits." "I disdain to have any parents," says Pride, who wants none of their favors, deluding himself with the hope of generating himself as the "demi-god" of the dominion of the Imaginary.[20] But

Wrath, who has already murdered them—"I had neither father nor mother . . . I was born in hell"[21]—realizes the impossibility of the project as he finds himself returning to the site of the murder, to become his own victim in the "Impossible Real."

This oedipal drama (of suicidal attempt at self-generation) is also the essence of the mad poet's adventure, which consists in the compulsive reenactment of the self-reflexive story which springs into life and dies away under his possessed hand. Its protagonist, the poet, generates the woman who "had . . . been [with him] in the beginning" and without whom "there would have been no beginning" (61) in order to make love to her and thereby re-effect his beginning, for the consummation of which he is punished by the annihilation of both. In consequence of the symbiotic merging with her, the woman disappears and the poet goes mad with despair, which is nothing but the repetition of the very event which he seeks to undo by way of compulsive reenactment: their relationship of sex and mutual conception manifests, on the one hand, its underlying oedipal wish for self-generative omnipotence and, on the other hand, the manner of its self-destructive realization in the textual performance. The poet's transgressive relationship with the woman from "*a mad play by a Greek*" (59) who pleads to be born in his dreams represents the transgression of the boundary between signifier and signified, that is, between the signifier that she is and the "diabolic," regressive compulsion and object that she signifies. The woman is "of the devil"—or *is* the devil in disguise, who manipulates the *semiotic* charms of his sensuous signifier (his feminine disguise) in order to finally attain an unmediated expression. The devil attains his goal by inducing the poet to liberate the language-bound imaginary representation of his desire from the symbolic boundaries of his text, which sustain both the desire and the representation. In consequence, the metaphor of the woman collapses—she disappears—and its signified emerges to annihilate the poet as well: "'Welcome,' said the devil to the madman" on admitting his depleting client to the pits at No Self place, exhibiting his imperialistic identity behind the seductive woman's mask. "'Cast your eyes upon me. I grow and grow. See how I multiply. See my sad, Grecian stare. And the longing to be born in my dark eyes. Oh, that was the best joke of all'" (69). And as the devil inflates, the disempowered poet deflates: "I am only ten pounds now. I am lighter. Six pounds. Two pounds . . ." (73) And so he shrinks until he becomes a disembodied "flying voice," which is no other than "that still small voice that speaks in the night" to which "[i]t is wicked to listen" (72), with which the possessed poet identifies to the point of self-annihilation.

The mad Greek play from which the woman comes may of course be *Oedipus Rex*, as the oracle in the lead of the pencil intimates, but her seven duplicates, with their mad black hair and their ritualized suffering, also bring to mind the raging women of *The Bacchae*,[22] whom Dionysus cured of their madness by initiating them to his "new religion." The Dionysian motif plays a central role in the story, illustrating the pre-oedipal dynamics of merging and boundary blurring which subverts the paternal, Apollonian principle of the well-delineated form. The Dionysian is also the governing principle in the art of black magic practiced by the Faustian poet. The Alchemical tradition, according to Cavendish, identifies the magician with the founder of the "new religion," whose practice is interpreted as a symbolic procedure of self-authentication: "The magician's ordinary self is 'a mob of wild women, hysterical from uncomprehended and unsated animal instinct,' " whose "disorderly rabble" Bacchus, the "true self," transforms through ecstatic inner-fermentation into "harmonious movements."[23] The suggested allusion to *The Bacchae* explains, therefore, why Dr. Faustus chooses the Dionysian method for curing the woman of her "sickness of never having sinned and of never having done well" (60), which is the sickness of unreality suffered by all signs which repress, but fail to displace their dissociated subject's "unsated animal instinct."

The Apollonian-Dionysian antinomy manifests itself to dramatize the splitting oedipal conflict (over the transgression versus the assertion of boundaries) in the oppositions of sun-moon, day-night, sight-blindness (associated with voice), objectivity-subjectivity, distinct–ephemeral forms, etc. The poet's subversive disposition as a devotee of the "new religion" is suggested by the fact that he performs his necromantic business in the "*lunatic blackness*" of the night from which his images come, away from the "*harsh sun*" whose "beams . . . twisted his images into the *hard lines of light*" (60). Indeed, the "harsh sun" is the poet's bitter enemy, whose blinding light dispels the penumbral reality of all magic, but whose foreclosure di-spells the signification of reality—which leaves the poet no self place in which to be.

Defensive Fencing and De-fencing

The fascination with the transgression of laws and boundaries is reflected not only in the symbolic adventures of the protagonist of "The Mouse and the Woman," but also in their author's narrative and performance. As in "A Prospect of the Sea," Thomas employs here the associative technique of the literalization of metaphor to obtain a vicarious share of his protagonist's transgressive experiences, as well as a distancing framing technique which ensures the delineation of his often chaotic narrative. In both stories, he frees his narrative voice to indulge in self-enchantment, but within limits that are set by a mise-en-abyme structure. However, whereas the narrator of "A Prospect of the Sea" could afford to be swept by his protagonist's chaotic stream of consciousness—having reasons to trust that it should lead him to a relatively safe place—the fatal course of the poet's story in "The Mouse and the Woman" seems to require that its narrator take means of precaution against over-identification. To prevent a dangerous blurring of boundaries, he locks his protagonist up in a madhouse, within the boundaries of which the latter may enact his author's wildest transgressive fantasies. Correlatively, in order to make sure that his pencil should not be diabolically entranced, but may still produce the terrible delights of transgression, he uses a narrative structure and techniques of voice and focalization which reflect this ambivalent disposition.

The text is organized as a complex mise-en-abyme structure consisting of four diegetic levels: the frame-story or scene of the asylum, the scene of the reminiscing poet's consciousness, the retrospective story of his (self-destructive) creative process, and the content of his poetic text. The frame-story, like the walls of the lunatic asylum, serves as a defensive alienating structure which distances and delineates the psychotic reality evoked in the intradiegetic narrative. Its boundaries are clear, and so is the distinction between the poet's and the protagonist's perspectives. The intradiegetic levels, by contrast, constitute a foregrounding chaotic structure (or non-structure) which is mimetic of the protagonist's chaotic consciousness and effective in depriving the reader, too, of his reality testing with respect to the represented world. The retrospective story is narrated in a technique of combined speech, which makes it impossible to distinguish between the sane and the mad poets' voices, and hence between the protagonist's text and the context of its narration. Thus, for example, the event, in section 4, of the poet's meeting the woman "alive" for the first time on the beach, after having "put the pencil" with which he has written her story "down" (61), may be taking place in the poet's text or in its delirious context. It may also be a metaphor—but then whose metaphor is it? The mad reminiscing poet's or the reminisced one's? Or perhaps the narrator's? And does it signify the same thing in each case? Is it a romantic metaphor for the creative process or for its psychotic consequences? The combined speech gives no clue. Another example is the protagonist's nocturnal visit to the sleeping girl who clenches her fist over his ephemeral self, which has turned into a flying voice. The visit might be either the retrospective poet's delirium, evidence of which is to be found on the kitchen floor "painted all over with the grotesque figures of birds and girls" (77), or the reminiscing poet's hallucination, inspired by the sight of the girl in the asylum garden beckoning to the sparrows. A partially preventive remedy against the viscissitudes of diegetic perplexity is offered in the non-focalized frame story, in the form of a self-reflexive game of perspective (in the non-technical sense) which lays bare as if to dispel the psychotic literalization of metaphor. The reassuring presence of the asylum wall provides the figurative axis for an emphasized distinction, by way of ironic juxtaposition, between the perspectives of the mad inside and the sane outside of the story: "the asylum trees [waving] green hands . . . to the world outside" (58) in response to the birds' "whistl[ing] the coming in of spring" shows how the mad inside's vision of things literalizes that which, from the external point of view, seems only a harmless metaphor.

The most effective laying bare of the "crazy" device is brought about by the thematization, in the opening section, of the material phenomena of voice. Voice is evoked here as that which links between the inside and the outside of the body, and, in the present case, also between the inside and the outside of the story. The transition from the intra- to the extradiegetic story is performed through a foregrounding shift from ordinary to combined speech and from non- to internal focalization, which takes place in the gradual course of a narrative zooming in on the reminiscing poet's howling voice and its expressive source and effect. The narrative moves through a series of alternating auditory and visual images from the distant sound of the madman's voice "in the top room" to its source in his face in the open window and then closer, to his open mouth, then to his mind as he listens to it and finally to the memory-contents conjured by it into visual presence. The shift from the auditory to the visual illustrates the magic function of the image-making voice, whereby the poet-protagonist enchants himself into an auto-suggestive incantatory trance of reminiscing:

> Opening his mouth wide, he bayed up at the sun, *listening* to the inflections of his voice with a remorseless concentration. With his *unseeing* eyes fixed on the green garden, he *heard* the revolution of the years as they moved softly back. Now there was no garden. *Under the sun the iron bars melted.* Like a flower, a new room pulsed and opened (58–59).

The poet's voice melts the boundaries of his reality, symbolized by the bars of the window and the sun, which he "unsees" as the mnemonic contents reverberated by the *semiotic* inflections of the voice encroach upon his field of perception. The transition to combined speech in the passage, effected by the gradual liberation of the mental images from their subordination to their perceptual context, foregrounds them to the effect of conferring on the "combined voice" the magic power to enchant the reader, too, into the retrospective world. One might say, in other words—such that transgress the boundary between the metaphorical and the literal—that the mad and the sane poet's voices unite in this passage to melt the diegetic boundaries between the sane inside and the mad outside of the story; to turn it, as it were, outside in.

A Greek Tragedy

The force that drives the poet's oracular pencil predetermines the classically tragic structure of his story. Blinded by the intensity of his desire, the protagonist forgoes his intuition of the consequences of realizing it; he enacts the symbolic message of the oracle and suffers the pain of its inevitable "tragic recognition." The tragic sequence is condensed in the poet's first, oracular dream in section 2, which prefigures the oedipal destiny unfolded in the story—of the poet's compulsive acting out the contents of his dream. The dream anticipates the two, poetic and psychotic, phases in the enchanted poet's adventure of symbolization and desymbolization, while elucidating the psycho-symbolic, or sexual-textual relation between the story's levels of representation and performance. The poetic and the psychotic phases correspond to the sequence of oracular enigma and resolution which the dream dramatizes, and which symbolizes the transition from the suggestive representation, or *reverberation*, of the repressed in poetic enchantment to its unmediated "return" in psychosis.

In the first part of the dream, the mysterious woman emerges to signal the enigmatic inscription of the poet's astrological fate, which she and her seven duplicates "[spell] on the sky" (59) by the deictic gesture of their hands. The mystery of the woman and her enigmatic message are the source of her seductiveness as a *semiotic* signifier: the poet will be captivated by her spell out of a hermeneutic desire to know what it is that she is spelling for him in the sky. That this is indeed the case is suggested by the second part of the dream, where the astrological enigma is solved by the dramatization of its fatal decryption by the dreamer, who Real-izes, in the Lacanian sense, his hermeneutic desire for its castrating maternal signified. Giving way to its return, the feminine signifiers disappear and

> [w]here the women were was an avenue of trees. And the trees leant forward and interlaced their hands, turning into a black forest. He had seen himself, absurd in his nakedness, walk into the depths. Stepping on a dead twig, he was bitten (59).

The symbolic meaning of this obviously sexual scene is suggested by an allusion to a Welsh folklore story cited by Pratt.[24] The avenue of trees into which the woman's seven duplicates turn connotes the seven apple trees associated with Olwedd, "'the laughing Aphrodite of Welsh legend'" (who smiles at the poet a little later as "the creams of the sea ran . . . over her feet" and "[t]he spray brushed her naked body" [63]). That lady is met by Merlin, a late incarnation of Dylan the sea-son, when he goes to reclaim his promised property, the British Island. The quest for the girl and her apple represents, according to Pratt, "the bardic search for the Logos, for the maiden who guards it or for the tree which bears its derivations."[25] "The Welsh search for Genesis," Pratt emphasizes the context, is mainly "*for the source of verbal life*"—which is also the source of the poet's story and the woman's metonymical (indexed) signified. We learn this by what happens when the questing poet follows the index to its "corpo-Real" source, the knowledge of which is death. That death and the law which sentences (or phrases) it are symbolized by the "*dead*," and a few lines later the "*toothed*" "*twig*" on which the dreamer steps and gets himself "bitten." The "toothed twig" condenses, with psychological adequacy, the primal sin and its instantaneous punishment: the teeth belonging to the devouring mother are attributed to the dead twig, later the "*talking thorn*" (70), which is thus at once the phallic, prohibitive tree and its punitive correlative, the God-sent serpent who, while seducing him, bruises Adam's heel, or—why not?—Oedipus's foot, which was nailed, upon his father's indirect command, as a preventive punishment for his prospective sin. The same drama is enacted in the poet's two other anxiety-dreams. In the second dream (section 8), God and his cloudy throne dissolve into a nest of snakes whose hissing suggests the sound of water in which the poet drowns, seeing his aborted genesis—his abjection or maternal castration, that is—in the image of "a bottle of foetus" (66). The dissolution concretizes the abortive process of desymbolization (of the decoded paternal symbol) which brings about the poet's de-subjectification in the third and more obvious castration dream about the ultimate crushing of the desubstantiated "flying voice" (72).

THE MECHANISM OF HER DELIRIUM

The source of the poet's hermeneutic temptation to decipher the riddle of his origins is the indeterminacy of the woman's *semiotic* signification: "He remembered *the pitch of her voice*, though not what she said" (59). In order to help him find out, his dream zooms in on the source of the voice, and ends with a close-up on the face of the woman, who dominates, as it turns out, not only the perceptual field of her oneiric representation, but also its performance:

> Then there was her face again. There was nothing . . . but her tired face. And the changes of the details of the dream . . . the levers of the trees and the toothed twigs, these were the mechanisms of *her* delirium (59–60).

The mechanism of her seduction is the manipulation of the indeterminacy of her symbolic context, which magnetizes the desiring imagination. For desire works in the "lunatic blackness" (60) of the ambiguity which it creates as a condition for its realization—by way of neutralizing the subject's faculty of judgment.

The woman is born as a signifier that is *also* a being of flesh and blood by dint of the positive, integrative ambiguity generated by the "eucharistic" alchemy of poetic enchantment. That alchemy draws on the tension between sameness and difference in the metaphorical condensation, as is concretized in the depiction of the symbolic black mass which the poet holds at breakfast after waking from "her" dream. Contemplating her irresistable materiality, "[h]e saw her flesh in the cut bread; her blood, still flowing through the channels of her mysterious body, in the spring water" (61). At this point, the black sacrament is productive (of signification), because its symbolic limits and limitations are recognized: the metaphorical *com*-union is possible precisely because the discrete identities of the bread and the water on one side and of the flesh and the blood on the other are retained while as if merging to create the penumbral space of a *contained* paradox. The paradoxical tension between the simultaneously blurred and sustained boundary between signifier and signified generates the illusion of the realization of the signified desire. This optical illusion draws on the materiality of the sacramental signifier, which *almost* summons its signified into presence—by lending it its materiality. This "almost" sustains the woman as a fetishistic signifier within the bounds of the metaphorical *as-if.* But her creator, who cannot, or would not, contain the metaphorical paradox (and the desire which sustains it), will not content himself with a fetishistic substitute, and will venture to attain *the thing itself*—through a black practice of the sacrament of marriage.

His diabolical seduction to lie with his fetish (in section 9) is followed by a domestic argument (in section 11) concerning the question of the woman's clothing, in which the poet is still trying to assert his limits. Despite the woman's manipulative pretence of indignation, the poet insists on "cover[ing] up [her] nakedness" which, he soundly intuits, is "not good to look upon" (68). For him, "[s]he had lost none of her beauty with the covering up of her nakedness" (63), but had in fact gained it thereby, because, as it turns out, the woman *is* her clothes, while her nakedness is the diabolic absence—the "Impossible Real"—which she clothes with her metaphorical being. But "the terrible curve of her breast" (64) showing through her innocent domestic clothes (wherein she "swept [the floor] as a child sweeps the floor of a doll house" [67]) blinds him to this sound intuition, and, mistaking the negativity of the naked signified for a desired immanence, he strips the woman of her self only to face her diabolic Impossibility. The sexual consummation of their relationship represents the ultimate crossing of the linguistic barrier which has both separated and united them, and which has maintained their respective existence as the subject and the object of a language-bound desire. And once "[t]he last barrier fell away" (68), the tide of disjunctive, negative ambiguity rushes in to submerge the poet in the confusion of the psychotic "uncanny": "Real things kept changing place with unreal" (70). After the collapse of her metaphor, the woman grows more and more evasive, until she finally disappears. The poet tries to regain control over the situation and restore the chaotic contents of his delirium back into the text, "so that they might stand hard and clear upon the paper. But the words would not come" (66). Or alternatively, he "wrote upon the block of paper, not knowing what he wrote, and dreading the words that looked up at him" (73). Unable to detain the woman, he at least tries to control her loss by symbolizing it. Solemnly,

> He turned over the block of paper and upon the last page wrote in a clear hand:
>
> 21
>
> The woman died.
>
> 22
>
> There was dignity in such a murder. And the hero in him rose up in all his holiness and strength. It was just that he who had brought her forth from darkness should pack her away again . . . [but going down to the beach to drown his ever so solemnly ritualized sorrow], [t]here . . . she lay and smiled . . . (75–76).

For once the poet abandons his creative power to the lunatic ebb and flow of *her* delirium, the harsh sun would not lend him the hard lines of light which would fix her and make him master of his fate and the possessive woman.

A SYNOPTIC INTERLUDE (THE MISSING DOG)

> And this is all there was to it: a woman had been born, not out of the womb, but out of the soul and the spinning head. And he who had borne her out of darkness loved his creation, and she loved him. But this is all there was to it: a miracle befell a man. He fell in love with it, but could not keep it, and the miracle passed. And with him dwelt a dog, a mouse, and a dark woman. The woman went away, and the dog died. (73)

. . . which is why it is omitted from the title of the story, which is all about how an Imaginary woman went away because the Symbolic Dog died, and the mouse gnawed its way into the miraculous space of her representation to prove its Impossibility. The dog was the only one who could detain her, by keeping its watchful starry eye on the Edenic couple: "*green Sirius*, an *eye* in the east" (70), is the Dog Star which, in Egyptian astrology, rises and sets with the *sun* during the period of the floods.[26] And the sun, which is also an eye in the East, is "the old effigy of *time*" (74)—that "All-Seeing" "Chronos"[27] who gives and takes life—as well as "the eye of *God*" (76) that spies on the sinful couple who has inverted His name in their bedeviled dislectic rituals . . .[28] ("Within this circle is J-a's name / Forward and backward anagrammatised" [*Doctor Faustus*].)[29]

The synoptic quotation accounts for the poet's maddening loss of the woman as well as reality by foreclosing the Symbolic order that sustains both. The process is symbolized by the associative chain which begins with the missing dog:

> He buried the dog at the end of the garden. "Rest in peace," he told the dead dog. But the grave was not deep enough and there were rats in the under-hanging of the bank who bit through the sack shroud (74)

to awaken the pangs of conscience and the reflexive consciousness.

A PROTO-GRECIAN TRAGEDY

> I am covetousness. Begotten . . . in a leather bag[,] . . . might I now obtain my wish, . . . you and all, should turn to gold, that I might lock you safe into my chest. (*Doctor Faustus*).[30]

The protagonist dooms himself by yielding to the temptation to attain an internal knowledge of his origins instead of symbolizing them from without, which would give him some control over them. He is tempted despite his better judgement, which voices itself at the critical, liminal moment between wishful dreaming and waking into reality, a moment which the woman's voice seeks to subject to the projective mechanism of her delirium. Like Faustus's "Old Man," the voice of the reality principle and its Symbolic legislation emerges to try to break the enchantment, provoking a little psychomachia: "What she said . . . spoke in the wind *whose brother rattled the panes like an old man*" (59). The wind and its brother seem to be trying to say the same thing, namely, the oedipal meaning of the dream, but to different purposes: while the first invites to its transgressive realization (the poet later "understood what the wind that took up the woman's cry had cried in his last dream. 'Let me be born,' it had cried" [62]), the second signals the prohibition of that realization by calling attention to its fantasmatic limits (by rattling its symbolic window panes). The identity of the intruder is revealed beyond doubt in the poet's second dream, where his (wishfully) dead father appears as an old man. His business here, in the first dream, will be made clear by the direct suggestion of his relation to the woman in the scene of the poet's last meeting with her, in which she will be wearing a dark coat "on which the single hairs from old men's heads lay white on black" (74) (this white-on-black format seems to be standard in the devil's inverted texts, such as the pattern of the stars in the sky). The position of the usurped Peeping Tom at the window is a wishful inversion of the "primal scene," in whose imaginary space the dreamer submerges himself in order to inhabit his origins rather than seeing them from outside. But the jealous ghost will not content himself with witnessing his usurpation, and will continue to haunt the transgressor with guilty delusions of being watched and to rattle his fantasy till it breaks. For what is foreclosed from inside is bound to attack from outside, in paranoic delusions and chaotic ontological confusion. The Father's means will be, as I have suggested in the "Interlude," *time* and *sight*, the differential properties of the Symbolic sun and the inevitable agents of loss and its tragic recognition, which is only a matter of time—the viscious, circular time of tragedy.

For the time being, however, the poet continues to invert the oedipal power hierarchy. He does so by subjecting the paternal elements—time, God's authority and the space of His creation—to his wishful enterprise. Thus, when, upon waking from his first dream "he heard the clock" in the "[c]andle light[, which] threw the shadows . . . into [the very] confusion" that prevails in his twi-lit consciousness, the poet, "no longer [able to] listen to the speaking of reason," "let the dream dictate its rhythm," subjecting the clock to the beating of the wishing heart: "But now the steady tick tock tick sounded like the heart of someone hidden in the room" (60). Similarly, when he begins to suspect that the woman is "of the devil," he reasons: "Her beauty could not have sprouted out of evil. God . . . had formed her for his mate as Eve for Adam . . . 'God at my side', he said" (65). Finally, the covetous fantasizer incorporates reality into the space of his fantasy by means of an imperialistic projective gesture which, by blurring the boundaries between them, subverts their ontological hierarchy. Thus, while substantiating the woman of his dreams, he has "the things of the surrounding world . . . wrought out of their own substance into the shapes of his thoughts" (75), and turns them into *signifiers* of the woman's reality: the starry sky is her text, the wind carries her voice, the clock echoes her heartbeats, etc.

The topological aspect of the oedipal transgression—the turning inside out of fantasy or outside in of reality and the symbolically corresponding inversion of the "primal scene" to the effect of inhabiting rather than seeing it—foregrounds its ultimate pre-oedipal motivation and its "oral" dynamics. Clearly, it manifests the wish to restore the narcissistic omnipotence over the undifferentiated, projective space of the maternal world by reestablishing the archaic, Imaginary sovereignity of the pleasure principle—but only for the purpose of *not having to master*. All the poet wants is, precisely, to enter his fantasy and let go; to be contained in its reality without having to sustain it, and himself, by a controlling act of self-conscious symbolization. The hallucination fulfills this regressive wish, which is the wish for "being" without "doing" anything.

The psychotic is a tired narcissist. He is tired of generating himself by words, of constantly delineating his existence, of the never ending struggle to internalize the Symbolic rules of the game of inhabiting a world that is not there; tired of having to re-create the world as a space for being and knitting the symbolic grid to hold his own "holding environment"; tired of reproducing his dead mother (while sucking up to his father), of inventing the "good mother" that never was ("good enough"). The hell with all this work! says Marlowe's Sloth, and then resumes: "I'll not speak another word for a king's ransom" (*Doctor Faustus*):[31] Let the world bear *me* of its *own* accord, says the "bottled foetus" (66), drowning in the sea of smiling Aphrodite; let it nurse me, let it feed me, let it bring my Mummy back! And let *her* do the job that is *her* job . . . And so she does: "She moulded his image that evening. She lent light and the lamp was dim beside her who had the oil of life glistening in every pore of her hand"(67). The poet re-creates the woman who "had been with him from the beginning" so that she may generate him, but renounces his authorial rights over her creation, conferring them on nature and on God, so that she may be authenticated: if at first she is born like Athena, "out of the soul and the spinning *head*" (62) of the would-be Jupiter, later she is yielded by the sea like Aphrodite, and God creates her for the poet "as Eve for Adam out of Adam's *rib*" (65). For such is the narcissist's paradoxical wish (and the wish, I presume, of any poet): like an overly ambitious alchemist, he wishes his manufactured gold to be real gold; to find, rather than invent, the lost thing itself.

The poet's creative project is to establish a signifying space that is positive and affirmative by controlling the potentially subversive otherness of the external and the internal realities. Unlike the poetic text, which admits the negativity of these othernesses into its integrative heterogeneous space, the poet's fantasy, which departs from its textual boundaries, is an attempt to project a homogeneous space that encroaches on its context. But by thus excluding its otherness and suppressing its negativity, the fantasy dooms itself to an eventual destruction by their insistent return. Or in other words: the delirious poet tries to establish the unity of Eden that never was nor can be—without the tree. He aims for the Impossible; for the impossibility of repressing the negative maternal, or the negative *of* the maternal, while foreclosing the very law which makes this repression possible—in order to constitute his fantasy as an *autonomous* Imaginary space. To this effect, he prepares the conditions for ensuring the "absolute" reality of the woman and her metonymical space, and the latter's imperviousness to the impingement of any differential factor that might deauthenticate her/it. "He had come to the cottage on the hill that the being within him might ripen and be born away from the eyes of men" (62), so that none may doubt her existence, and to make sure that nothing might subvert it from within, he shut the hole in the kitchen wall to prevent the mouse from gnawing its way into its metaphorical space. The mouse is the abject, the corrosive alien that subverts representation. It is a figure of castration[32] which the text associates with the negative maternal as well as with the woman and her negative, the devil: "*A mother rat* . . . suckled its young" (61); "The rats . . . came out in the dark . . . The dark woman, too, had risen out of the depths of darkness" (61), and "her foot lay on his like a mouse" (65) until that ominous metonymy, too, should collapse. For when the *time* comes for the corporeal consummation of the Edenic affair (in section 9), the mouse is bound to come out, to symbolize the collapse of the representation of the affair into its underlying negativity (section 10). As "[t]he last barrier [falls] away" (68), it steps into the moon-lit room to herald the devil's laughter as he reveals himself to the poet and initiates him into the hell of that negativity, which is the hell of knowing his condition without being able to do anything about it. The mouse is the agent of the hellish experience of the "Real"—of the psychic disintegration from which, the poet knows, "nothing on the earth could save him" (69), and this despite the reflexive consciousness of the boundaries which have been foregrounded, precisely, by their transgression. The inevitable but evasive presence of these boundaries heterogenizes his perceptual field, haunting it with the negativity of loss and guilt, but they are never fixed so as to delineate a positive form. Reflecting on this diabolical epiphany, the poet admits to himself that, in effect, "[h]e had known at the ringing of the first syllable [of the woman's talk] in his ears . . . that the mouse would come out" (69), because with no symbolic grid to fix her, the reality of the woman/fantasy can only be transient. Her black magic depends on the ebb and flow of the lunatic imagination and on the evasive moon, which wanes to leave the chaotic scene of a ruinous, empty beach "where a sea flowed over" (75): "The secret of that alchemy that had turned a little revolution of the unsteady senses into a golden moment was lost as a key is lost in undergrowth" (73). The alchemy which harmonizes the clock with the desiring heart no longer works, and "[t]here was contradiction in heartbeat and green Sirius, [the dog's or God's] eye in the east. He put his hand to his eyes, hiding the star," and went down to the beach to look for the woman again. "But she had gone, and all the mystery of her presence has left the cottage" (70).

Mad with despair at the notion of "her life" being "only a life of days"(74), the poet expresses his "to-morrow's anger" by a voodoo ceremony which he directs against time, the dispelling gaze of the solar eye and God's jealous, evil eye:

> Consider now the old effigy of time, his long beard whitened by an Egyptian sun . . . Watch me belabour the old fellow. I have stopped his heart. . . . Consider the sun for whom I know no image but the old image of a *shot eye* (74–75).

The last that is seen of the poet, he is still trying to blind himself to his fate by telling himself stories. To give meaning to his psychic suicide, he rationalizes the death of the woman and idealizes her as one who "had shown him that it was wonderful to live . . . and how pleasant the blood in the trees" (76). By so doing, he can reconcile himself to his predicated death: "And now . . . he must close his eyes and die." But his fate will not let him control it *now*, by making up stories to beguile away its tragic recognition. "He opened his eyes, and looked up at the stars. There were a million stars spelling the same word. And the word of the stars was written clearly upon the sky." The unbearable meaning—or meaninglessness—of the Word is suggested in the penultimate section, 24, in the metaphorical description of the madman's deserted kitchen. Accompanying the scene of "broken chairs and china" and "the grotesque figures of birds and girls" painted all over the walls of the foetal fantasy, runs "the sound [-track] of the mouse's nails scraping upon wood" (76–77).

The Prodigal Son

> Earth, gape! Oh no, it will not harbour me.
> You stars that reigned at my nativity,
> Whose influence hath allotted death and hell,
> Now draw up Faustus . . .
> Into the entrails of yon labouring cloud,
>
> . . . .
>
> So that my soul may but ascend to heaven.
>
> . . . .
>
> Oh God, . . . have mercy on my soul[.]
>
> (*Doctor Faustus*)[33]

The earth would not harbour the poet, who, like Faustus and the Wandering Jew, is doomed to the eternal hell of bearing the recognition of the tragic word of the stars that reigned in his nativity. And so he flies to heaven (in section 14), to seek reconciliation with his paternal enemy, who sits "in an alcove carved in a cloud."

> 'Speak to me, your son. Remember how we read the classic books together on the terraces. Or on an Irish harp you would pluck tunes until the geese, like the seven geese of the Wandering Jew, rose squawking into the air. Father, speak to me, your only son, a prodigal. . . . You are a wise old man.' (71).

The advice he is seeking from the "wise old man" concerns not only his dramatized condition, namely, the concrete and extreme condition of having lost the woman and gone mad, but also the narcissistic predicament which seems to drive both him and his author to their shared imaginative adventure:

> 'Father,' he said, 'I have been walking over the world, looking for a thing worthy to love, but I drove it away and go now from place to place, moaning my hideousness, hearing my own voice in the voices of the corncrakes and the frogs, seeing my own face in the riddled faces of the beasts' (Ibid.).

In this confession, the poet acknowledges his authorship over the riddle which he has projected onto the expressionless face of the oracular beast (the Sphynx), and whose contents he has realized by what he now condemns to be his self-pitied narcissistic "hideousness." His plea for his father's advice and acceptance expresses the narcissist's agonized longing for reality, which he cannot help driving away. It is the plea to be released from the Self-reflexive prison house of the split self, which is bound up with the longing—so movingly expressed in the realistic reference by which the dreamer tries to revive the old man—to be fathered, or parented, after all.

But the contrary inclination must be the stronger, after all: "Coming closer to him and staring into his face, he saw the stains of death upon *mouth* and *eyes* and a nest of *mice* in the tangle of the frozen beard." What he sees is, once again, a *reflection* of his own, willful blindness, and the muteness of the mouth which accommodates a nest of mice at the disintegrating source of the voice. He sees, in other words, the reflection of his ambivalence and the primal sin and its punishment in the old effigy of the father, who sits in his alcove like a crucifix to symbolize the fate of the holy son. For, by killing the father, the prodigal son condemns himself to exile from (what is, after all) "His dominion" (that "exceeds the mind of man"), to slouch about as an eternal outcast in the intertextual company of Oedipus and the Wandering Jew.

Conclusion

The return, at the end of the narrative, to the fenced scene of the asylum is reassuring. The familiar scene of birds and the girl who beckons to them may suggest that the story might not have taken place at all, and has been no more than a projection of the looney from the top room. The latter is still immersed in his initial voodoo ceremony which, from the present perspective, may appear somewhat less dramatic: incarnating the dog he has never quite managed to bury, he bays at the sun as if trying, in this way, to turn it into a moon. A similar distancing irony marks the scene of the three crazy old women dancing "on a square of lawn" "to the music of an Italian organ from the world outside" (77), which is a pathetic, domesticated version of the mad Greeks with their ritual treading on a "ruler of turf" (59).

But Thomas's defensive irony in the frame-story is not condescending, nor is it necessarily sedative. A counter-(self-) irony displayed in the first section is directed against the aloof disposition of the sane outside which he generally assumes in the frame-story. In commenting on the aspect of the madhouse under the sweet spell of the "imported" spring, Thomas mocks the defensive illusions of the sane, who cling to secure appearances: "Children in print dresses might be expected to play, not noisily, upon the lawns. The building too had a sweet expression, as though it knew only the kind things of life and the polite emotions" (58). The ensuing refutation of this illusion is a hair-raising demonstration of the only too real "uncanny": "In a middle room sat a child who had cut off his double thumb with a scissors." The contrast between the harmless and rather dull anthropomorphization of the sweet-looking building and the terribly effective evocation of the psychotic child's literalized mental image is designed, it seems, to ironize the complacent, aesthetic approach to poetry—an approach which Thomas would not let his reader maintain when he invites him to share his experience of the magic and the horror of the living metaphor.

CONCLUSION

A Confession of the Speaking Subject

(or Who Is Afraid of Dylan Thomas?)

What can I say? I'm exhausted. And as identification is a central part of the problem, let Dylan Thomas speak for me, for a change, through a confessional letter in which he analyzes what has finally exhausted *him*.

> What can I say?
>
> Why do I bind myself into these imbecile grief-knots, blindfold my eyes with lies, wind my brass music around me, sew myself in a sack, weight it with guilt and pig-iron, then pitch me squealing to sea, so that time and time again I must wrestle out and unravel in a panic, like a seaslugged windy Houdini, and ooze and eel up wheezily, babbling and blowing black bubbles, from all the claws and bars and breasts of the mantrapping seabed?
>
> Deep dark down there, where I chuck the sad sack of myself, in the slimy squid-rows of the sea there's such a weed-drift and clamour of old plankton drinkers, such a mockturtle gabble of wrecked convivial hydrographers tangled with polyps and blind prawns, such a riffraff of seabums in the spongy dives, so many jellyfish soakers jolly & joking in the smoke-blue basements, so many salty sea-damaged daughters stuffing their

wounds with fishes, so many lightning midnight makers in the luminous moon of the abysmal sea, and such fond despair there, always there, that time and time again I cry to myself as I kick clear of the cling of my stuntman's sacking. "Oh, one time the last time will come and I'll never struggle, I'll sway down here forever handcuffed and blindfold, sliding my woundaround music, my sack trailed in the slime, with all the rest of the self-destroyed escapologists in their cages, drowned in the sorrows they drown and in my piercing own, alone and one with the coarse and cosy damned seahorsey dead, weeping my tons."

What can I tell you? Why did I bray my brassy nought to you from this boygreen briny dark? I see myself down and out in the sea's ape-blue bottom: a manacled rhetorician with a wet trombone, up to his blower in crabs.

Why must I parable my senseless silence? my one long trick? my last dumb flourish? It is [not] enough that, by the wish I abominate, I savagely contrive to sink lashed and bandaged in a blind bag to those lewd affectionate raucous stinking cellars: no, I must blare my engulfment in pomp and fog, spout a nuisance of fountains like a bedwetting [?whale] in a blanket, and harangue all land-walkers as though it were their shame that I sought the sucking sea and cast myself out of their sight to blast down to the dark. It is not enough to presume that once again I shall weave up pardoned, my wound din around me rusty, and waddle and gush along the land on my webbed sealegs as musical and wan and smug as an orpheus of the storm [sic]: no, I must first defeat any hope I might have of foregiveness by resubmerging the little arisen original monster in a porridge boiling of wrong words and make a song and dance and a mockpoem of all his fishy excuses.

The hell with him. (*Letters*)[1]

Or shall I "pardon" him again, as he "presume[s]"? No, I must first resubmerge him (or myself?) in his mock-porridge of fishy excuses for "haranguing" me with all his "nuisance," for by his perverse logic, there is no redemption without abjection, no birth without a murder, no affirmation without radical negation. So I should say the hell with him, or rather: to hell *with* him, for how can I do it otherwise, but by subjecting myself, once again, to that nuisance of being compelled to reenact, "time and time again," his obsessive indulgence of "fond despair," that ambivalent pendular motion between "fond" and "despair," between negation and affirmation? Let me repeat, then, one more time, alas!, the motions of that same old ambivalence . . .

The meaning of Thomas's confessional letter transcends, in my reading of it, its self-referential context and specific purpose—of seducing its addressee to "pardon" its unpardonable performance—[2] extending to Thomas's poetic enterprise and its communicative context. Thomas at once summarizes and enacts here the ambivalent dynamics of abjection which mark his poetic works, while emphasizing its "exhausting" obsessive, dissociative aspect and its underlying negativity. His analysis, although distortive in its negative totalization, is insightful and touches, in its implied reference to the reader's experience, on the major difficulty in assessing the quality of his work. The critical question which Thomas answers in his self-deprecating letter is whether his poetic art compensates for the intense negativity which it expresses, or, in other words, whether it sublimates the negativity of its underlying psychological predicament to an aesthetic or poetic meaning effect. The pertinence of this question is testified by the extreme, contrasting views of different readers on the issue. Thomas's letter voices the essential claims of his hostile readers while accounting for the sympathetic readings of his work. It also accounts for my own ambivalent, if on the whole positive response. The depressive content of the letter presents its writer as a decadent suicidal "stuntman," whose morbid self-indulgence, anti-communicative infantile aggressiveness, and "fishy" deceptiveness—the deceptiveness of a charlatan, or of a "Houdini" "blindfold[ed]" with his own "lies"—anticipate the charges laid against him by many readers, including Kenneth Rexroth, David Holbrook, George Steiner, and others.[3] And it is from the perspective of this charge that the letter explains what Thomas takes to be the mistaken admiration of readers like Moynihan, Nowottny, and others for the "musical orpheus,"[4] in whose guise Thomas as it were pretends to transform Houdini's intense negativity in sublime poetic and religious acts of affirmation. However, the direness of the judgment suggested by the self-deprecating rhetoric of the letter seems to be ambiguated by its self-delighting rhetoric, which suggests the author's faith in the aesthetic effectiveness of his performance. This ambiguity anticipates, more or less, my own ambivalence in relation to Thomas.

But the reader-response hypothesis which Thomas's letter projects goes beyond the question of the specific evaluative response, and comes to bear on the basic *process* of response that may be inherent in the signification of his poetic texts as such. This process may be experienced variously according to personal taste and temperament. In a more general way, the letter bears on the role of the reader as the *other subject* of the text, that is, on the intersubjective, identificatory dynamics of transference and counter-transference which involve the reader as the projected other and as an actual subject respectively. As such, this projected hypothesis foregrounds the objective aspect of subjectivity which I have been exploring in this text, namely, that of the constitution of the subject as a process that is activated in and through the poetic text.

My interpretation of Thomas's letter is largely congruous with David Holbrook's analysis of the nature and the reception of his work in general.[5] That analysis seems to coincide with the manifest content of the letter as well as with the critical judgment which colors it. Highly sensitive to the dissociative aspect of Thomas's work, Holbrook diagnoses what he generally deems to be its symbolic failure as symptomatic of the poet's suicidal "schizoid predicament,"[6] namely, the predicament of a suspended psychic birth whose attempted achievement is doomed by hate-ridden, splitting ("paranoid schizoid")[7] defensive strategies. Holbrook's purpose of investigating what he once defined as Thomas's "not-poetry" is largely to explain its strong impact, as reflected in the "immense industry" of Dylan Thomas criticism.[8]

Holbrook's analysis has been useful for me for a variety of reasons. In the first place, his psychoanalytic approach is very close to my own, and allows him to discern issues of texuality and intersubjectivity which will be the focus of this chapter. Yet despite the similarity of his reading and my own, his critical approach and judgment are very different from mine. Indeed, assessing these similarities and differences will serve as the basis for a sharper formulation of my own view, and provide the occasion for re-addressing, by way of conclusion, the major theoretical issues which I have been exploring in the course of my reading of Thomas' work.

Before introducing my reading of Thomas's letter,[9] I want to formulate my understanding of Holbrook and its application in this context. Holbrook's analysis of Thomas in *The Code Of Night* is one of the most pertinent I have encountered. It touches with great insight and personal involvement on what seem to me to be the central issues with which Thomas contended in his poetry, with varying degrees of success. His reading is weakened, however, by his tone, and by the attitudes it betrays. Contrary to his explicit claim, Holbrook's reading is biased by an unchecked hostility which manifests itself in a reductive pathologizing approach to Thomas's work. He himself addresses the problem of such bias in relation to his earlier work on Thomas, *Llaregubb Revisited*, which is a vehement attack on Thomas. He reassesses that attitude in *The Code of Night* in the light of his psychoanalytic account of what he sees as defensive reader-responses to the threatening aspect of Thomas's works.[10] *The Code of Night* sets out to overcome his own defensiveness by trying to read what he still regards as Thomas's generally unsuccessful poetic work as empathically and objectively as possible. He wants to "hear" the human plea expressed in it, and avoid the pitfalls of defensive distortions and reductionist psychologism.[11] Yet the success of this attempt is limited because the compassion and the objective distance to which Holbrook aspires are not really there. In this respect there is no real difference in approach between his two books. Hence I treat them as a continuum. Nevertheless, something of Holbrook's objection to Thomas clearly corresponds to an aspect of my own ambivalent response to Thomas, which I express in this chapter in a rhetorical exaggeration that conforms to the spirit of Thomas's letter and to Holbrook's approach. My debate with Holbrook in this chapter is therefore, up to a point, also a debate with myself, in the course of which I attempt to sort out my own response to Dylan Thomas.

Clearly, Thomas's letter traces the "orphic" itinerary paved by his "dialectical method," while providing a catalogue of the sea-prospects through which it takes its thematized course in many of his self-reflexive works. It clearly confirms, in other words, that Thomas knew as well as any what he was about, and *why*—a question which he rhetorically repeats here in order to eliminate the "fishy excuses" for doing the very thing he is thereby repeating: purgative self-abjection for the purpose of an undeserved redemption (he *says*), for the purpose of being excused ("pardoned") for his inexcusable being . . . a babbling, black bubble-blowing, slippery fish![12] A self-indulging death-dealer selling his obsessive stuntman's number of rhetoricized suicide—the skillful, dazzling verbal acrobatics whereby he displays (but does not dispel) "the wish [he] abominate[s]," but which he cherishes even more! And so, a morbid Houdini in sublime Orpheus's disguise, he must once again rid himself, once and for all, of the "engulfment" which is his identifying excuse, that is, his very reason for being the kind of poet that he is—by being just that!

There he is, our "convivial hydrographer," devotee of the lost "claws and bars and breasts" of the "abysmal sea"; a professional surviver ("escapologist") who lives off the "one long trick" of perpetuating the "mantrapping" narrative of his abortive origins. Fascinated by death, he lives *off* it, literally: "time and time again" he dives toward the fondly desperate site of "*senseless silence*" at the sea-blue bottom of signification, to get his kick out of its danger and then kick back at it and clear of its cling and, by the newly gained momentum (or fresh flow of adrenalin, that Shklovskian "sensation of life" which marks liminal experiences), bubble up again with a birthday flourish of his orphic trombone. "Time and time again" he tries himself out, that "subject on trial," repeating the abject's *fort-da* game with his own being—and with the reader's—spinning and unravelling the language that sustains us both . . . Until he gets tired, naturally: "'Oh, one time the last time will come and I'll never struggle." For why should he, anyway? "*Why* must [he] parable [the] senseless silence" of his "stinking" underwater "cellars" if, in the final analysis, the wish he abominates is the one he cherishes most? And why must *I*, if this is really the final analysis, partake of this morbid ordeal, in which death overrides pleasure, let alone choose its suicidal performer for substantiating my thesis about the genesis of the speaking subject?

The answer to the first question is clear: the fish wants to be humanized by obtaining the "landwalkers'" undeserved "pardon." He seeks the confirmation of his self-denied right of birth by the gaze of those "others," his readers, whom he abuses. But what is the abuse? What is it, exactly, that he needs to be "pardoned" for? For "*spouting*" his "*fountain[ous]*" "*nuisance*" at them like some "*bedwetting [?whale] in a blanket*," or, to put it plainly, for pissing them off with his aggressive, regressive "harangu[ing]," which he permits himself on the "presumption" of their pardon (at least one more time . . .), on account of his cute rhetoric. Indeed, to an unpardoning eye his letter might seem the epitome of the cute, infantile coquetry of a destructively self-indulgent narcissistic sucker who, as Holbrook basically feels, drains you emotionally while giving you very little in return,[13] other than the negativity of his rotten cadavers and broken syntax. Readers have complained that they experienced this intense negativity in Thomas's poetry, in what they feel to be the raw thematization of his abject hatred in a contorted verbal performance, where he mutilates language to the point of actual meaninglessness, linguistic or emotional. "[H]e hits you across the face with a reeking, bloody heart, a heart full of worms and needles and thorns, a werewolf heart," Kenneth Rexroth writes,[14] and Holbrook, who feels contaminated, proclaims Thomas to be "*very dangerous*," because "he evoke[s] such hate and insecurity."[15] What evokes this hate and insecurity in Holbrook and in everyone else is, he explains, Thomas's aggressive suspension or destruction of meaning in his poetry. Holbrook believes that Thomas deliberately (unconsciously) withholds self-expression, and thus confronts the reader with a confusing, frustrating invitation to an impossible communication.[16] While fascinating the "pardoning" gaze of the "others," as Thomas himself confesses, he "cast[s him]self out of their sight"!

Holbrook explains Thomas's evasiveness—or fishlike slipperiness—as a paranoic defense against the "impinging" (or devouring) gaze of the (m)other, which the "schizoid individual" achieves through the strategy of splitting.[17] That strategy is manifested, by Holbrook's analysis, in the various forms of meaninglessness in Thomas's poetry, which occur on the thematic, as well as the verbal and emotional levels of expression. For Holbrook, Thomas's "dialectical method" as the latter introduces it, is a deconstructive technique which employs ambiguity to suspend meaning and in this way to avoid the self-exposure involved in taking a clear subjective position.[18] But Thomas's most common way of suspending or destroying meaning and communication is, according to Holbrook as well as according to himself in his letter, one which combines verbal obscurity and emotional inauthenticity. Holbrook regards the obscurity of Thomas's "unnecessarily difficult," "incohate" language as a regressive defense against the integrative expression of his archaically abused "true self." This defensive strategy is complemented by the compensatory projection of a "false self,"[19] through the spectacular rhetorical acrobatics ("verbal pyrotechnics," "fireworks")[20] which mark much of Thomas's performance and which, to the extent that they do bear some kind of intelligible meaning, are, for Holbrook, devoid of emotional authenticity.[21] The same falseness also manifests itself to Holbrook, on the thematic level, in Thomas's grandiose impersonations as the priestly Bard or prophet (Christ, Noah, the Druid heron-priest), as well as in the "manic" gestures with which he enchants himself into these self-dramatizing roles.[22] The combination of obscurity and falseness is alluded to by Thomas, who confesses to "blare" his "dumb flourish" "in *pomp* and *fog*"—or, for our purposes, the other way around: to compensate for the fogginess of his obscure language, he displays his pompous pose of Orpheus, who "weaves up" in that "empty" guise, to disguise the *double* murder effected by the stuntman's acrobatics!

And there is a double murder here, in this acclaimed sabotage of the *inter-subjective* interaction. The evasive subject's strategy of absenting himself (by splitting) undermines his self-realization in relation to the others, whom he thus annihilates as well. Indeed, it is precisely this fishy falseness and fogginess that constitutes the "engulfment" that derealizes the "schizoid individual," or his experience of himself and of others, and of which, therefore, the stuntman would rid himself through the obsessive rhetorical procedure of his confessional letter. His ultimate and most desperate wish is to be real (-ized), and that is *why* (again) he admits that it is through the gaze of the *cheated* other that he (now as always) seeks his redemption from the cheering audience—an audience which buys the rhetorical tricks of a nihilistic fraud (a poetic imposter, as George Steiner sees him[23]). That nihilistic fraud is what Orpheus *is*, if he is reduced to a Houdini: for Houdini, unlike Orpheus, dives for no Euridice, but for the sake of diving (and making a living out of it), because, as he says in his poem, "[a]fter the first death, *there is no other*"![24] And so, as Kristeva says of his kind, the abject "never stops harking back to the symbolization mechanisms," performing his one number of symbolizing and de-symbolizing "in order to find in a *process* of eternal return, and not in the *object* that it names or produces, the hollowing out of anguish in the face of nothing"[25]—and *nobody*! The anaesthetic of a slow suicide, in short—*that* is the "fishy excuse" for the abuse of language that deconstructs us as subjects; for the obsessive indulgence of suffering which brings no catharsis, but only negates whoever might be there to "pardon"—subject and other transitively . . . "Schizoid suicide," as Holbrook names it, involves the symptomatic abuse of the "true self" by the "false" one, who gets all the pardon. For whatever pardon may be obtained from those idiots, the gullable landwalkers, is unredeeming, as its object is not really Thomas, but an empty mask. This is, surely, a bad excuse for haranguing them with all that regressive nuisance by a bedwetting critter—of which he is literally dying to get rid: "the hell with him" . . . *Fort!* And then *Da!* A little "black bubble" pops up to disturb the smooth surface of the cartoon sea-prospect and contradict the nonsensical "silence": "it is *fond*, the despair . . . ," it seduces, embodying, in its marked vitality of poetic grace and humor, the promise of the return of the merman, who weaves up alive and kicking again—and therefore is pardoned, as he ultimately "presume[s]"?

. . . But not by Holbrook, for whom neither Thomas's "gallows humour,"[26] nor his infantile charms (to which he is by no means susceptible), compensate for the disturbing experience of his generally "unmeaning"—because *immature*—poetry.[27] For Holbrook, poetic meaning lies in the mutually reflective confirmation of mature, integral selves engaged a Buberian "I-Thou" communication,[28] and not in the depersonalizing paranoid-schizoid hide-and-seek games of an angry bedwetter.[29] And yet—and here comes the answer to the second question, of the readers' motivation for exposing themselves to Thomas's abusive poetry—it is precisely in the infantile aspect of what he regards as Thomas's metaphorical irresponsibility that Holbrook recognizes the power of his poetry over its pardoning readers.[30] That power, he clarifies, has nothing to do with pleasure. This becomes clear if one conjures an image of the wan, wet and plankton-poisoned landwalkers as they cheer at their surging Orpheus. It is, as Thomas's letter confirms, a deeper, darker power that is at work: "[Thomas's] appeal consists in the [unconsciously] calculated disarming irresponsibility—the child's amoral attitude to its expression," says Holbrook.[31] In Holbrook's view, it is precisely through that amoral attitude, which avoids a decent relation between two discrete selves, that "Thomas seeks [and manages] to draw us into a [*different*] kind of relationship to him."[32] Something of the nature of this relationship is suggested in the letter by the depiction of the tantalizing evasiveness of its writer, who "cast[s him]self out of [the readers'] sight" "as though it were *their* shame that [he] sought the sucking sea." By thus manipulatively withholding true expression of his "self," Holbrook argues, Thomas binds his readers to him in a relation of guilt which stems from fear in the face of the helpless infant-crying-in-the-night who indulges his self-undoing: "what [one hears] is the *cry of a baby*, and the 'regressed libidinal ego.'" "In responding to his work, we are trying to 'meet' the scream we hear," for "to leave such an individual in [his] anguished need . . . would feel too dreadful."[33] And so we rush out to save him, and thereby fulfill the transferential role he assigns us: according to Holbrook, the communicative failure of Thomas's unnecessarily difficult and deliberately perverse[34] language is a strategy of manipulating the reader into the role of "mothering" him—by symbolizing and sublimating *for* him. By supplying or completing the absent meaning in his poems, we as it were confirm, in the way of an overly "creative reflection" (or maternal "mirroring"),[35] his self-denied being or "incomplete personality."[36] The reader is compelled, in other words, to reenact the role of an unassimilated mother by making sense of a language which knows no "other," which does not recognize its addressee as subject but forces him, instead, to invent himself by assuming a "false" defensive role against an annihilating communicative vacuum (a "dreadful gulf of non-communication").[37]

But the question still remains as to what it is, in Thomas's rethoric, that makes the reader yield to this transferential manipulation, and to accept this unrewarding relationship. The answer is, once again, in the particular nature of Thomas's manipulative "non-communication"—that combined "schizoid" strategy of "*pomp* and *fog*," or the other way round. Through the foggy (*semiotic*) obscurity of his language, he disarms the readers of their symbolic control, bypasses or shatters the integrity of their subjective position, and so gets hold of their guts, drawing them into a symbiotic identification with his regressive plea. And so, says Holbrook, if "we are likely to begin by seeing ourselves looking in a mirror as if to confirm [our] identity," we end up finding "ourselves drawn through the mirror into a world where our whole relationship with experience is threatened with inversion."[38] Fascinated by the reverberation of a bottomless oceanic memory in the "woundaround music" of the fish, the susceptible reader follows the merman toward its whirlpooling center in the decentering wound of their being. What, under these circumstances, can they do to save themselves from this deconstruction, but embrace his false *pomp*-pose of Orpheus (or any other of his grandiose prophetic-poetic personae) and his theatrical gestures of false sublimation? Bewildered by their own regressive chaos, which they are compelled to confront in this identificatory relationship, readers will do anything to find a tangible, determinate Symbolic meaning to hold on to in the poems, even if it rings false—like the empty "palavers of birds" twittered by the "*webbed*," "*sea-legged*" musical Orpheus! And if they cannot find such a meaning, they will take laborious pains to furnish mad interpretations for mute texts, to give them meanings that are "simply not there," and then say that the linguistic challenge in Thomas's poetry is exciting![39]

Like Thomas's aggressive poetic gesture, the "false" "mothering" interpretative gesture of the prone reader is, therefore, a defensive response that is ultimately motivated by fear and hate rather than by genuine sympathy. It would be "dreadful" not to adhere to Thomas's regressive plea because, says Holbrook, it "would expose *us* . . . to threats of annihilation ourselves." And "when an individual . . . evokes such responses in us, our reaction is a *controlling response*. This person threatens the core of our own being, and is therefore so dangerous that he must be controlled at all costs." "This reaction in others was exploited by Dylan Thomas. . . . Some individuals fell into the role of mothering him; others sought to control him by annihilation, or by trying to beat him into normality."[40] So the pardoning readers are not such good mothers at all. . . . They are not really different from those violently hostile readers, who dismiss Thomas altogether as a poetic charlatan, because, subject to the same threat of dangerous identification, they cannot bear to face his desperate, self-defeating, hate-driven poetic struggle for self-generation. So they, too, annihilate him, as mentioned earlier, by their *overly* "creative reflection"; what their blind other's gaze confirms is not the subject of the poems, whose desperate plea is too hard for them to take, but their own, "bad" or "impinging" mother's narcissistic projection. Therefore, those who take on the transferential role of the reader which is embodied for them in Thomas's poetic language do not really understand him, nor his poetry.[41] For the truth, or meaning of Thomas's largely "unmeaning" poetry lies, for Holbrook, precisely in that threatening, existential plight which undermines it as poetry, and which, if empathically "heard," has the value of teaching us something beyond its pathological aspect, about "what [it is] to be human."[42] In order to learn this lesson, which is ultimately a lesson in compassion that requires emotional and introspective honesty, one needs, he suggests, to go *beyond* Thomas's ("not-") poetry and resist its rhetorical effects: "The reader thus has to resist being drawn into the falser roles, in which such a schizoid individual seeks to involve him. He needs, like a psychotherapist, to *arm* himself by conscious insight" against Thomas's "dangerous," "*disarming*" charms. "[The reader] can then afford to "creatively reflect" Thomas's poetry—and if he does," says Holbrook, "I believe he may find himself able to understand more of the meaning of madness."[43] The critical reader ought—to clarify Holbrook's position further—to follow his example and *really* "mother" the *infant crying* beyond Thomas's poems ("I have admitted 'mothering' Thomas," he says)[44]—and in so doing, I would add, to send their *speaking subject* to hell . . .

For what Holbrook is doing by focusing on what he sees "beyond" Thomas's poetry, even as he dismisses the poetry itself, is a repetition of the very same abjection which he attributes to Thomas's "uncritical" readers (his former self included), and this, as it emerges from the spirit and the tone of his argument, for the very same reason that he attributes to them.[45] Despite the impressive honesty which he reveals in the revision, in *The Code of Night*, of his earlier, overtly hostile response, his psychoanalysis of Thomas in his later book seems to me a "controlling response" that is no less aggressive than the manifest resentment that had caused him to drive Thomas off the stage of poetry in the first study. It is a disturbing contradiction to his claim to a compassionate approach. In terms of "mothering," I would add, he is the worst mother of all. But mothering is not really the issue here. I do not think our role as readers is that of the psychotherapist, and therefore it is not our business either to "really mother" the subjects of the poetic texts we read or to deepen our understanding of madness through their "case" study—if this means to dismiss their work as art. Indeed, regardless of how much one universalizes its object's "human predicament," such an approach is reductively pathologizing. It is unfair to the poet and to the reader alike, because it denies the poet's more or less valuable achievement as well as his gift to the more or less patronizing reader.

The point is not that Thomas does not elicit the responses to which Holbrook refers, nor that Holbrook's analysis of the intersubjective dynamics at work in the encounter with the subject of Thomas's poetry is inaccurate. To the contrary: there *is* often something disconcerting and at times even deeply upsetting in Thomas's work—as I have experienced it during my long and intensive dwelling on and with him. I agree with Holbrook that the dissociative tension in his poetry is sometimes a reason to be afraid of Dylan Thomas, because, as he says, "it raises in . . . us the harsh fact of the existence of an 'inner reality' with which we cannot perhaps ever come to terms . . . nor alter it at will."[46] But the fact that Thomas compels us to experience this inner reality and the way in which he does this are by no means a reason to reject his poetry as such, nor, necessarily, its poetic value.

Holbrook's predominant criterion for poetic writing as well as for criticism is authenticity, which he associates with integrity in the full sense of the word—of integration as well as truthfulness. This is implicit in his notions of true and false selves and articulations, and of good and bad maternal reflection ("mothering"). A similar, but also very different criterion is implied by my own notion of the sense of reality in poetic mimesis and in relation to tone in poetry, discussed in chapters 3 and 4. The main difference between our ideas of poetic authenticity is that Holbrook's is absolute while mine is relative; relative, that is, to the reality of the poem as a dynamic, generative artifact. The authenticity of successful poetry as I see it is the synthetic, "alchemical" product of the textual intra- and intersubjective dynamics, and not, as Holbrook seems to be suggesting, the univocal, truthful representation of a given subjective reality. This difference and its broader meta-poetic implications may partly account for the differences in our responses to Thomas at large. Generally speaking, it seems to me that Holbrook disregards, or indeed, refuses, that which pertains to the dynamic, performative aspect of poetry, which I take to be the very essence of poetic language. What I am referring to are the two time-bound, translinguistic effects of poetic defamiliarization: the deconstruction of subjective position in the face of symbolic indeterminacy and its displacement by a productive (integrative) dialectical process of response; and the pleasurable aesthetic product of this process, namely, the binding experience of enchantment, which subjects the negativity of indeterminacy and deconstruction to the affirmative and compelling, cohesive force of desire.

Holbrook's static notion of poetic signification emerges from the distinction which he draws between Thomas's "unmeaning" poetry and his psychologically revealing utterance. From his point of view the latter does signify, but only as a pathological symptom through which we can hear the "true" Thomas. Indeed, Holbrook's blind, or deaf spot here is precisely his failure to hear Thomas's utterance—not as a symptomatic representation, but as a productive gesture that transforms the reality which it initially represents. His mishearing may be associated with his strictly *symbolic* notion of poetic meaning and with what one might call his essentialist conception of subjectivity. For Holbrook, poetic meaning is the determinate—intended and immediately accessible—expression of a more or less pre-integrated self, whose a priori being as such preconditions the very possibility of the "truly metaphorical language" of poetry. The accessibility of truly poetic language is, according to Holbrook, a function of its integrated subject's *achieved* process of socialization, which manifests itself in the conformity of his language to the shared associative network of the given traditional culture. Thomas's language is poetically "unmeaning," for Holbrook, because it is "unpossessible," "ambiguous," and anti-socially idiosyncratic ("Thomas . . . does not write in English"[47]), and as such it signifies no more than the psychic schism underlying its symbolic failure and the dire implications of this failure for the creative potential of its subject. Such language signifies the "schizoid individual's" incapacity for effective symbolization, which is predestined by the fact that he "cannot get on 'good terms with himself,' because he failed to be on good terms with his mother in the first place, who is the origin of the first symbol and all symbols."[48] This analysis implies that Thomas is doomed to fail in fulfilling his potential for self-realization through his poetic creation; for poetic language, in Holbrook's restrictive view, can only represent, but not constitute, its subject. To the extent that poetic creation does have some kind of subjectifying function, that function is, for Holbrook, limited to the confirming "reflection" of a pre-existent identity: "A true core to himself . . . [Thomas] did *find* from time to time in some of his poetry," but on the whole, he says later, "we may, I think, deduce that Dylan Thomas's 'linguistic doing' was a substitute for having anything inward to say, with . . . its roots in being."[49] The productive option of generating, rather than finding subjectivity through poetic signification, is not really available in Holbrook's conception of poetic language, whose meaning he identifies with the "intended," univocal position of its speaker, who must "have something to say" that is grounded in his "true" "being."

This essentialist perspective, which underestimates the integrative properties of the act of signification, does not allow for the possibility of generating "being" as well as "something inward to say" through the poetic "doing," for such "doing" can yield no more than false meaning and equally false subjectivity and/or obscurity and ambiguity ("pomp" and/or "fog," or the other way around). Thus, the effect of Thomas's "dialectical method" is, for Holbrook, one of meaningless ambiguity, because he cannot conceive of its potential function—as Thomas saw it—of containing oppositions in motion. Thomas saw the dialectical flow, or "warring stream" of his conflicting images as a means to achieve a "momentary peace" between them, "a contradictory peace" within the poem.[50] For Holbrook this is absurd: "Thomas seeks for 'peace' in a 'war'"! The oxymoronic "contradictory peace" and "warring stream" epitomize Thomas's way of suspending meaning or "preserving the chaos of the regressive self" as a defense against integration.[51] Holbrook's deprecation of the value of the integrative "peace" embodied in the oxymorons may also be accounted for by the "momentary" nature of that peace, which cannot be authentic by his standards.

Concretely speaking, do *I* see that kind of integrative "peace," say, in the conclusion of "Poem on His Birthday"? I am not quite sure. From my analyses in chapters 2 and 3, it would apear that the answer is first yes and then no (in chapters 2 and 3 respectively). In fact, in the revision, in chapter 3, of my response to "Poem on His Birthday," the fault I find with Thomas's "manic" tone and the mimetic failure associated with it, is very much in line with Holbrook's impression of the dissociated nature of the "magical incantation" of the poem.[52] But does the manic tone annihilate the aesthetic quality of the poem because it betrays the denied psychic truth of depression underlying it? Not necessarily, because *both* the depression and the manic joyfulness which represses it are real, as the sequence of my two—enchanted and disenchanted—readings suggests. Indeed, Thomas's effort to dispel his despair is a meaningful authentic gesture which animates his wishful poem not only with the tension of manic dissociation, but also with the tension of desire. It is a gesture that *binds* desire by containing the melancholic or "schizoid" split within the linguistic bounds of the other-bound, communicative poem. The extent to which it succeeds in integrating the split to the effect of poetic mimesis remains undecided, but here Kristeva's notion of poetic mimesis is no less relevant. Indeed, the perceptibility of the genuine effort invested in the act of faith that is the poem lends it, in this particular case, a movingly expressive quality, which the exuberant play of sound and images insures against an otherwise possible pathetic effect. The too loud, too bright sun blooms there because we want the light (or, as Holbrook would put it, because we are induced to identify with the desperate need for it), but *also* because it is magically beautiful. This brings back to mind Thomas's Houdini, whose "sullen art"[53] is as serious as can be, both existentially and technically, which is why I do pardon him again.

Holbrook's attitude toward poetic enchantment in Thomas's work is clearly marked by his characteristic, uncompromising demand for truth. He regards that distinctive aesthetic effect as a mark of an escapistic tendency on the part of the poet, which he compares with his habit of drinking alcohol. For example, Thomas's "magical incantations" in "Poem on His Birthday," like his time-negating attempts to "marvel [his] birthday [a]way" in "Poem in October," are, in his view, "an attempt to deny reality" in "an act of composing orally an artificial entity . . . which stands instead of the real world, in order to change and redeem it—redeem it not from 'sin' or 'evil', but *from being real*."[54] What Holbrook seems to overlook in devalorizing the poet's intent "to cast a magic light over the real world"[55] is, precisely, the role of that light and the *semiotic* devices that project it in generating the poem as a *shared* intimate "transitional space." The difference between our approaches is reflected in our readings of the *theme* of the visionary light in "Poem on his Birthday" where, according to my reading, the creation of the light as a "transitional space" is evoked through the speaker's voyage from the dark confinement of melancholia toward liberating faith. This process, as I have shown, is anticipated in the poet's vision, where "love unbolts the dark." Holbrook, by contrast, interprets the unbolting of love as a withdrawal from its reality into schizoid isolation, "love being a dangerous threat."[56] This reading is symptomatic of Holbrook's reduction of Thomas to the "schizoid predicament," which precludes the very possibility of transformation in, if not through, his poetic performance.

Holbrook's reading of Thomas's other birthday poem, "Poem in October," by contrast, is affirmative. I refer to it in order to point out a subtle but telling difference between our otherwise quite similar responses. Holbrook singles out "Poem in October" because of its speaker's readiness to face reality. Here Holbrook feels, as I do, that "dissociation has been overcome," and he explains it by the conjecture that Thomas has overcome "the impulse to over-indulge in nostalgia" for the "tall tales" of childhood's imaginative vision, and is ready to face the reality of time which separates the child he was from the adult that he is now: "There could I marvel / My birthday / Away but the weather turned around" and lead the poet to the peak of the poem in the here and now of his reality, where he "stood *there then* in the summer noon," rejoicing in his "heart's truth" which he differentiates from the "the true / Joy of the *long dead* child."[57] What Holbrook overlooks in his interpretation, I think, is the metaphorical meaning of the geographical "there"—the peak of the "high hill" which is *unrealistically* summery in the realistic October scene. The luminous high hill signifies another "parables / Of sun light," or "tall tale," in the series of fantasies which characterized the child's "unrealistic" vision, and hence a nostalgic recuperation of the child by way of identifying, or indeed, merging with him.[58] The truth of the dead child becomes that of the adult poet's heart as he introjects and impersonates him, and thereby revives him—within the tall tale of the poem. It is in this magic revival, which involves the nostalgic bridging of the distance between past and present rather than a differentiation between them, that I see Thomas's dissociation overcome in "Poem in October." There is a paradox at work here with which Holbrook might disagree. In both of these birthday poems, the poet needs to "marvel [his] birthday away" in order to come to terms with its implications; to beguile the time in order to both sing in its chains and accept them.

Holbrook's psychoanalysis of the orality of enchantment in Thomas seems pertinent enough, except for its pathologizing character, which turns the poet's articulations into predatory gestures. He attributes the oral aspect of Thomas's de-realizing strategies and his addiction to alcohol alike to a regressive longing for symbiotic immersion, the implications of which are dangerous for the susceptible reader: "We are drawn into a state something like the undifferentiated state of the infant before his necessary 'disillusion,' and forfeit our own 'self-interest' and reality-sense."[59] This telling description may throw some light on Holbrook's unsusceptibility to Thomas's charms, which he dismisses—and misses—precisely because he *refuses* to submit himself to the risks and the pleasures involved in the trans- or prelinguistic interaction to which Thomas's poetry invites its reader.

But Holbrook is not the only one who is afraid of enchantment, as we saw very clearly in "The Mouse and the Woman" and in "A Prospect of the Sea," and it is here, I think, that the reason to be afraid of Dylan Thomas lies. Thomas's own fear of it, or his conflictual attitude toward it, is, for me, what generates the most disturbing effect of his work, which is his obsessiveness. There is often a sense that he is in some kind of desperate competition with his imagination, which he does not trust not to turn wild and chaotic. Like the boy who is afraid of his fantasies in "A Prospect of the Sea," who must constantly tell himself that "this is [only] a story," Thomas is constantly checking his imaginative spontaneity, arresting its flow by means of his sometimes excessive formalism or formulaic expression. At times he overworks his language so that it may stop the flood, as it were, almost sculpting it by charging his "overweighted imagery," as Thomas himself formulates it,[60] to the paradoxical point of impoverishing it. The supercondensed language leaves no air; the close associative clusters and sound patterns make it too material, too objectlike to function symbolically. "The last thing my poems do is flow," he himself complains (and Holbrook quotes, to illustrate a similar point), and "when the words do come, I pick them so thoroughly of their *live* associations that only the *death* in the words remains."[61] The live associations are sometimes deadened in the overschematic symbolic structures which Thomas sets as a kind of safety grid against the dangers of the chaotic imaginary. This is manifest in the abstract, archetypal polarizations of the terms of ambivalence with which he maps his experiential world, which I discussed in chapter 3. These "controlling" strategies reflect the fear that motivates them, and account for the reader's transferential "controlling response." But the ultimate object of this fear is not the enchantment itself, but the "inner reality" which underlies it, as Thomas's stories so effectively dramatize. In the journey to the origins which takes place there, one can actually see the controlling Thomas in competition with his imagination over who will get there first—the boy's desire, which will symbolize the beginning in a fantastic image, or his fear of it, which will destroy the fantasy? the critical mouse who gnaws at the fantasy, or the imaginary woman, who figures as a woman only as long as she can hide her true nature as the devil of compulsion? It is the fear of that woman, that she might strip herself of the clothing that she is, that makes Thomas sometimes kill her—in the faceless devil's name (or namelessness, rather). For the fear of the enchanting image is the fear of the breaking of the enchantment, and the way to render oneself immune to it is not to be enchanted. This is, indeed, Holbrook's strategy: like the cautious author of "The Mouse and the Woman," who shuts up his mad poet in the lunatic asylum on account of his Faustian sin, Holbrook controls the risks of enchantment in Thomas "unhealthy," "immoral" poetry by reducing its subject to his pathology, drawing, for this de-aesthetization, on the authority of mental health morality.

But have *I* been altogether free of that same fault in my own psychoanalysis of Thomas? *Can* one be, in a psychoanalytic reading of this kind?

What is certain is that on reading "The Mouse and the Woman" I, too, was a little afraid of the disenchanting mouse. And here the question arises, as to whether both Holbrook and I are not more afraid of it than Thomas himself, who, once having set up his securing narrative structure, does permit himself to slide along on the inflection of his mad-poet's voice, to a pleasurably aesthetic symbolization of his madness?

The End of the Story?

The preoccupation with the war between "the wish [he] abominates" and its aesthetic sublimation in Thomas's work, on the one hand, and the attempt to determine its consequences, on the other, is reflected in the narratives within which different readers have organized their responses. Each of these narratives projects a "history" of the subject of the poetry in accordance with a particular conception of him as such. Holbrook's narrative coincides with Thomas's biography. It explains the fate of what he sees as Thomas's aborted attempts to be born through his poetic creation by a psychological determinism, originating in his "schizophrenogenic" family background,[62] and consummated by Thomas's ultimate suicide by alcohol. William Moynihan objects to such identification of the poet with the biographical man (and to Holbrook's reading in general),[63] advocating George Whalley's "theory of 'symbolic extrication' which 'holds that the poet extricates himself from situations of intolerable reality in the process of poetic creation.'"[64] Accordingly, the narrative which he projects in *The Craft and Art of Dylan Thomas* draws on the mythical narratives whereby Thomas extricates himself from the biographers' narratives. Relating to the chronological evolution of Thomas's work rather than to his life, Moynihan traces in it a development toward an "affirmation" of life through a "reconciliation of life and death" in a "temporary . . . synthesis,"[65] which conforms to Northrop Frye's dialectical "Biblical rhythm" of Creation, Fall, and Regeneration.[66] In this dialectical sequence, "the anguish of a creation whose end is decay, and of a fallen world characterized by a fatal marriage to sex and time and by the opposition of flesh and spirit, becomes reconciled in a gigantic body which creates and recreates deathlessly."[67] Moynihan observes the same affirmative process in Thomas's performance as well, in which he traces an increasing clarity and directness of expression, and a greater thematic and symbolic coherence in the organization of his recurrent materials.[68] The consummation of this development is epitomized, for Moynihan, at the end of the "Author's Prologue" to the *Collected Poems*, where the author's regenerative reconciliation of life and death is thematized in the symbolic impersonation of Noah.

My own narrative, in its "switchback" oscillation between enchantment and disenchantment, combines the directions taken by both narratives mentioned above. In my reading of "Poem on his Birthday" in chapter 2 I sailed with the Christ-poet through the maternal orphic deeps toward his new testament with Noah's Creator. That Symbolic testament was facilitated by the eucharistic procedure of *semiotic* enchantment, thematized by the growth of Christ's mustardseed into a loud sun which brought Heaven down to earth. In chapter 3 we fell back again into the deeps of melancholia, whose silent lurking I now heard, like Holbrook, underneath Thomas's "manic" incantation in that religious poem. In this context, I explored the "diabolic" dissociative dynamics of the reincarnation of the maternal abject in the poet's forked world and tongue. In chapter 4 we climbed Heaven's Hill again, on the enchanted bilateral ladder of nostalgia toward its futured antecedent in childhood. In chapter 5, in the reading of "A Prospect of the Sea," I tried to show how climbing this bilateral ladder spans the history of the climber. In the second part of the chapter, we explored the option of falling off that ladder into Hell by consequence of opting for an actual recuperation of the nostalgic object. My reading of "The Mouse and the Woman" as an anatomy of enchantment and disenchantment may be seen as a kind of *post-mortem* which ends my narrative with a disenchanted note.

By following this oscillating course, my story reenacts what it is about, that is, what I see as constituting, or rather setting in motion, the subject of Thomas's poetic texts. The genesis of subjectivity as I have "heard" and experienced it while reading Thomas consists, precisely, in the process of signifying that same ambivalence which he enacts—and generates. It is, in other words, neither a true nor a false self, neither a self-cured patient nor a poetic persona, neither Houdini nor Orpheus, but the subject of that "exhausting" "sequence of creations, recreations, destructions, contradictions" ("inevitable, because of the . . . contradictory nature of the motivating center"), whereby Thomas, whom I am quoting, "tr[ies] to make that momentary peace which is a poem,"[69] and in the course of which Houdini may (or may not) *become* Orpheus.

Does he??

Because if so, I would ask in Holbrook's name, how do I account for the fact that I have concluded this pendular narrative of mine, which started off with a birthday celebration, with the anatomy of a psychic suicide? Is it the power of gravitation, which determines the direction of my final textual analysis because it is also the predominant one, by the "final analysis" of the stuntman's exhausting number? Or is it, perhaps, the gravity of an obsessive psycho- or any other analysis, which, in its insistence on reducing things to their final cause, misses their actual, phenomenal essence?[§] Possibly, for the force of Thomas's poetry at its best is, precisely, in that it overcomes the power of gravitation. My first encounter with Dylan Thomas supports this possibility. When I first read "The Mouse and the Woman," at the age of sixteen, I did not think that the word in the stars signified the tragic determinism of the death drive. I believed, rather, that the word was a word of redemption, and neither the protagonist's madness nor his author's fear of it made it occur to me, even for a moment, to determine *what* that spelled word was—and thereby dispel its benevolent indeterminacy.

[§]"I shall explain. A thin veneer of immediate reality is spread over natural and artificial matter, and whoever wishes to be in the now, with the now, on the now, should please not break its tension film. Otherwise the inexperienced miracle-worker will find himself no longer walking on water but descending upright among staring fish." Vladimir Nabokov, *Transparent Things*.

Notes

CHAPTER ONE
THE GENESIS OF THE SPEAKING SUBJECT

1. I wish, at this starting point, to acknowledge my indebtedness for this inspiration. The scope and depth of Kristeva's understanding of the psychology of the poetic utterance and the magnitude of its influence on my thinking have become increasingly clear to me as I tried to work out my own understanding of it and of Thomas's poetry. Therefore, to the extent that it reflects its own writing-process, this book unfolds the evolution of a reading not only of Thomas, but also of Kristeva.

2. Julia Kristeva, "The Speaking Subject," in *On Signs*, ed. Marshall Blonsky (Oxford: Basil-Blackwell, 1985), 210–220; *Revolution in Poetic Language*, trans. Margaret Waller (New York: Columbia University Press, 1984). Though Kristeva focuses here on the "revolutionary" nature of the modern text, many aspects of her theory seem to apply to poetic language in general.

3. For the sake of convenience, and since the question of gender is not addressed in this book, the conventional third person masculine will be generally used in theoretical reference to the speaking subject. A comment on the problematic issue of gender (which is *not* dealt with) is to be found at the end of this chapter.

4. Julia Kristeva, *Black Sun: Depression and Melancholia*, trans. Leon S. Roudiez (New York: Columbia University Press, 1989), 5–6, 9.

5. The following introduction of the intersubjective perspective is based on George E. Atwood and Robert D. Stolorow, *Faces in a Cloud: Intersubjectivity in Personality Theory* (Northvale, N. J.: Jason Aronson, [1979] 1993), and on Robert D. Stolorow, George E. Atwood, and Bernard Brandchaft, eds., *The Intersubjective Perspective* (Northvale, N. J.: Jason Aronson, 1994).

6. Atwood and Stolorow, *Faces in a Cloud*, 178.

7. Ibid., 177; Stolorow and Atwood, "Towards a Science of Human Experience," in Stolorow, Atwood, and Brandchaft, *The Intersubjective Perspective*, 15.

8. Ibid., 20.

9. Stolorow and Attwood, *Faces in a Cloud*, 176–78.

10. See Donna M. Orange, "Countertransference, Empathy, and the Hermeneutical Circle," in Stolorow, Atwood, and Brandchaft, *The Intersubjective Perspective*, 181–85.

11. Orange, 181.

12. Hans Georg Gadamar, *Philosophical Hermeneutics*, trans. D. E. Linge (Berkeley: University of California Press, 1976), 9. Quoted by Orange, 182.

13. Wilhelm Dilthey, *Meaning in History* (London: Allen and Unwin, 1961), 191, quoted by Stolorow, Atwood, and Brandchaft, in "Towards a Science of Human Experience," in *The Intersubjective Perspective*, 17.

14. Though these mechanisms are predominantly bound with the earliest "oral" phase, they may be lived out in relation with other—anal and genital—erotogenic zones and other functions. "*Projection*" is an "operation whereby qualities, feelings, wishes or even 'objects', which the subject refuses to recognize or rejects in himself, are expeled from the self and located in another person or thing." "*Introjection*" is the imaginary process "whereby the subject transposes objects and their inherent qualities from the 'outside' to the 'inside' of himself." In "Instincts and Their Vicissitudes," Freud's "most explicit text on this point," and in "Negation," projection and introjection are associated with the original determination of the boundary between "inside" and "outside" as correlatives of unpleasure and pleasure. Thus, the subject-to-be projects what is "bad" inside him and introjects what is "good" outside. "*Incorporation*" is a "process whereby the subject, more or less on the level of fantasy, has an object penetrate his body and keeps it 'inside' his body. . . . Incorporation provides the *corporal* model for introjection and identification." (J. Laplanche and J-B Pontalis, *The Language of Psycho-Analysis*, translated by Donald Nicholson-Smith [London: Hogarth, 1983], 349, 230–31, 211.) The corporal aspect of incorporation distinguishes it from introjection as it was first introduced by Sandor Ferenczi and then interpreted by Abraham and Torok and by André Green. These writers stress the psychic and symbolic element in introjection as a real, integrative assimilation that contributes to the growth of the ego, as opposed to the false, fantasmatic internalization—rather than assimilation—into the (fantasy of) the body in incorporation. Green distinguishes between "instinctual," "imaginary," and "symbolic" introjections (*On Private Madness* [Madison, Conn.: International Universities Press, 1986], 268–69). The "imaginary" introjection of affects and representations and the "symbolic" introjection of verbal and perceptual communications as Green presents them apply to the processes of sublimation and the intersubjective dynamics of symbolization and intertextuality discussed in this book. "*Excorporation*," the correlative of incorporation, is Green's term for the more archaic, corporal model of

projection. Preceding the constitution of the "outside" as a "projective plane," excorporation is an ejection that resembles exorcism, "of which the motor discharge is the behavioural manifestation—cries, tears . . ."—and perhaps also some forms of textual articulation? (Green, *On Private Madness*, 87).

15. Kristeva, *Tales Of Love*, trans. Leon S. Roudiez (New York: Columbia University Press, 1987), 21–48.

16. Kristeva, *Tales of Love*, 26–27, 34–35, 40–43; *Black Sun*, 23. The cohesive function of the archaic paternal agency is designated by its definition as "unitary feature" (*Tales of Love*, 46–47).

17. Kristeva, *Tales of Love*, 46–48.

18. The gender of the "imaginary father" is an ambiguous issue, given that primary identification originally occurs through the mother-child relationship and prior to sexual differentiation. "For Freud," Kristeva says, "such a 'father' is the same as 'both parents,'" and so is he also for Kristeva, to the extent that he is a "non-object" representing the cohesive "unitary feature" and the imaginary plenitude of wish-fulfilling fantasy (see *Tales of Love*, 26, and n. 6 there). Kelly Oliver (*Reading Kristeva: Unravelling the Double-bind* [Bloomington and Indianapolis: Indiana University Press, 1993]) reads Kristeva's notion of the archaic father as referring, essentially, to a "maternal function" (dismissing Kristeva's "insistence that it is called a 'father'" as "a holdover from traditional psychoanalytical theory"), which thus "challenges the priority given to the paternal function in traditional psychoanalytical theory," (15, 69, 70). Indeed, one might object to the attribution of both law and love to the paternal, and join Oliver in maintaining that the love that facilitates the child's transition from the mother's body to the subjectifying (symbolic) realm of desire is maternal—if, that is, we allow the maternal to represent anything but symbiosis and its negative somatic correlative, abjection. For after all—and here lies Kristeva's improvement on the Lacanian model, according to Oliver—it is through the discourse of maternal love that the early capacity for symbolization is inherited. Acknowledging this fundamental fact, and making good use of the observations made by object relations theories that center around it, Kristeva nevertheless insists, like André Green, on the importance of postulating a triangular oedipal structure—with a mediating *paternal* "other"—in order to account for the signification of the dyadic relation. Oliver criticizes this as a reactionary element in Kristeva (for which she accounts by Kristeva's at times Christian imagination), claiming that "[t]here is nothing inherent in human life that this third party be a father or paternal" (129).

19. Jacques Lacan, *Écrits: A Selection*, trans. Alan Sheridan (New York: Norton, 1977), 269; Kristeva, "The Speaking Subject," 215.

20. *The Seminar of Jaques Lacan, Book II: The Ego in Freud's Theory and in the Technique of Psychoanalysis* 1954–1955, trans. Sylvana Tomaselli, ed. Jacques-Alain Miller (Cambridge: Cambridge University Press, 1988), 44.

21. See note 4.

22. The provisional nature of self-integration is suggested in Klein's theory of the early phases of the ego's organization. The "paranoid-schizoid" and the "depressive" phases which mark the emerging subject's strategies of coping with his innate, fragmenting ambivalence are also "states" or "positions" between which the subject oscillates throughout his life. In her introductory comment on Klein's 1935 paper, "A Contribution to the Psychogenesis of Manic-Depressive States," (in *The Selected Melanie Klein*, ed. Juliet Mitchell [Harmondsworth: Penguin, 1986]), Juliet Mitchell points out that Klein's use of the concept of *position* there marks a shift from a developmental to a structural notion ("a 'position' is an always available state, not something one passes through" [Mitchell, 116]). (See 17–18 of this chapter).

23. On the *semiotic* see esp. *Revolution in Poetic Language*, 25–30. On the dialectic of the *semiotic* and the *symbolic* see ibid., 23–123 and 22–25 of this chapter.

24. "Among School Children," in *Selected Poems and Two Plays of William Butler Yeat*, ed. M. L. Rosenthal (New York: Macmillan, 1978), 117.

25. See Winnicott, *Playing and Reality* (Harmondsworth: Penguin, 1985), 1–30.

26. Raanan Kulka, introduction to the Hebrew translation of D. W. Winnicott, *Playing and Reality*, trans. Yossi Milo (Tel-Aviv: Am Oved, 1995), 12, 24.

27. Ibid., 23.

28. The term "autism" is applied here in its non-clinical sense, to designate the non-relating muteness of the melancholic, "autoerotic" introversion.

29. Kristeva, *Tales of Love*, chapter 1, "Freud and Love: Treatment and its Discontents," 21–56.

30. Freud, "On Narcissism: An Introduction" (1914), *PFL* vol. 11: 69.

31. Freud, "The Ego and the Id" (1923), *PFL* vol. 11:370.

32. Ibid.

33. Kristeva, *Tales of Love*, 43; my emphasis.

34. The paternal pattern or *schema* is "metaphorical" in its symbolic function rather than semantic content: "*Metaphor* should be understood as a movement toward the discernible, a journey toward the visible. *Anaphora, gesture, indication,* would probably be more adequate terms for this sundered unity, in the process of being set up, which I am presently conjuring. Aristotle refers to an *epiphora*: a generic term for the metaphorical motility previous to any objectivation of *a* figurative meaning . . ." (ibid., 23, 30.)

35. See note 22.

36. Hanna Segal, *Introduction to the Work of Melanie Klein* (London: Karnac Books and the Institute of Psycho-Analysis, 1988), 80.

37. Klein, "Notes on Some Schizoid Mechanisms," in Mitchell, 182, 191; "Mourning and its Relation to Manic Depressive States," ibid., 151–52; "A Contribution to the Psychogenesis of Manic-Depressive States," ibid., 132.

38. Klein, "A Contribution to the Psychogenesis of Manic-Depressive States," 132–34.

39. Klein, "Mourning and its Relation to Manic Depressive States," 152–53.

40. Kristeva, *Black Sun*, 23–25, 50–51.

41. Ibid., 27–28.

42. The maternal "abject" and the "Thing" designate aspects of the maternal pre-object in the different contexts of Kristeva's *Powers of Horror: An Essay on Abjection* (trans. Leon S. Roudiez [New York: Columbia University Press, 1984) and *Black Sun*, respectively. While the maternal abject configures the unseparated subject's disposition of repulsion and paranoia in relation to the archaic maternal, on whom he projects the negativity of and in relation to the separation, Kristeva's Thing is an ambiguous concept which configures both terms of the subject's primary ambivalence. It is the unsymbolized "center of attraction and repulsion" whose positive and negative aspects manifest themselves in different states: the "*erotic Thing*" is an idealized (sublimated) imaginary or affective representation of the maternal container ("place" or "pre-object" rather than object), and is thus dominated by the pleasure principle. The "melancholic Thing," by contrast, is governed by the death drive: configuring the paranoid anxieties of the archaic separation which a fragile primal repression fails to eliminate, it is the "focus of my hatred . . . [a] mere nothing . . . that contains my dejecta . . . a waste . . . not . . . a significant object but the self's borderline element. For those who are depressed, the Thing like the self is a downfall that carries them along into the invisible and unnamable. Waste and *cadavers* all" (*Black Sun*, 13–15; my emphasis). These attributes are also those of the maternal abject in *Powers of Horror* (see especially, 3–4), the term I use in opposition to the "Thing" in its sublimated, nostalgic, or "eroticized" aspect.

43. In her "Notes on Symbol Formation" (1957), Hanna Segal refers to the internal reproduction of the mourned object or instinctual aim in effective sublimation and symbol formation. The renunciation of the object, she writes, "can be successful, like the first situation [of the giving up of the breast] if the object to be given up can be assimilated in the ego, by the process of loss and internal restoration. I suggest that such an assimilated object becomes a symbol within the ego" (quoted in Segal, *Introduction to the Work of Melanie Klein*, 76).

44. Freud, "Mourning and Melancholia," in *PFL* vol. 11; Kristeva, *Black Sun*.

45. "Mourning and Melancholia," 262; *Black Sun*, 12–13.

46. Kristeva, *Black Sun*, 17, 20.

47. Freud, "Mourning and Melancholia," 258, 260.

48. Kristeva, *Black Sun*, 47.

49. Jakobson, "Closing Statement: Linguistics and Poetics," in *Style in Language*, ed. Thomas A. Sebeok (Cambridge, Mass.: MIT Press, 1960), 350–77; Shklovsky, "Art as Technique," (1917), *Russian Formalist Criticism: Four Essays*, trans. Lee T. Lemon and Marion J. Reis (Lincoln: University of Nebraska Press, 1965). The notion of defamiliarization is discussed in more detail in chapter 3.

50. Donald Davidson, "What Metaphors Mean," in *Philosophical Perspectives on Metaphor*, ed. Mark Johnson (Minneapolis: University of Minnesota Press, 1981), 200–220; my emphasis. See also note 20 of chapter 2.

51. Kristeva, *Powers of Horror*, 51–53.

52. Kristeva, *Revolution in Poetic Language*, 28.

53. On this symbolic failure and the related theory of the sign, see Kristeva, *Powers of Horror*, 51–53.

54. On "empty" and "full" speech, see Kristeva, *Black Sun*, 51–55, and "La parole deprimée," in "La voix: Actes du Colloque d'Ivry (1988), ed. R. Lew and F. Sauvagnat (Paris: la Lysmaque, 1989). See also Lacan, "The Function and Field of Speech in Language," *Écrits* 30–113, esp. 45–46.

55. On concatenation and transposition in psychoanalysis, language aquisition and poetry, see Kristeva's *Black Sun*, 40–41.

56. Kristeva, *Tales of Love*, 26.

57. Holbrook, *The Code of Night* (London: Athlone Press, 1972), 1.

58. "Vision and Prayer," *CP* 139.

59. Dylan Thomas, *A Prospect of the Sea*, ed. Daniel Jones (London: Dent, 1979), 92–94.

60. *CP* 6.

61. Kristeva, *Black Sun*, 132; *In the Beginning Was Love: Psychoanalysis and Faith*, trans. Arthur Goldhammer (New York: Columbia University Press, 1987).

62. Particularly relevant and revealing among the many critical discussions of Thomas's "sacramental poetry" is Eleanor J. McNees's, in chapter 4 of her book *Eucharistic Poetry: The Search for Presence in the Writings of John Donne, Gerard Manley Hopkins, Dylan Thomas and Geoffrey Hill* (London and Toronto: Associated University Presses, 1992). McNees expounds on Thomas's "sacramental" poetic strategies for instigating "real presence" by "exploding [the] ordinary logic of language" to the effect of transcending it toward the unnamable or, in Paul Ricoeur's terminology, by playing with "'limit-language' of paradox, metaphor, and pun" and of distorted syntax to "evoke the 'limit-experience' of incarnation or indwelling spiritual presence" (111, 194; 21 and n. 14). Addressing the controversial question of Thomas's religiosity, McNees indicates the metaphorical or mimetic nature of his "sacramental" poetics in its modern context of the absence of doctrinal faith. Tracing a process of conversion in the development of Thomas's poetry, she points out his attempt, in his

early poetry, to imitate the creative Word for the purpose of "resurrecting," or calling forth, the presence of his own self and the world (rather than God or Christ; 113). Later, she claims, Thomas comes to incorporate religious language and typology in order "to displace dogma and renew active faith" (131), while in the last phase of his poetry, she suggests, appropriation gives way to a reciprocity, i.e., to Thomas's "sacrificial" submission to the Christian myth instead of subjecting it to his own, self-magnifying poetic use. McNees interprets this last development as an expression of the acceptance of the religious requirement of self-sacrifice (see 140), which she sees reflected in Thomas's "Poem on His Birthday." My own position, as I show in my analysis of the same poem, is that Thomas's poetry is "sacramental" in the metaphorical sense, which makes it more generally applicable to poetic signification.

63. The representation of the subject's inherent rupture and the "redemptive" oral dynamics of its sublimation in the logic of the Christian sacrifice and in its reenactment in the Christian sacrament of the eucharist is discussed in Kristeva's *Black Sun*, 130–35.

64. See Oliver's critique of what she sees as instances of the "recreation of the Christian imaginary" in Kristeva's writing (125–33), which she interprets as "a symptom of Kristeva's nostalgic relationship to Christianity" (128); of "the melancholic atheist mourning the death of God" (132).

65. Letter to Henry Treece in *The Collected Letters of Dylan Thomas*, ed. Paul Ferris (London: Dent, 1985), 281. Thomas's idea of his deconstructive "method" will be discussed in more detail in chapter 2.

66. "In the Direction of the Beginning," in *A Prospect of the Sea*," ed. Daniel Jones (London: Dent, 1979), 93.

67. Ibid.

68. "I, In My Intricate Image," *CP* 30; my emphasis. Note: all the emphases in the quotations from Dylan Thomas's works are my own.

69. "In the Beginning," ibid., 20.

70. The poetic rearticulation of the creative Word is referred to in "Poem on his Birthday," where the represented world expresses "more triumphant faith / Than ever since *the world was said*" (ibid., 158).

71. Jakobson, "Closing Statement: Linguistics and Poetics," 355; my emphasis.

72. Kristeva cites Benveniste, *Le Vocabulaire des instutions indo-européennes* (Paris: Minuit, 1969), vol. 1, 175, in *In the Beginning Was Love*, 30–31.

73. Michel de Cérteau, "What We Do When We Believe," in *On Signs*, ed. Marshall Blonsky (Oxford: Basil-Blackwell, 1985), 192–202.

74. John Malcolm Brinnin, *Dylan Thomas in America* (Boston: Little, Brown, 1955), 28.

75. In his introduction to *On Private Madness*, André Green expresses the belief "that what [has] changed since Freud was probably less the population of analysands than the analysts' way of listening to them. . . . above all, it [is] the ear of the analyst that [is] no longer the same. Nowadays one's hearing is more sensitive to picking up conflicts that are laden with archaic potential, which perhaps passed unnoticed in the past. Today—even if we do not all formulate it in the same way—we are sensitive to the process of symbolization" (11).

76. *On Private Madness*, 60. That hero is diagnosed by Green as a "borderline," a prototype which Kristeva takes up in *Powers of Horror*, to qualify the postmodern subject's existence at the limits of abjection and subjectivity ("At the limit of primal repression." 7, 9, 10).

77. This notion is forcefully developed in Kochhar-Lindgren's *Narcissus Transformed: The Textual Subject in Psychoanalysis and Literature* (University Park: Pennsylvania State University Press, 1993). Kochhar-Lindgren analyzes what he regards as the Thanatic self-reflexivity of contemporary Western discourse, with its loss of faith in the imaginary (the fictive) and its obsession with immediacy, in terms of the transformative disillusionment of the mythical Narcissus. Through readings of psychoanalytical and literary works—by Freud, Lacan, and Kristeva, and modern and contemporary fiction—he traces the "entextualization" of the subject and his death-driven narcissistic vicissitudes of annihilating autoerotic negativity, and concludes with a redemptive credo that accords with Kristeva's extolment of "erotic narcissism." The only way to move beyond narcissism, he suggests, is from within it; to be liberated from the "otherless," autoerotic logic of narcissism, which is the deadening, tautological logic of (self-)identity, one must renounce subjective identity and, adhering to a third party, embody oneself in discourses whose fictionality is acknowledged—as is the truth of the desire that animates them and of the other toward which that desire is addressed.

78. Kristeva, *Revolution in Poetic Language*, 48; my emphasis.

79. *CP* 129–39.

80. The obsessiveness of this preoccupation in our culture points to an existential anxiety that exceeds, I think, ethical and political considerations as well as intellectual fashion.

81. *CP* 124–25.

82. Freud wrote in a letter to Fliess (1897): "Can you imagine what 'endopsychic myths' are? They are the latest products of my mental labour. The dim inner perception of one's own psychical apparatus stimulates illusions, which are naturally projected outwards, and characteristically into the future and a world beyond. Immortality, retribution, the world after death, are all reflections of our inner psyche . . . psycho-mythology" (*The Origins of Psychoanalysis: Letters to Wilhelm Fliess, Drafts and Notes 1887–1902*, [New York: Basic Books, 1954], 237).

83. Felman, "To Open the Question," in *Literature and Psychoanalysis*, ed. Shoshana Felman (Baltimore: Johns Hopkins University Press, 1982), 6.

84. *CP* 155–58.

85. *CP* 35.

86. Walter Benjamin, "On Language as Such and on the Language of Man," in *Reflections: Essays, Aphorisms, Autobiographical Essays*, trans. Edmund Jephcott, ed. Peter Demetz (New York: Schocken, 1986).

87. *CP* 150–51, 95–97.

88. Benjamin, "On Language as Such and on the Language of Man," and also in "The Task of the Translator," in *Illuminations*, trans. Harry Zohn, ed. Hanna Arendt (London: J. Cape, 1970), 69–81.

89. *A Prospect of the Sea*, 3–12, 58–77.

90. R. B. J. Kershner, *Dylan Thomas: The Poet and His Critics* (Chicago: American Library Association, 1976), ix; Jacob Korg, *Dylan Thomas* (New York: Twayne Publishers, 1992), ch. 9, "Thomas in Retrospect," 143–49.

CHAPTER TWO
POEM ON HIS BIRTHDAY

1. The motif of mother riding appears as a suggestive symbol of separation in the Welsh *Mabinogion*, where it is associated with the character of Rhiannon, the Great Queen, Great Mother, and horse-goddess, whose name is also borne by an ambiguous maternal character in Thomas's work, "The Visitor" (in *A Prospect of the Sea*, ed. Daniel Jones [London: Dent, 1979]). In *The Mabinogion*, Rhiannon is the rider of a magic horse and the hero's mother, who takes long to give him birth and loses him soon afterwards, as he is kidnapped while she is asleep. Her six irresponsible baby-sitters plot to save their skins by claiming that she murdered the baby (in her sleep, again), and her consequent punishment is "to sit every day by the mounting-block near the gate and tell her story to anyone who might not already know it," as well as "to offer to carry guests and stangers to the court on her back" (*The Mabinogion*, trans. Jeffrey Gantz [Harmondsworth: Penguin, 1976], 61). It is interesting that the murder which separates mother and son (who develops extraordinarily well elsewhere), is a verbal rather than an actual one, which mainfests, perhaps, a psychological insight into the phenomenon of abjection as the first psychic act of separation. Similarly, the fact that the alleged murder takes place during Rhiannon's sleep suggests an awareness of the grain of unconscious truth underlying the blood libel.

2. Eratosthenes of Alexandria quoted by Emmet Robins, "Famous Orpheus," in John Warden, ed., *Orpheus: The Metamorphoses of a Myth* (Toronto: University of Toronto Press, 1985), 13.

3. Warden, 91.

4. "*dolce parlare*," ibid., 90; ibid., 93–94.

5. "*Orphica comparatio*," ibid., 97; ibid., 90, 94.

6. Robert K. Burdette, *The Saga of Prayer* (The Hague: Mouton, 1972).

7. See the sower's parable and the comparison of the Logos to the sun, as depicted in Matthew 13 and Mark 4. These, and their relevant narrative context—Jesus' sea journey with his disciples—will be discussed in more detail in the close analysis of the poem.

8. See note 7.

9. The same process, essentially, is depicted in Thomas's poem "Vision and Prayer" (*CP* 129–40). The more explicit birth imagery in that poem foregrounds the "corrective" dynamics of return to origins involved in the poetic "act of faith."

10. Burdette, 82.

11. For reference on "empty" and "full" speech, see note 54 in chapter 1.

12. Marcel Proust, *The Past Recaptured*, trans. Andreas Mayor (New York: Random House, 1971), 134.

13. On the "helio-tropical" light of the sun (-flower), see Jacques Derrida, "White Mythology: Metaphor in the Text of Philosophy," *New Literary History* 6, no. 1 (Autumn 1974): 51.

14. Burdette, 14–15.

15. "Chanter: that pipe or bagpipe, with finger-holes, on which a melody is played" (*OED*).

16. *CP* 140.

17. See "Le démon littéraire," in *Folle vérité: vérité et vraisemblance du texte psychotique*, ed. Julia Kristeva (Paris: Seuil, 1979), 204.

18. "Mais c'est seulment ceux qui n'ont pas d'yeux ni d'oreilles pour le véritable sens de la parole ('Aux autres les paraboles(-)') qui l'intendent ainsi comme allusion, double sens, secret" (ibid.).

19. Jacques Lacan, "The Freudian Thing," in *Écrits: A Selection*, trans. Alan Sheridan (New York: Norton, 1977), 122–23.

20. In his essay on "What Metaphors Mean," Donald Davidson discusses the deictic function of metaphor as a transverbal signifier. Starting from a view of metaphor that is essentially similar to Christ's alluded "speech-act poetics" of his parables, Davidson claims that "metaphors mean what the words, in their most literal interpretation, mean, and nothing more," 201. ("What Metaphors Mean," in *Philosophical Perspectives on Metaphor*, ed. Mark Johnson [Minneapolis: University of Minnesota Press, 1981], 200–221). To justify the assumption that metaphors cannot be paraphrased, Davidson claims that "what [a metaphor] makes us see" beyond its literal meaning is not a "specific cognitive content" (ibid., 216–17). Consequently, the relation of metaphor to what it shows is not a linguistic propositional one, but a pragmatic relation: a metaphor "does not say and it does not hide, it *intimates*" (ibid., 217). And "intimation is not meaning," but a translinguistic effect, which "makes us notice," or "calls to our attention," or *points out of language* to, something that is neither "finite in scope" nor "propositional in nature," for which "words are [therefore]

the wrong currency" (ibid., 217–18; my emphasis). As for the translinguistic domain to which the indexed thing belongs, Davidson does not give a clear indication. His illustrations for the deictic function of metaphor designate an obvious semiological domain: "If someone draws a finger along a coastline on *a map*, or mentions the beauty or the deftness of a Picasso *etching*, how many things are drawn to your attention?" (ibid., 219; my emphases). But the semiological domain to which metaphors—and, for that matter, *semiotic* signifiers in general—point their fingers extends beyond the obviously cultural one, to the psychosomatic one, of perceptions and sensations and their psychobiological signal and representation system.

21. *The Collected Letters of Dylan Thomas*, ed. Paul Ferris (London: Dent, 1985), 281.

22. Kristeva, *Powers of Horror: An Essay on Abjection*, trans. Leon S. Roudiez (New York: Columbia University Press, 1982), 1.

23. Indeed, some of Thomas's readers charged him with being incommunicative (see chapter 6). The psychological explanation given by one such reader is particularly relevant with regard to the problem (which this poem, at least, certainly solves). David Holbrook explains what he feels to be the motivated incoherence in many of Thomas's poems as a paranoid-schizoid defense strategy of "preserving chaos in self-defense" (Laing), that is, of maintaining a state of inner split and fragmentation as a defense against annihilation (see Holbrook, *The Code of Night* [London: Athlone, 1972], 20).

24. The "impossible object" of phobic hallucination, Kristeva writes, is "the maternal phallus, which is *not*" (*Powers of Horror*, 42).

25. Kristeva discusses the sublimative process of narrative unfolding and prosodic cohesion in her analysis of Nerval's orphic textual journey in "El Desdichado" (*Black Sun*, trans. Leon S. Roudiez [New York: Columbia University Press, 1989], 159–62). In that poem too, as she points out, the poet's "having assimilated an unnamed Eurydice into his song and the chords of his lyre . . . adopts the pronoun 'I' as his own" (159). In *Powers of Horror* she explains the subjectifying aspect of the narrative binding and Symbolic "detour-taking": "a narrative is, all in all, the most elaborate attempt, next to syntactic competence, to situate a speaking being between his desires and their prohibitions, in short, within the Oedipal triangle" (140).

CHAPTER THREE
INCARNATE DEVIL IN THE GARDEN OF EDEN

1. Victor Shklovsky, "Art As Technique" (1917), *Russian Formalist Criticism: Four Essays*, eds. Lee T. Lemon and Marion J. Reis (Lincoln: University of Nebraska Press, 1965), 12.

2. Julia Kristeva, *Revolution in Poetic Language*, trans. Margaret Waller (New York: Columbia University Press, 1984), ch. 8, 57–61.

3. Julia Kristeva, "Le vréel," in *Folle vérité: Vérité et vraisemblance du texte psychotique*, ed. Julia Kristeva (Paris: Seuil, 1979), 11.

4. An exact definition of Lacan's enigmatic notion of the "Real" is impossible. Moreover, as Laplanche and Pontalis note in reference to his less enigmatic notion of the "Symbolic," "to attempt to contain [its] meaning . . . within strict boundaries—to define it—would amount to a contradiction of Lacan's thought, since he refuses to acknowledge that the signifier can be permanently bound to the signified" (*The Language of Psycho-Analysis* [London: Hogarth, 1983], 440). Therefore, one can only interpret, that is, bind another, new signified to the term.

The evasiveness of the meaning of the Real in Lacan's language is in line with the evasiveness which he attributes to its referent in relation to language (and experience) in general, both of which allow for an adequate definition only by way of negative attribution. Thus, reconciling apparently divergent tendencies in Lacan's presentation of it, Malcolm Bowie explains the Real as "that which is radically extrinsic to the procession of the signifiers . . . it is the irremediable and intractable 'outside' of language; *the indefinitely receding goal towards which the signifying chain tends*. . . . As a result of this view, the Real comes close to meaning 'the ineffable' or 'the impossible' in Lacan's thought" ("Jacques Lacan," in *Structuralism and Since*, ed. Malcolm Bowie [Oxford: Oxford University Press, 1979], 133–34).

As the goal of the movement of the signifiers, the Real as I understand it, suggests two (im-) possibilities: either the *object* of the desire which propels speech, namely "*being*" as the real-ization of the (incestuous) desire for (the "original") integrity, whose impossibility makes it into an *ideal*; or the *truth* which it signifies, namely, the reality of the impossibility or the *lack* of that object—"the lack of being properly speaking" ("Desire, Life and Death," in *The Seminar of Jacques Lacan, Book II*, trans. Sylvana Tomaselli, ed. Jacqus-Alain Miller [Cambridge: Cambridge University Press, 1988], 223), which is, ultimately, the reality of "castration" underlying and *misrecognized* by the "Symbolic" and the "Imaginary." These two possibilities are pointed out by Bowie though within a different categorization. According to Bowie, "two apparently divergent general tendencies may be discerned in Lacan's presentation of [the] notion [of the Real]. First, the Real is that which is there . . . and inaccessible to the subject, whether this be a *physical object* or a *sexual trauma*" (133. See also ch. 5 of Lacan's *The Four Fundamental Concepts of Psychoanalysis*, trans. Alan Sheridan, ed. Jacques-Alain Miller [Harmondsworth: Penguin, 1987]). Secondly, however, the Real is the "*primordial chaos* upon which language operates" in its creation of the world of things by words. As I see it, sexual trauma (or its retroactive signified) and the primordial chaos belong to the category of lack/castration, while a physical object, or the access to its experience, belongs to the order of ideal recuperation of "being". The "impossible real" suggests both ideal being and lack, as it emerges from Lacan's following formulation, which at once affirms the Real as a presence, by way of a double negation, and negates it: "the lack of the lack makes the real, which emerges only there, as a cork. This cork is supported by the term of the impossible." (ibid., ix).

5. See note 4.

6. Susan K. Deri, *Symbolization and Creativity* (New York: International Universities Press, 1984), 46.

7. Francis Jeanson, *La foi d'un incroyant* (Paris: Seuil, 1963), 24; my emphases.

8. The phatic function of language is, according to Roman Jakobson (after Malinovski), its emphasis on ensuring or sustaining communication or "contact" between the addressor and the addressee ("Closing Statement: Linguistics and Poetics," in *Style in Language*, ed. Thomas A. Sebeok (Cambridge: Cambridge University Press), 355–56).

9. David Holbrook, *The Code of Night* (London: Athlone, 1972), 1. Holbrook borrows the term from R. D. Laing (*The Divided Self* [London: Tavistock, 1960]) to designate the sense of unreality and existential anxiety, which marks what he diagnoses as Thomas's "schizoid predicament."

10. Shklovsky, "Art As Technique," 13, (1917), (in *Russian Formalist Criticism: Four Essays*, ed. Lee T. Lemon and Marion J. Reis [Lincoln: University of Nebraska Press, 1965] see 11 ff.).

11. Deri, 33. On Gestalt theory and symbol formation, see 29–42.

12. Shklovsky uses the word "vision" in "Art As Technique" (18) to designate the mode of perception of the signified constituting the poetic effect. His focus on the *signified* and on the perceptual *effect* of the poetic "technique," as well as the mystical connotation of the word he uses to describe it, reflect, in my reading, a strong *anti*-Formalist pull in his "Formalist" text. Though he expresses his commitment to Formalism by declaring emphatically that "the object is not important," as what is important is the "artfulness of the object" (12), what is really important for him, to judge by the general spirit of the essay, is precisely the immediate sense of the object's "*essence*" (11; my emphasis)—the "stoniness" of the stone' (12)—rendered available by the "artfulness" of the signifier. This impression is yielded as strongly in his "The Resurrection of The Word" (in *Russian Formalism*, ed. Stephen Bann and John E. Bowlt [Edinburgh: Scottish Academic Press, 1973], 41–47)—a title in itself suggestive by its nostalgic allusion—where he declares that "the aim of Futurism is the resurrection of *things*—the return to man of sensation of the *world*" (41; my emphases).

13. The same schematic impression is sometimes generated in other, less successful poems, in the use of archetypal metaphors, which are not defamiliarized and assimiliated enough to generate a concrete personal experience, and in the vitalist preoccupation with the "naked forces of life."

14. *CP* 126.

15. The term "basic trust" is originally E. H. Erikson's. Winnicott's "good enough" mother provides a "good enough" environment for the child's development by actively adapting herself to the child's needs of adjustment and individuation. She does this by fulfilling the "feminine" function of "being" there for him (in contrast with neglecting, on the one hand, and intrusive or "impinging" "male" "doing," on the other). The trust or confidence created by such an environment guarantees the child's confidence or trust in others and in his own (introjected sense of) "being," and preconditions his capacity for symbolization (see Winnicott, *Playing and Reality*, 127–29. On male and female "doing" and "being," see 93–95). It should be noted that, from the dynamic and less optimistic perspective of this essay, the goodness and the effect of such an environment is more limited than Winnicott allows, given that the early maternal environment is never "good enough." . . .

16. Didiér Anzieu, "Machine a décroire: sur un trouble de la croyance dans les états limites," in *La croyance (Nouvelle Révue de Psychanalyse* no. 18) (Paris: Gallimard, 1978), 159.

17. D. W. Winnicott, "Fear of Breakdown," *International Journal of Psychoanalysis* 1 (1974): 103–7.

18. Winnicott, "Mind and its Relation to the Psyche-Soma" (1949), in *Collected Papers* (London: Tavistock, 1958), 253–54.

19. Shklovsky, "Art As Technique," 11–13. See also "The Resurrection of the Word," 41–42.

20. See note 10.

21. Shklovsky, "Art As Technique," 13.

22. According to David Holbrook, most of Thomas's poetry is emotionally dissociated and forces the reader to give it its absent meaning. This claim will be discussed in chapter 6.

23. Walter Benjamin, "On Language As Such and on the Language of Man," in *Reflections: Essays, Aphorisms, Autobiographical Essays*, trans. Edmund Jephcott, ed. Peter Demetz (New York: Shocken, 1986), 323.

24. Ibid., 325. Also relevant here is Benjamin's notion of "translation" as presented in "The Task of the Translator" (*Illuminations*. Tr. Harry Zohn, ed. Hanna Arendt. London: J. Cape, 1970). Benjamin's conception of origin and translation in both essays is discussed in chapter 4.

25. Ibid., 325–26.

26. T .S. Eliot, "*Burnt Norton*," in *Four Quartets* (London: Faber & Faber, 1959), 14, 16; my emphasis.

27. Freud, "Negation," (1925), *PFL* vol. 11, and André Green's reading of it in "The Borderline Concept," in *On Private Madness* (Madison, Conn.: International Universities Press, 1986).

28. Freud, "Negation," 440.

29. John Milton, *Paradise Lost*, Book 1, l.

30. Freud, "Negation," 438.

31. Benjamin, "On Language," 327; my emphasis.

32. Freud, "Negation," 438.

33. Kristeva, *Black Sun: Depression and Melancholia*, trans. Leon S. Roudiez (New York: Columbia University Press), 43–44.

34. Freud, "Negation," 438.

35. Benjamin, "On Language," 328.

36. Ibid., 327–28.

37. Freud, "Beyond the Pleasure Principle" (1920), *PFL* vol. 11.

38. Freud, "Negation," 441.

39. Benjamin, "On Language," 330–31.

40. William T. Moynihan, *The Craft and Art of Dylan Thomas* (Ithaca: Cornell University Press, 1968), 222.

41. Moynihan, 232.

42. "In The Beginning," *CP* 20.

43. Moynihan, 231.

44. Ibid., 233.

45. *CP* 33.

46. "Le mal est sans pourquoi," André Green, "Pourquoi le mal?" (1988), in *La folie privée: Psychanalyse des cas-limites* (Paris: Gallimard, 1990), 369.

47. As in Lady Macbeth to her "spot," *Macbeth* V.i.38.

48. The logic of the "supplement" subverts, by way of inversion, the hierarchical relation between the apparently central and marginal elements of that order (see, for example, the application of that logic to the relation between speech and writing in Jacques Derrida's *Of Grammatology*, trans. G. C. Spivak [Baltimore: Johns Hopkins University Press, 1976], part 2, esp. "That Dangerous Supplement," 141–57).

49. The ambiguity of the creation and its "inborn" knowledge (inscribed in the split subject's primary ambivalence) are suggested by Thomas's straightforward origin poems, "In the Beginning" and "Before I Knocked": "In the Beginning . . ./ The substance forked . . . / And, . . . / Heaven and Hell mixed as they spun"; "Before I knocked[,] . . . Ungotten [,] I knew night and day." (*CP* 20, 6–7).

50. W. B. Yeats, *A Vision* (New York: Macmillan, 1977).

51. This performative task is also in line with Benjamin's idea of the literary work, of which the "essential quality is not statement or the imparting of information," but the transmittance of "the unfathomable, the mysterious . . . 'poetic' something" which he qualifies by way of analogy to "an unforgettable life or moment even if all men had forgotten it," whose recognition pertains to the "realm" of "God's remembrance" ("The Task of the Translator," in *Illuminations*, trans. Harry Zohn, ed. and intr. Hanna Arendt [London: J. Cape, 1970], 69–70).

52. The notion of the "purifying" chain of translations is introduced in Benjamin's essay "The Task of the Translator." Reading that essay in the light of the essay on the origin of language, as I will do in chapter 4, suggests an essential similarity between the role of the translator and that of the poet (despite Benjamin's explicit distinction between them on p. 76 of his essay on translation).

53. Dylan Thomas, "Poetic Manifesto," *Texas Quarterly* 4 (Winter 1961): 45; my emphasis.

54. "Now," *CP* 46.

55. A "mantrapping seabed" from which he must extricate himself, appears in Thomas's draft of a letter to Princess Caetani (*The Collected Letters of Dylan Thomas*, ed. Paul Ferris [London: Dent, 1985], 915), discussed in chapter 6.

56. In "Poem on his Birthday," however, the rage is redemptive: in the first part, the poet-protagonist's "*Terror rage[s] apart*" his visionary underwater "blind cage," "and [then] love unbolds the dark." In the second cathartic cycle, the disillusioned poet prays "faithlessly unto Him" like "*the last / Rage shattered waters* [that] kick / Masts and fishes to the still quick stars," and ends up sharing the "triumphant faith" of the exulting sea.

57. "Do Not Go Gentle into That Good Night," *CP* 159.

58. "I, In my Intricate Image," *CP* 30–33.

59. *A Vision* (New York: Macmillan, 1977). Book I: "The Great Wheel," 67–184, esp. 71–86.

60. Freud, "Negation," 439.

61. "Antithetical identity" is an impossible contradiction in terms, because identity implies identification with another. It designates, therefore, the subject's wishful attempt to generate an impossible, autonomous self.

62. Julia Kristeva, *Powers of Horror*, trans. Leon S. Roudiez (New York: Columbia University Press), 55.

63. In his discussion of borderline personalities, André Green makes the distinction between *having* and *being* a boundary, and defines the borderline subject as a "moving border." (*On Private Madness*, 62–63).

64. Kristeva, *Powers of Horror*.

65. Ibid., 54.

66. See the bearded witches in *Macbeth* (I.iii.45–47) and the configuration of the unsexed, or sexually self-ambiguated Lady Macbeth (I.v.42).

67. Kristeva, *Powers of Horror*, 14, 48–49.

68. Ibid., 49.

69. E.g., "Before I knocked," and "I, In my Intricate Image," (*CP* 6–7, 30–33).

70. "The Visitor," in *A Prospect of the Sea*, ed. Daniel Jones (London: Dent, 1967), 25.

71. Thomas, *Letters*, 915.

72. Kristeva, *Powers of Horror*, 53–54.

73. Ibid., 54.

CHAPTER FOUR
UNDER THE SIGN OF LOSS, A RECUPERATION

1. Freud, "Mourning and Melancholia," *PFL* vol. 11:257.

2. *CP* 150–51 and 95–97.

3. Gaston Bachelard, *The Poetics of Reverie: Childhood, Language, and the Cosmos*, trans. Daniel Russell (Boston: Beacon Press, 1969), 97–141.

4. "Inhibitions, Symptoms and Anxiety," *PFL* vol. 10:237–333.

5. Ibid., 330, 331, 244.

6. Ibid., 331.

7. Ibid., 330.

8. The articulation of *Fort, Da*—meaning, away and there—accompanied a game with a cotton reel and a piece of string tied around it which Freud's baby grandson used to play when his mother was away. The game concretized, for Freud, the infant's access to symbolization and its relation to maternal absence. The child used to throw the reel over the edge of his cot, chasing it away by crying something like "*Fort*!" and then draw it back again, welcoming its return with a joyful "*Da!*" Through this playful simulation, the child came to master, according to the grandfather's interpretation, the reality of the experience of his mother's absence ("Beyond the Pleasure Principle," *PFL* vol. 11:283–287).

9. *CP*, 24.

10. "Inhibitions, Symptoms and Anxiety," 293–94.

11. Ibid., 331.

12. "Beyond the Pleasure Principle."

13. "A Refusal To Mourn The Death, By Fire, Of A Child In London," *CP* 94.

14. David Holbrook, *The Code of Night* (London: Athlone, 1972), 193.

15. *CP* 62.

16. Holbrook, *The Code of Night*, 191.

17. Freud, "Mourning and Melancholia," 257–61.

18. Ibid., 262.

19. Ibid., 258.

20. Ibid., 262.

21. "*The Seed-At-Zero*," *CP* 37–38.

22. Freud, "Negation," *PFL* vol. 11:437.

23. Stéphane Moses, "L'idée d'origine chez Walter Benjamin," in *Walter Benjamin et Paris*, ed. Heinz Wisman (Paris: Cerf, 1986), 811; my emphasis. This and the forthcoming quotations from this essay are in my translation.

24. Ibid., 810.

25. Ibid., 811.

26. Ibid., 815. In his elaboration of the notion of the "double determination" of the return to/of origins, Moses refers to and cites from Benjamin's first version of his introduction to *The Origin of Greek Tragic Drama*, in *Gesammette Schriften*, ed. Rolph Tiedenann and Hermann Schweppenhauser (vol. 7:3, 1974), 935.

27. "This nucleus is best defined as the element that does not lend itself to translation." Thus "the primary concern of the genuine translator remains elusive." "The Task of the Translator," in *Illuminations*, trans. Harry Zohn, ed. Hanna Arendt (London: J. Cape, 1970), 75.

28. Ibid., 76, 77.

29. The challenge of "*ripening* the seed of pure language in a translation" is met when "the life of the [original] attains in [it] to its ever–renewed latest and most abundant *flowering*." Ibid., 77, 72; my emphases.

30. "There Was a Savior," *CP* 118.

31. T. S. Eliot, "Burnt Norton," 13; my emphasis.

32. Ibid.

33. Ibid., 14.

34. "There Was a Savior," *CP* 118.

35. "Poem on His Birthday," *CP* 156.

36. *CP* 36.

37. "Incarnate Devil" was written and revised in 1933 and 1935, and "Today, This Insect" in 1930 and 1936 (see Ralph Maud, *Entrances to Dylan Thomas's Poetry* [Pittsburgh: University of Pittsburgh Press, 1963], 129, 131), so the comment would be in the editing, if not also in the revision.

38. *CP* 36, and William Moynihan, *The Craft and Art of Dylan Thomas* (Ithaca: Cornell University Press, 1968), 247.

39. See note 70.

40. C. G. Jung, "The Psychology of the Child Archetype," in Kerényi and C. G. Jung, *Essays on a Science of Mythology*, trans. R. F. Hall (New York: Harper and Row, 1963), 83.

41. Bachelard, 102.

42. *A Prospect of the Sea*, ed. Daniel Jones (London: Dent 1979), 8.

43. Bachelard, 74.

44. John Ruskin coined the term (in "Of the Pathetic Fallacy," in *Modern Painters*, Vol. 3, 1856) to describe the tendency of poets and painters to "credit nature with the feelings of human beings." He discards this "error" as "morbidly" distortive in the case of those whom he considered as "second rank" poets (such as Wordsworth, Coleridge, Keats and Tennyson), who, overpowered by their feelings, as he claimed, were unaware of projecting them. "After Ruskin, and perhaps because of him, the use of the fallacy declined markedly" (*The Princeton Encyclopaedia of Poetry and Poetics*, eds. Preminger, Warnke, and Hardison [Princeton: Princeton University Press, 1974]).

45. See D. W. Winnicott, "Establishment of Relationship with External Reality," in *Human Nature* (London: Free Association Books, 1988), 106–9.

46. Bachelard, 128.

47. "Dylan Ali Mor" ("the son of the sea") is a figure in Welsh mythology (see Annis Pratt, *Dylan Thomas's Early Prose* [Pittsburgh: University of Pittsburgh Press, 1970], 65). The figure of Dylan in *The Mabinogion* is a typical "divine child." Dylan, which means sea, was born and "dropped" by Aranrhod as she stepped across a magic wand whereby her uncle Math wished to test her acclaimed virginity. Immediately following his baptism, the abandoned child "made for the sea, and . . . took on its nature and swam as well as the best fish. He was also called Dylan son of Ton," which means wave (*The Mabinogion*, trans. Jeffrey Gantz [Harmondsworth: Penguin, 1976], 106).

48. See 27–28 of C. Kerényi, "The Primordial Child in Primordial Times," in C. G. Jung and C. Kerényi, *Essays on a Science of Mythology*, 25–69, paraphrased by Bachelard, 132–33.

49. Bachelard, 133.

50. Ibid; original emphasis.

51. Ibid., 99–100.

52. Ibid., 121.

53. Ibid., 100.

54. Ibid., 119.

55. Ibid., 100.

56. Ibid., 101.

57. Winnicott's distinction between "being" and "doing" (*Playing and Reality* [Harmonsworth: Penguin, 1985], 94–99) refers to different modes of object relating, which involve the "female" and the "male" aspects of the personality. The "feminine" mode of "being" draws on the internalized experience of the undifferentiated maternal object (the breast as a "subjective object" of identification), and is not "backed by drive." The mode of "doing" presupposes separation and is instinctually driven.

58. Bachelard, 100.

59. Ibid., 129; my emphasis.

60. Ibid., 108; my emphasis.

61. Ibid., 112, 104; my emphasis.

62. Ibid. 104–5.

63. Ibid., 111, 112, 109, 110, my emphasis.

64. Ibid., 111.

65. Ibid.

66. Ibid.

67. Julia Kristeva, "The Speaking Subject," in *On Signs*, ed. Marshall Blonski (Oxford: Basil-Blackwell, 1985), 215.

68. Bachelard, 111.

69. Winnicott, *Human Nature*, 110 (my emphasis).

70. The "mirror role" of the mother is, according to Winnicott, that of affirming the child's identity or "reality," by way of giving him a confirming reflexive feedback through facial expression (see *Playing and Reality*, 130–38.).

71. Kerényi, "The Primordial Child in Primordial Times," 61.

72. See C. G. Jung, "The Psychology of the Child Archetype," 93.

73. Ibid., 83.

74. On the solar "metaphor of metaphors" and its "helio-tropical" light, see Derrida's "White Mythology: Metaphor in the Text of Philosophy," *New Literary History* 6, no. 1 (1974): 51.

75. *CP* 111–15.

76. *CP* 70.

77. ". . . and the unseen eyebeam crossed," T. S. Eliot, in "Burnt Norton," 14.

78. "A Process In The Weather Of The Heart," *CP* 5.

79. Marcel Proust, *The Past Recaptured*, trans. Andreas Mayor (New York: Random House, 1971), 133.

80. Ibid., 132; my emphasis.

81. Such *semiotic* continuity, which marks the internal quality of the experience, is distinct from the *symbolic*, syntactic continuity drawn between the experience and its self-conscious context.

82. Proust, 139.

83. Ibid., 138.

84. Bachelard, 116, original emphasis; my emphasis.

85. "Once It Was the Colour of Saying," *CP* 82.

86. Bachelard, 116–18.

87. Ibid., 117, 123.

88. Ibid., 119; my emphasis.

89. Ibid., 118; my emphasis.

90. Ibid., 127; my emphasis.

91. C. G. Jung, *Memories, Dreams, Reflections* (Glasgow: Collins, 1982).

92. Ibid., 295–99.

93. Thomas, *A Prospect of the Sea*, 51–57.

94. Annis Pratt, *Dylan Thomas' Early Prose: A Study in Creative Mythology* (Pittsburgh: University of Pittsburgh Press, 1970), 73–74.

95. Thomas, *A Prospect of the Sea*, 6.

96. Pratt, 73.

97. Susan Deri chose to borrow the term "dual-union" from I. Hermann ("Clinging—going-in-search") to qualify the earliest mother-child relationship, because by distinction from "symbiosis," it "allows for the objective twoness of the relationship as well as implying a unity" (*Symbolization and Creativity* [New York: International Universities Press, 1984], note 6).

CHAPTER FIVE
THE LOVER, THE POET, AND THE LUNATIC

1. See note 4 to chapter 3 on Lacan's ambiguous notion of the "Impossible Real." In this context I refer to the aspect of the "Impossible," i.e., the impossibility, or lack of "being" in reality which the Symbolic and the Imaginary "misrecognize," and which psychosis "forecloses"—in order to reenact and real-ize in hallucination.

2. "Traumatic" is used here in the Freudian sense of the retroacted provocation of instinctual excitations associated with infantile experiences or primal fantasies. See J. Laplanche and J-B Pontalis, *The Language of Psycho-Analysis* (London: Hogarth, 1983), 467–69.

3. This same persona sails out of "Poem on His Birthday" and embodies the same reconciled disposition in many other of Thomas's poems, and notably his "Author's Prologue" to the *Collected Poems.*

4. "The 'Cogito' of the Dreamer," in Gaston Bachelard, *The Poetics of Reverie: Childhood, Language and the Cosmos*, trans. Daniel Russell (Boston: Beacon Press, 1969), 143 ff.

5. The notion of paradox is central to Winnicott's conception of human creativity and the "transitional phenomena" which enhance and manifest it. In his introduction to *Playing and Reality* he writes: "My contribution is to ask for a paradox to be accepted and tolerated and respected, and for it not to be resolved. By flight to split-off intellectual functioning it is possible to resolve the paradox, but the price of this is the loss of the value of the paradox itself," ([Harmondsworth: Penguin, 1985], xii).

6. "This Side of the Truth," *CP* 98–99.

7. Annis Pratt, *Dylan Thomas's Early Prose: A Study in Creative Mythology* (Pittsburgh: University of Pittsburgh Press, 1970), 71–72.

8. The French translation of Freud's title, "Instincts and Their Vicissitudes" (*PFL* vol. 11), "Pulsions et destins des pulsions" (*Métapsychologie* [Paris: Gallimard, 1968]), is useful in the context of this chapter.

9. Pratt, 42.

10. On the metonymical and the metaphorical axes of language, see Roman Jakobson, "Two Aspects of Language and Two Types of Aphasic Disturbances," in Roman Jakobson and Morris Halle, *Fundamentals of Language* (The Hague: Mouton, 1956, part 2, 55–82), 76–82.

11. The original phrase in Proust is "The true paradises are the paradises that we have lost" (*The Past Recaptured*, trans. Andreas Mayor [New York: Random House, 1971], 132).

12. Pratt in *Dylan Thomas's Early Prose*, 74–75, citing Robert Graves, *The White Goddess* (New York: Vintage Books, 1948), 98.

13. Introduction to *The Collected Letters of Dylan Thomas*, ed. Paul Ferris (London: Dent, 1985), ix.

14. "Replies to an Enquiry," quoted by Andrew Sinclair in *Dylan Thomas* (New York: Holt, Reinhart and Winston), 220.

15. Letter to Pamela Hansford Johnson (Dec. 1933), in Thomas, *Letters*, 73.

16. David Holbrook discusses this point in chapter 7 of *The Code of Night* (London: Athlone, 1972), 123 ff, where he quotes Thomas's complaint, in a letter to Pamela Hansford Johnson (9.5.1934), about his picking his words "so thoroughly of their live associations that only the *death* in the words remains" (*Letters*, 130, original emphasis).

17. T. S. Eliot, "*Burnt Norton,*" in *Four Quartets* (London: Faber & Faber, 1958).

18. I,i,52–61; I,v,124–25, in Christopher Marlowe, *The Complete Plays* (Harmondsworth: Penguin, 1980).

19. Ibid., I,i, 31–48.

20. Ibid., II,i,116.

21. Ibid., II,i,141, 145.

22. Euripides, *The Bacchae and Other Plays*, trans. Philip Vellacott (Harmondsworth: Penguin, 1954).

23. Cavendish, *The Black Arts* (London: Pan Books, 1969), 194.

24. Pratt, 78–79. Pratt quotes Robert Graves' *The White Goddess*, 31.

25. Pratt, 95.

26. Ibid., 82; Cavendish, 311.

27. C. G. Jung, *On the Nature of the Psyche*, trans. R. F. C. Hull (Princeton: Princeton University Press, 1973), 107–8.

28. This inversion and its ominous satanic context are suggested in Thomas's letter to Pamela Hansford Johnson (May, 1934), where he writes: "In the beginning was a word I can't spell, not a reversed Dog . . . but a word [that] . . . speaks out sharp & everlastingly with the intonations of death and doom." This fatality, however, is attenuated by Thomas's self-irony, in the letter, with regards to his mystifying attitude to words and their power, whose magic has the effect of desubstantializing reality and derealizing his emotions. "I love your word, the word of your hair . . . ," he writes to his friend, and then becomes frustrated by his failure to give adequate verbal expression to his love: "O oracle in the lead of the pencil," he sighs: "wishes, always wishes. Never a fulfillment of action, flesh" (*Letters*, 136).

29. *Doctor Faustus*, I,iii,8–9.

30. Ibid., II,i,127–30.

31. Ibid., I,ii,168–69.

32. Pratt reads it as a phallic symbol (144).

33. *Doctor Faustus*, V,ii,166–76.

CONCLUSION
A CONFESSION OF THE SPEAKING SUBJECT

1. Dylan Thomas, *The Collected Letters of Dylan Thomas*, ed. Paul Ferries (London: Dent, 1985), 915–16.

2. The letter (an incomplete draft) was addressed to Princess Caetani, a friend, patroness and publisher of Thomas, shortly before his death (on or around August 26, 1953), when Thomas was in great financial and emotional trouble. "He was writing, not about his financial problems, but about the problem of why he wrote her such contorted letters. His method was to write a letter that was even more contorted than usual" (Paul Ferris, *Dylan Thomas: A Biography* [New York: Dial Press, 1977], 295).

3. See note 4.

4. Rexroth, Holbrook, Steiner, Nowottny, and Moynihan are cited and discussed later on in the text. Let me now bring some additional examples of opposing opinions of other readers in the controversial "industry" of Dylan Thomas. These readers relate to the question of clarity and obscurity in Thomas's poetry and to the sublimatory aspect of its thematic and emotional content, which are relevant to this chapter.

While Edith Sitwell (1936) "know[s] of no young poet of our time whose poetic gifts are on such great lines," (quoted by Marshall W. Stearns, on p. 113 of "Unsex the Skeleton: Notes on the Poetry of Dylan Thomas" [1944], in E. W. Tedlock, *Dylan Thomas: The Legend and the Poet* [London: Mercury Books, 1963], 113–31), Goeffrey Grigson reads Thomas's writing as an uncontrolled, unsublimated, "mechanic" and obsessive expression, or rather expulsion, of emotional waste ("How Much Me Now Your Acrobatics Amaze," [1947], in Tedlock, 155–67). Thomas's poems, he writes "live, sprawl loosely, below the waist . . . [they] break out . . . with [a] meaningless hot sprawl of mud." His "automatic muddle," "with only the frailest ineptitude of structure," "suggests the disinfection of psychological ordure" (160–65). Donald Davie shares something of this view when he charges Thomas with obscurity and incoherence, regarding what he considers to be the symbolic failure of Thomas's poems (their "pseudo-syntax" and their progression through repetition rather than in a syntactic sequence) as reflecting the poet's "loss of confidence in the intelligible structure of the conscious mind, and the validity of its activity" (*Articulate Energy* [London: Routledge and Kegan Paul, 1955], 125–29). By contrast, it is seeking the proof for "the poetry's coherence," and justifying "faith in Thomas's meaningfulness," that motivates Ralph Maud to write his *Entrances to Dylan Thomas's Poetry* (Pittsburgh: University of Pittsburgh Press, 1963], see p. 14). Robert Lowell does not attribute clarity to Thomas, but neither does he find fault in its absence: he sees Thomas as "a dazzling obscure writer who can be enjoyed without understanding" ("Thomas, Bishop and Williams," *Sewanee Review* 55 no. 3 [Summer, 1947], 493–96, quoted in H. H. Kleinman, *The Religous Sonnets of Dylan Thomas* [Berkeley and Los Angeles: University of California Press, 1963], 6). Elder Olson, in *The Poetry of Dylan Thomas* (Chicago: University of Chicago Press, 1954), justifies part of the obscurity of Thomas's poetry as resulting "from the sheer unfamiliarity of the world which he presents to us." Thomas's enormously powerful, seemingly "unlimited" "imagination," he writes, "permits him to enter into areas of experience previously unexplored or to unveil new aspects of perfectly common experiences," and "there is no familiar way of expressing something in itself so unfamiliar" (12). (For Maud, by contrast, the apparent obscurity is an effective strategy of defamiliarizaion of familiar experiences: "Thomas writes about common things in a most uncommon way . . . [whereby] he brings to the front of the mind what was always at the back of it" [8].) But though strangely articulated, says Olson, Thomas's "mighty" imagination, "sweeps us up with it, like an angel, and forces us to endure the visions of another world thronged with enchantments and horrors. This is a great natural force" (14).

However, Olson emphasizes, it is not only Thomas's "natural genius" that renders him effective, but also his verbal art, which gives us "the immediate presence of strange things," making them "very real indeed." Indeed, the effect of Thomas's verbal magic is so forceful and immediate that it suspends our disbelief: "He arouses our emotions before we have time to doubt" (14–15).

Grigson compares Thomas to "a child learning to talk," who "work[s], as a child works, *towards* form and coherence" (163; my emphasis). E. Glyn Lewis, who attributes to Thomas's poetry a "formal excellence with a quality of magnanimity and greatness," counters this claim by saying that for Thomas "poetry is not so much a means of expression" (of ordered, preconceived ideas), but "an activity of the spirit"; "it is the process of discovery itself, so that the excitement of our reading derives as much from the quest as from the ultimate vision" ("Dylan Thomas" [1948], in Tedlock, 168–85, 171). This process is, for Robert Horan, properly creative, as the imagination at work in it "is remarkable to the degree that it transforms, actively, rather than describes, passively, the objects of [Thomas's] attention" ("In Defense of Dylan Thomas" [1945], in Tedlock, 132–40, 133).

Though finding a restricted range of emotion and a limited capacity for empathy in Thomas's self-centered poetry, Olson generally classifies the poet and his poetry as belonging to the "serious," "lofty," "heroic," rather than the melodramatic kind (22–23). That seriousness is mocked by Hugh Gordon Porteus, who, experiencing Thomas's poetry as an unconducted tour of Bedlam, sums up the poet's enterprise as an invention of "an *idiom*, consisting of a few tricks of verbal and metaphorical violence, like an infectiously engaging lisp or stutter, as found in the repertoire of a successful social clown" ("Map of Llareggub" [1939], in Tedlock, 91–95, 92). For D. S. Savage, however, that clown (still alive when this assessment was made) has a chance of becoming "worthy to be classed with Dante, Shakespeare or Milton" ("The Poetry of Dylan Thomas" [1946], in Tedlock, 141–47, 147). And as for his verbal art, David Daiches values Thomas as "a remarkably conscientious craftsman. . . . No modern poet in English has had a keener sense of form and has handled stanzas and verse paragraphs . . . with more deliberate cunning." "[A]t his best," he says, "he is magnificent" ("The Poetry of Dylan Thomas" [1956], in *Dylan Thomas: A Collection of Critical Essays*, ed. C. B. Cox [Englewood Cliffs, N.J: Prentice-Hall, 1966], 14–24, 15, 24).

Many readers regard Thomas as a profound religous poet. For Kleinman, his poetry is "a deeply moving statement of religious perplexity concluding in spiritual certainty" (10), and for W. S. Merwin, Thomas's poetry is "the office of celebration . . . the statement of vocation of a great religious poet" ("The Religous Poet" [1954], in Tedlock 236–47, 246). For Sister Roberta Jones, Thomas achieves "union with Christ" (in "Vision and Prayer"): "This blinding light of mystic insight, this realization of Christ's redemption is an affirmation out of nothingness of self, that He saves each one who admits Him, is perhaps the gift only of the creative genius or saint" ("The Wellspring of Dylan," *English Journal* 55, no. 1:82; quoted in Holbrook's *The Code of Night*, 64). Robert M. Adams, however, approaches Thomas's "so called 'religous sonnets'" with less reverence ("Crashaw and Dylan Thomas: Devotional Athletes" (1958), in C. B. Cox, 130–39). He feels "intensity . . . to be the chief value of [Thomas's] style . . . [who accordingly] uses language percussively, like a pianist playing with his forearm, creating a furious, barbaric, dissonant clangor which has all sorts of intensity." "Thomas," Adams concludes, "quite properly welcomed the chance to judge for himself how close poetry can come to the psychopathic and still survive" (136, 139).

5. I will be referring mostly to Holbrook's *The Code of Night* but also to his earlier *Llareggub Revisited: Dylan Thomas and the State of Modern Poetry* (London: Bowes & Bowes, 1962).

6. Holbrook's "schizoid diagnosis" is based on Harry Guntrip's psychoanalytic works (see *The Code of Night*, n.2). He develops his analysis also drawing on works by Winnicott, Fairbairn, Laing, and Melanie Klein.

7. Melanie Klein, *Developments in Psychoanalysis* (London: Tavistock, 1952) quoted in Holbrook , *The Code of Night*, 257.

8. Holbrook, *Llareggub Revisited*, 96; *The Code of Night*, 19.

9. Holbrook briefly addresses the letter himself on pages 141–42 of *The Code of Night*. However, my reading, which is consisent with his, is based on his general analysis of Thomas.

10. See note 5. Holbrook's professed motivation for writing *Lareggub Revisited* was that "[he] felt that only by a rejection of Thomas's poetry, his attitude to poetry, and the attitudes of his audience to poetry, could this essential activity of the civilized consciousness, poetry, regain health, prestige and effectiveness" (*Lareggub Revisited*, 16). His reason for revising that work is introduced in *The Code of Night*, 27, 66, 122.

11. Holbrook , *The Code of Night*, 3, 24, 66, 259–61.

12. Thomas "invented a babble-language which concealed the nature of reality from himself and his readers" (Holbrook, *Lareggub Revisited*, 128).

13. Fixated in the early oral situation of the infant as "mouth ego," the "schizoid individual" that Thomas is for Holbrook is characterized by "the libidinal attitude . . . in which *taking* predominates over giving" (*The Code of Night*, 27). In this light Holbrook formulates the critical question concerning Thomas's poetry: "The problem is to judge how far we can allow ourselves to be maddened by such poetry, and how many compensatory rewards and satisfactions we get that make up for this" (ibid., 65).

14. "From the Introduction to *The New British Poets*," in John Malcolm Brinnin, ed., *A Casebook on Dylan Thomas* (New York: 1960), 128 (quoted by Moynihan in *The Craft and Art of Dylan Thomas* [Ithaca: Cornell University Press, 1968], 2).

15. Holbrook , *The Code of Night*, 60.

16. E.g., ibid., 6, 103, 107, 112.

17. Ibid., 45.

18. "The development of the poem is negative . . . he must kill the symbolic existence of each image as he proceeds to the next, in case the images breed integration between them, or begin to bring life to the 'central aspect' of his deeper self. *That center, and the poetry, must be kept dead*" (ibid., 138–39).

19. Ibid., 99, 245, 19. Holbrook refers to Laing's observation of the need of schizoid patients "*to preserve chaos in self-defense* against the dangers of integration" (ibid., 20). This corresponds to Winnicott's notion of non-integration in defense against disintegration in "Fear of Breakdown," to which I have referred in chapter 3.

20. Ibid., 60 (quoting Aneirin T. Davis, *Dylan: Druid of the Broken Body* [London: Dent, 1964], 9); Holbrook , *Llaerggub Revisited*, 183.

21. Holbrook , *The Code of Night*, 68, 133–34, 142, 189.

22. Ibid., 58–59, 132.

23. George Steiner, "The Retreat from Word," *Kenyon Review* 23 (Spring 1961): 207 (quoted by Moynihan, 4).

24. "A Refusal to Mourn the Death, by Fire, of a Child in London," *CP* 94.

25. Julia Kristeva, *Powers of Horror*, trans. Leon Roudiez [New York: Columbia University Press, 1982], 43.

26. Holbrook, *The Code of Night*, 142 (in reference to Thomas's letter.)

27. Holbrook, Ibid., 84, 104, 257; *Llareggub Revisited*, 128, 161, 183, 238–39.

28. Holbrook , *The Code of Night*, 8.

29. Ibid., 28–29 (on relevant schizoid phenomena).

30. Holbrook , *Llareggub Revisited*, 163, 238.

31. Ibid., 98.

32. Holbrook , *The Code of Night*, 19.

33. Ibid., 19, 114.

34. Ibid., 99.

35. The term "creative reflection" is Winnicott's (see ibid., 7).

36. Ibid., 19, 103, 122.

37. Ibid., 104, 113.

38. Ibid., 65.

39. Ibid., 122. The "linguistic excitement" is Winifred Nowottny's, in her interpretation of Thomas's "There was a Saviour" (*CP* 117–18) in *The Language Poets Use* (London: Athlone, 1962), 187 ff (Holbrook, *The Code of Night*, 113).

40. Ibid., 19, 60–61.

41. Holbrook , *Llareggub Revisited*, ch. 5; *The Code of Night*, 69.

42. Holbrook , *The Code of Night*, 2.

43. Ibid., 71–72, my emphasis.

44. Ibid., 260.

45. For the justification of such a conjecture, see Holbrook's *The Code of Night*, 114–15.

46. Ibid., 60.

47. Ibid., 113.

48. Ibid., 20.

49. Ibid., 61, 134; my emphasis.

50. A letter to Henry Treece (23.3.38), in Thomas, *Letters*, 282.

51. Holbrook , *The Code of Night*, 138.

52. Ibid., 132.

53. "In My Craft or Sullen Art," *CP* 120.

54. *The Code of Night*,132.

55. Ibid.

56. Ibid., 131.

57. Ibid., 201–2.

58. See chapter 4. In his discussion of "Fern Hill," his favorite Thomas poem, Holbrook is more ready to accept the idea of nostalgic merging. "The effect of the poem on us," he says, "is to recapture for us the energy and vision of childhood, and to help us infuse our own adult attitudes with something of the visionary power of the child, indeed to see that we only see a meaningful world *because* of that first irresponsible vision" (ibid., 210).

59. Ibid., 117.

60. Letter to Richard Church (9.12.35, in Thomas, *Letters*, 205); in *The Code of Night*, 140.

61. Letter to Pamela Hansford Johnson (9.5.34, in Thomas, *Letters*, 128–35), quoted in and commented on in Holbrook, *The Code of Night*, 124; original emphasis.

62. A "schizophrenogenic" family is such that is "likely to produce schizophrenia in its members," Holbrook , *The Code of Night*, 38, n.3. Holbrook relates Thomas's "schizoid" disturbances to his being the son of a narcissitically disturbed father and a "schizoid mother" who suffered the trauma of having given birth to a dead baby, *The Code of Night*, 35–44.

63. Moynihan, 2–10. Moynihan refers to Holbrook's reading in *Lareggub Revisited.*

64. George Whalley, *Poetic Process* (London: Routledge, 1953), 104–5, cited by Moynihan, 7.

65. Moynihan, 216.

66. Northrop Frye, *Anatomy of Criticism* (Princeton: Princeton University Press, 1957), cited in Moynihan, 220.

67. Moynihan, 264.

68. Ibid., 222.

69. Thomas, *Letters*, 281–82.

Works Cited

Abraham, Nicolas, and Torok, Maria. *The Shell and the Kernel.* Edited and translated by Nicolas Rand. Chicago: University of Chicago Press, 1994.

Adams, Robert M. "Crashaw and Dylan Thomas: Devotional Athletes." In *Dylan Thomas: A Collection of Critical Essays*, edited by C. B. Cox, 130–39. Englewood Cliffs, N.J.: Prentice-Hall, 1966.

Anzieu, Didiér. "Machine a décroire: sur un trouble de la croyance dans les états limites." *Nouvelle Révue de Psychanalyse*, no. 18:151–67. Paris: Gallimard, 1978.

Atwood, George E., and Robert D. Stolorow. *Faces in a Cloud: Intersubjectivity in Personality Theory*. Northvale, N.J.: Jason Aronson (1979), 1993.

Bachelard, Gaston. *The Poetics of Reverie: Childhood, Language and the Cosmos.* Translated by Daniel Russell. Boston: Beacon Press, 1969.

Benjamin, Walter. "The Task of the Translator." In *Illuminations*. Translated by Harry Zohn, edited by Hanna Arendt. London: J. Cape, 1970.

——— *Gesammete Schriften*. Edited by Rolph Tiedemann and Hermann Schweppenhauser. Vol. 1:3, 1974.

——— "On Language as Such and on the Language of Man." In *Reflections: Essays, Aphorisms, Autobiographical Essays*, translated by Edmund Jephcott and edited by Peter Demetz. New York: Schocken, 1986.

Benveniste, Emile. *Le Vocabulaire des instutitions indo-europeénnes.* Vol. 1. Paris: Minuit, 1969.

Bowie, Malcolm. "Jacques Lacan." In *Structuralism and Since*, edited by Malcolm Bowie, 116–53. Oxford: Oxford University Press, 1979.

Brinnin, John Malcolm. *Dylan Thomas in America.* Boston: Little, Brown, 1955.

Burdette, Robert K. *The Saga of Prayer.* The Hague: Mouton, 1972.

Cavendish, Richard. *The Black Arts.* London: Pan Books, 1969.

Daiches, David. "The Poetry of Dylan Thomas." In *Dylan Thomas: A Collection of Critical Essays*, edited by C. B. Cox, 14–24. Englewood Cliffs, N.J.: Prentice-Hall, 1966.

Davidson, Donald. "What Metaphors Mean." In *Philosophical Perspectives on Metaphor*, edited by Mark Johnson, 200–20. Minneapolis: University of Minnesota Press, 1981.

Davie, Donald. *Articulate Energy*. London: Routledge and Kegan Paul, 1955.

Davis, Aneirin T. *Dylan: Druid of the Broken Body*. London: Dent, 1964.

de Cérteau, Michel. "What We Do When We Believe." In *On Signs*, edited by Marshall Blonski, 192–202. Oxford: Basil-Blackwell, 1985.

Deri, Susan K. *Symbolization and Creativity*. New York: International Universities Press, 1984.

Derrida, Jacques. "White Mythology: Metaphor in the Text of Philosophy." *New Literary History* 4, no. 1 (Autumn 1974): 5–74.

——— *Of Grammatology*. Translated by G. C. Spivak. Baltimore: Johns Hopkins University Press, 1976.

Dilthey, Wilhelm. *Meaning in History*. London: Allen and Unwin, 1961.

Eliot, Thomas S. "Burnt Norton." In *Four Quartets*. London: Faber & Faber, 1959.

Erikson, E. H. *Childhood and Society*. New York: Norton, 1950.

Euripides. *The Bacchae and Other Plays*. Translated by Philip Vellacott. Harmondsworth: Penguin, 1954.

Felman, Shoshana. "To Open the Question." In *Literature and Psychoanalysis*, edited by Shoshana Felman. Baltimore: Johns Hopkins University Press, 1982.

Ferenczi, Sandor, "Introjection and Transference" (1909). In *First Contributions to Psycho-analysis*. London: Hogarth Press, 1952.

Ferris, Paul. *Dylan Thomas: A Biography*. New York: Dial Press, 1977.

———, ed. *The Collected Letters of Dylan Thomas*. London: Dent, 1985.

Freud, Sigmund. "Beyond the Pleasure Principle" (1920). *Pelican Freud Library*. Translated by James and Alix Strachey. Harmondsworth: Penguin Books, 1976–85. (Henceforth *PFL*). Vol. 11:275–338.

——— "The Ego and the Id" (1923). In *PFL* Vol. 11:350–407.

——— "Inhibitions, Symptoms and Anxiety" (1926 [1925]). In *PFL* Vol. 10:237–333.

——— "Instincts and Their Vicissitudes" (1915). In *PFL* Vol. 11:113–43.

——— *Métapsychologie*. Paris: Gallimard, 1968.

——— "Mourning and Melancholia" (1917 [1915]). In *PFL* Vol. 11:251–68.

——— "Negation" (1925). In *PFL* Vol. 11:437–42.

——— "On Narcissism: An Introduction" (1914). In *PFL* Vol. 11:65–104.

——— *The Origins of Psychoanalysis: Letters to Wilhelm Flies, Drafts and Notes 1887–1902*. New York: Basic Books, 1954.

Frye, Northrop. *Anatomy of Criticism*. Princeton: Princeton University Press, 1957.

Gadamar, Hans Georg. *Philosophical Hermeneutics*. Translated by D. E. Linge. Berkeley: University of California Press, 1976.

Gantz, Jeffrey, trans., *The Mabinogion*. Harmondsworth: Penguin, 1976.

Graves, Robert. *The White Goddess*. New York: Vintage Books, 1948.

Green, André. *On Private Madness*. Madison, Conn.: International Universities Press, 1986.

——— "Pourquoi le mal?" In *La folie privée: Psychanalyse des cas-limites*, 369–401. Paris: Gallimard, 1990.

Grigson, Geoffrey. "How Much Me Your Acrobatics Amaze." In *Dylan Thomas: The Legend and the Poet*, edited by E. W. Tedlock, 155–67. London: Mercury Books, 1963.

Hermann, I. "Clinging—Going-in-search." *Psychoanalytical Quarterly* 45 (1976): 5–36.

Holbrook, David. *The Code of Night*. London: Athlone, 1972.

——— *Llareggub Revisited: Dylan Thomas and the State of Modern Poetry*. London: Bowes & Bowes, 1962.

Horan, Robert. "In Defense of Dylan Thomas." In *Dylan Thomas: The Legend and the Poet*, edited by E. W. Tedlock, 132–40. London: Mercury Books, 1963.

Jakobson, Roman. "Closing Statement: Linguistics and Poetics." In *Style in Language*, edited by Thomas A. Sebeok, 350–77. Cambridge, Mass.: MIT Press, 1960.

——— "Two Aspects of Language and Two Types of Aphasic Disturbances." In Roman Jakobson and Morris Halle, *Fundamentals of Language* part II, 53–82. The Hague: Mouton, 1956.

Jeanson, Francis. *La foi d'un incroyant*. Paris: Seuil, 1963.

Jones, Roberta. "The Wellspring of Dylan." *English Journal* 55, no. 1.

Jung, C. G. *Memories, Dreams, Reflections*. Recorded and edited by Aniela Jaffe. Translated by Richard and Clara Winston. Glasgow: Collins, 1982.

——— *On the Nature of the Psyche*. Translated by R. F. Hull. Princeton: Princeton University Press, 1973.

——— "The Psychology of the Child Archetype." In C. G. Jung and C. Kerényi, *Essays on a Science of Mythology*, translated by R. F. Hull, 70–100. New York: Harper & Row, 1963.

Kerényi, C. "The Primordial Child in Primordial Times." In C. G. Jung and C. Kerényi, *Essays on a Science of Mythology*, translated by R. F. Hull, 25–69. New York: Harper & Row, 1963.

Kershner, R. B. *Dylan Thomas: The Poet and His Critics*. Chicago: American Library Association, 1976.

Klein, Melanie. "A Contribution to the Psychogenesis of Manic-Depressive States" (1935). In *The Selected Melanie Klein*, edited by Juliet Mitchell, 116–45. Harmondsworth: Penguin, 1986.

——— *Developments in Psychoanalysis*. London: Tavistock, 1952.

——— Mourning and its Relation to Manic-Depressive States. In *The Selected Melanie Klein*, edited by Juliet Mitchell, 146–74. Harmondsworth: Penguin, 1986.

——— "Notes on Some Schizoid Mechanisms." In *The Selected Melanie Klein*, edited by Juliet Mitchell, 176–200. Harmondsworth: Penguin, 1986.

Kleinman, Hyman H. *The Religious Sonnets of Dylan Thomas*. Berkeley: University of California Press, 1963.

Kochhar-Lindgren, Gray. *Narcissus Transformed: The Textual Subject in Psychoanalysis and Literature*. University Park: Pennsylvania State University Press, 1993.

Korg, Jacob. *Dylan Thomas*. New York: Twayne Publishers, 1992.

Kristeva, Julia. *Black Sun: Depression and Melancholia*. Translated by Leon S. Roudiez. New York: Columbia University Press, 1989.

——— "Le démon litteraire." In *Folle vérité: Vérité et vraisemblance du texte psychotique*, edited by Julia Kristeva, 203–6. Paris: Seuil, 1979.

——— *In the Beginning Was Love: Psychoanalysis and Faith*. Translated by Arthur Goldhammer. New York: Columbia University Press, 1987.

——— "La parole deprimée." In *La voix: actes du colloque d'Ivry (1988)*, edited by R. Lew and F. Sauvagnat, 79–87. Paris: La lysimaque, 1989.

——— *Powers of Horror: An Essay on Abjection*. Translated by Leon S. Roudiez. New York: Columbia University Press, 1982.

——— *Revolution in Poetic Language*. Translated by Margaret Waller. New York: Columbia University Press, 1984.

——— "The Speaking Subject." In *On Signs*, edited by Marshall Blonski. Oxford: Basil-Blackwell, 1985.

——— *Tales of Love*. Translated by Leon S. Roudiez. New York: Columbia University Press, 1987.

——— "Le vréel." In *Folle vérité*, edited by Julia Kristeva, 11–35. Paris: Seuil, 1979.

Kulka, Raanan. Introduction to the Hebrew translation of D. W. Winnicott, *Playing and Reality*, translated by Yossi Milo. Tel-Aviv: Am Oved, 1995.

Lacan, Jacques. *The Seminar of Jacques Lacan: Book II: The Ego in Freud's Theory and in the Technique of Psychoanalysis 1954–1955*. Translated by Sylvana Tomaselli and edited by Jacques-Alain Miller. Cambridge: Cambridge University Press, 1988.

——— *Écrits: A Selection.* Edited and translated by Alan Sheridan. New York: Norton, 1977.

——— *The Four Fundamental Concepts of Psychoanalysis.* Translated by Alan Sheridan and edited by Jacques-Alain Miller. Harmondsworth: Penguin, 1987.

Laing, R. D. *The Divided Self.* London: Tavistock, 1960.

Laplanche, J., and J-B Pontalis. *The Language of Psycho-Analysis.* Translated by Donald Nicholson-Smith. London: Hogarth, 1983.

Lewis, E. Glyn. "Dylan Thomas" (1948). In *Dylan Thomas: The Legend and the Poet,* edited by E. W. Tedlock, 168–86. London: Mercury Books, 1963.

Lowell, Robert. "Thomas, Bishop, and Williams." *Sewanee Review* 55, no. 2 (Winter 1947):103–6.

Marlowe, Christopher. *The Complete Plays.* Harmondsworth: Penguin, 1980.

Maud, Ralph. *Entrances to Dylan Thomas's Poetry.* Pittsburgh: University of Pittsburgh Press, 1963.

McNees, Eleanor J. *Eucharistic Poetry: The Search for Presence in the Writings of John Donne, Gerard Manley Hopkins, Dylan Thomas and Geoffrey Hill.* London and Toronto: Associated University Presses, 1992.

Merwin, W. S. "The Religious Poet." In *Dylan Thomas: The Legend and the Poet,* edited by E. W. Tedlock, 236–47. London: Mercury Books, 1963.

Mitchell, Juliet, ed. *The Selected Melanie Klein.* Harmondsworth: Penguin, 1986.

Moses, Stéphane. "L'idée d'origine chez Walter Benjamin." In *Walter Benjamin et Paris,* edited by Heinz Wismann, 809–26. Paris: Cerf, 1986.

Moynihan, William T. *The Craft and Art of Dylan Thomas.* Ithaca: Cornell University Press, 1968.

Nabokov, Vladimir. *Transparent Things.* Harmondsworth: Penguin, 1975.

Nowottny, Winifred. *The Language Poets Use.* London: Athlone, 1962.

Oliver, Kelly. *Reading Kristeva: Unravelling the Double-bind.* Bloomington and Indianapolis: Indiana University Press, 1993.

Olson, Elder. *The Poetry of Dylan Thomas.* Chicago: University of Chicago Press, 1954.

Orange, Donna M. "Countertransference, Empathy, and the Hermeneutical Circle." In Robert D. Stolorow, George E. Atwood, and Bernard Brandchaft, *The Intersubjective Perspective,* 181–85. Northvale, N. J.: Jason Aronson, 1994.

Porteus, Hugh Gordon. "Map of Llareggub." In *Dylan Thomas: The Legend and the Poet,* edited by E. W. Tedlock, 91–96. London: Mercury Books, 1963.

Pratt, Annis. *Dylan Thomas's Early Prose: A Study in Creative Mythology.* Pittsburgh: University of Pittsburgh Press, 1970.

Preminger, A., F. J. Warnke, and O. B. Haridson, eds. *Princeton Encyclopaedia of Poetry and Poetics*. Princeton: Princeton University Press, 1974.

Proust, Marcel. *The Past Recaptured*. Translated by Andreas Mayor. New York: Random House, 1971.

Rexroth, Kenneth. "From the Introduction to the New British Poets." In *A Casebook of Dylan Thomas*, edited by John Malcolm Brinnin. New York: Crowell, 1960.

Ricoeur, Paul. "The Specificity of Religious Language." In *Semeia* 4 (1975).

Ruskin, John. "Of the Pathetic Fallacy." In *Modern Painters*, vol. 3, 1856.

Savage, D. S. "The Poetry of Dylan Thomas." In *Dylan Thomas: The Legend and the Poet*, edited by E. Tedlock, 141–47. London: Mercury Books, 1963.

Segal, Hanna. *Introduction to the Work of Melanie Klein*. London: Karnac Books and the Institute of Psycho-Analysis, 1988.

——— "Notes on Symbol Formation." *International Journal of Psychoanalysis* 38 (1957):391–97.

Shklovsky, Viktor. "Art as Technique" (1917). In *Russian Formalist Criticism: Four Essays*, edited by Lee T. Lemmon and Marion J. Reis, 5–24. Lincoln: University of Nebraska Press, 1965.

——— "The Resurrection of the Word." In *Russian Formalism*, edited by Stephen Bann and John E. Bowlt, 41–47. Edinburgh: Scottish Academic Press, 1973.

Sinclair, Andrew. *Dylan Thomas*. New York: Holt, Reinhart and Winston, 1975.

Stearns, Marshall W. "Unsex the Skeleton: Notes on the Poetry of Dylan Thomas." In *Dylan Thomas: The Legend and the Poet*, edited by E. W. Tedlock, 113–31. London: Mercury Books, 1963.

Steiner, George. "The Retreat from Word." *Kenyon Review* 23 (Spring 1961).

Stolorow, Robert D., George E. Atwood, and Bernard Brandchaft, eds. *The Intersubjective Perspective*. Northvale, N. J.: Jason Aronson, 1994.

Stolorow, Robert D., and George E. Atwood. "Towards a Science of Human Experience." in Robert D. Stolorow, George E. Atwood, and Bernard Brandchaft, *The Intersubjective Perspective*. Northvale, N. J.: Jason Aronson, 1994.

Tedlock, E. W., ed. *Dylan Thomas: The Legend and the Poet*. London: Mercury Books, 1963.

Thomas, Dylan. *The Collected Letters of Dylan Thomas*, edited by Paul Ferris. London: Dent, 1985.

——— *Collected Poems: 1934–1952*. Dent: London, 1973.

——— *The Notebooks of Dylan Thomas*. Edited by Ralph Maud. London: New Directions, 1967.

——— *A Prospect of the Sea*. Edited by Daniel Jones. London: Dent, 1979.

——— "Poetic Manifesto." *Texas Quarterly* 4 (Winter 1961): 45–53.

——— "Replies to an Enquiry." *New Verse* 11 (October 1964).

Warden, John, ed. *Orpheus: The Metamorphoses of a Myth.* Toronto: University of Toronto Press, 1985.

Whalley, George. *Poetic Process.* London: Routledge, 1953.

Winnicott, Donald W. "Fear of Breakdown." *International Journal of Psychoanalysis* 1 (1974):103–7.

——— *Human Nature.* London: Free Association Books, 1988.

——— "Mind and Its Relation to the Psyche-Soma" (1949). In *Collected Papers.* London: Tavistock, 1958.

——— *Playing and Reality.* Harmondsworth: Penguin, 1985.

Yeats, William Butler. *A Vision.* New York: Macmillan, 1977.

——— *Selected Poems and Two Plays of William Butler Yeats.* Edited by M. L. Rosenthal. New York: Macmillan, 1978.

Index

Abject: abjection of, 15; autoerotic ambiguity and, 15; fear of, 57; maternal, 15, 57, 195*n42*; reenactment of abjection by, 69; super-ego of, 86

Abjection, 15, 52, 76, 172; drama of, 56; dynamics of, 53; eroticized, 92; facilitation of meaning by, 30; limits of, 198*n76*; maternal, 17, 20, 23; mechanism of, 79; melancholia and, 15, 16, 17; negativity of, 15–16; non-space of, 52; of the not-yet-other, 88; oral dynamics of, 51–59; representations of, 57; reptilian incarnations of, 78; self, 72; separation as, 15; sublimation of, 22; truth of, 78

Abortion, 23, 27, 51; fantasy of, 56, 96; of meaning, 54; original, 54; return to site of, 53

Adolescence, 31; crises of, 102, 103, 136

Affect: signification and, 7–9, 8

Affirmation, 76

Aggression, 13, 14; introverted, 16; melancholia and, 16

Alterity, 11

Ambiguity, 70, 81, 91, 141, 173; autoerotic, 15; castrating, 144; of creation, 205*n49*; good/evil, 77, 89; of images, 112; incarnate, 76–79; negative, 64, 70, 75, 85, 134; ontological, 25; origin of, 81, 84; primal, 77, 78, 81, 89; sexual, 91; silence and, 57; of the subject, 57

Ambivalence: assimilation of, 13; conflicts of, 14; defensive, 3; development and, 13; economy of, 13; fragmenting conflict of, 16; manifestations of, 13; melancholic, 3; oppositional terms of, 55; polarized projection of, 13; pre-oedipal, 63, 139; primal, 16; primary, 3, 14, 17, 18, 19, 63, 91; splitting, 3

Anxiety, 40; of birth, 96; calming, 49; depressive, 40; existential, 51, 203*n9*; generation of, 13; longing and, 96; primal, 96; of time, 59

Autoeroticism, 11, 12, 19, 39, 41, 52, 81

Bachelard, Gaston, 30, 95, 102, 103, 104, 105–108, 122, 124, 135

"Before I knocked" (Thomas), 22

Beginning: aborted, 51; in the direction of, 22, 23; god of, 23; idealized, 98–99; journeys to, 23; maternal, 136; of melancholia, 100; pre-verbal, 26; representation of, 148; that never was, 22, 98–99

Being, 115; absence of, 42; actual, 10; antecedence of, 106, 115; autonomous, 6; and becoming, 9,

106, 107; dialectic of, 8; doing and, 107, 116, 139–142, 210*n57*; experience of, 9, 115; feminine mode, 104, 204*n15*; generation of, 183; imaginative, 104; integral, 6; integrity of, 2, 8; in the listening, 152; maternal-spatial conditions for, 105; meaningful, 48; positive, 10; in reality, 61; relational mode, 6, 11; semiological, 2; sense of, 4; separation into, 94; signifiable, 63; sources of, 106; space for, 10, 11; subjective, 4, 7, 8, 106; symbiotic mode, 6; symbolic origin of, 20; in the text, 29; in time, 94, 105, 107; unity of, 2, 26

Benjamin, Walter, 30, 73, 74, 76, 78, 84, 85, 93, 98, 99, 108, 206*n51*

Birth, 47; actual, 47; anxiety of, 96; imagery, 200*n9*; imaginary, 47; incomplete, 38; psychic, 38; scenes, 53

Body: psychosomatic, 50, 52, 63; signification of, 9; signifying, 69, 70

Boundaries, 84; antithetical, 89; assertion of, 155; being a/having, 206*n63*; blurred, 125, 132, 133, 142, 153, 155, 156; collapsing, 89; consciousness of, 134; crossing, 125; demarcation of, 6; of existence, 66; exploration of, 66; fantasy/reality, 132, 142–148, 153; incestuous transgression of, 134; inside/outside, 74, 133, 192*n14*; linguistic, 31, 84; meaning/matter, 97, 98; metaphorical/literal, 158; objective, 11; oedipal themes, 131–135; ontological, 134; paternal, 132; of poetic symbolization, 132; poetry/psychosis, 131; problems of, 131–135; of reality, 158; between self and other, 74; sexual, 133; signifier/signified, 131–135, 132, 153, 154, 161; sign/object, 153; of subject, 6; of subjectivity, 31, 131–135; symbolic, 31, 134, 137, 144; textual, 31, 132, 133, 142–148, 153; transgressing, 97

Castration, 153; fantasy of, 150; maternal, 54, 55, 134, 135, 146, 159; misrecognition of, 64; paternal, 20, 136, 146; reality of, 132, 202*n4*; risk of, 92; separation as, 7; sublimation and, 18; Symbolic father and, 17

Childhood: benign narcissism in, 127; Eden of, 31; images of, 121; maternal space of, 139; nostalgia and, 105–108; perception, 30; poetry and, 95; reflections on, 112; relations of, 104; reverie, 107, 120, 124, 135, 140, 144; transitional space of, 102

Christ, 25, 49, 69

Conflict, 85; of ambivalence, 14; animating, 57; archaic, 25; in creation, 78, 81; Heaven/Hell, 87; with language, 17; melancholic, 28; oedipal, 12, 14, 17, 18, 19, 20, 24, 25, 27, 28, 131–135, 139–142, 155; pre-oedipal, 12, 63, 102, 139, 145; primal, 87; resolution, 97; sexuality and, 143; signifier/signified, 87; Spirit/Matter, 87; splitting, 96

Conversion: cycles of, 41; as generative process, 42

Countertransference, 5, 174; intersubjective dynamics of, 32

Creation: biblical narrative of, 78–79; conflict in, 78, 81; evil, 80; knowledge of, 71; myth of, 22, 78; solipsistic view, 81; unity of, 64

Crucifixion, 53, 79, 86

Davidson, Donald, 18, 50, 69, 200*n20*

Daydreams, 104, 132, 139, 140
Death instinct, 11, 16, 30, 39
Defamiliarization, 66, 70, 95–96
Denial: dissociative strategies of, 62; manic, 14; melancholic, 14
Derrida, Jacques, 79, 82, 205*n48*
Desire: animating, 28; detour of, 57; dialectic of, 148; dissolution of, 16; dynamics of, 68; for future recuperation, 44; imaginative vitality of, 4; logic of, 10; nostalgia and, 12, 44; object of, 113; origin of, 95, 97; reproduction of onset, 6; for self-authentication, 151; signifier of, 125; sustaining, 113; symbolic thrust, 3; textual, 12; thrust of, 68
Dionysus, 39, 155
Discourse: intertextual, 9; on maternal love, 193*n18*; poetic, 67; textual, 9, 62
Disintegration: anxiety of, 68, 105; defense against, 68
Dissociation: affective, 17; defensive, 23; dynamics of, 69

Eden: boundaries of, 74; creation of, 80; fall from, 153; forgetting, 100; governance in, 72; "Incarnate Devil" in, 61–92; name-language of, 74; pre-linguistic, 85; pre-verbal, 143; repression in, 75; underlying evil in, 75; unity of, 85
Ego: antecathexes of, 16; foundation of, 12; growth of, 192*n14*; loss, 97; organization, 194*n22*; reality, 74
Eliot, T. S., 30, 73, 99, 150
Empathy, 5
Enchantment, 43–50; Eucharistic, 43, 44, 45, 46, 47, 48; language of, 124; maternal, 132; poetic, 46; psychosomatic, 48; self, 156; *semiotic,* 46, 50
Eros, 39, 76, 138, 139
Eurydice, 39
Excorporation, 6
Existence: boundaries of, 66; judgment of, 74; psychosomatic threshold of, 52; in space, 66; in time, 66
Experience, 3, 47; aesthetic, 31; affective, 4; authenticity of, 65; of being, 9, 115; dissociation from, 29; of grace, 41, 47; imaginative, 4, 45; intensity of, 103; liminal, 66; lived, 5; mystical, 44, 45; of reality, 63–64, 65, 107; religious, 41; somatic, 7; of subjectivity, 1, 4, 28; symbiotic, 7; transgressive, 155; unmediated, 143; of unnamed good, 72

Faith: act of, 78; detheologized, 72; grace of, 68; inspiration to, 45; loss of, 43; as object of poetics, 67, 68; production of, 72; in time, 113
Fantasy, 42; of abortion, 56, 96; of advent, 22; of castration, 150; conscious, 116; enactment of, 1–27; endopsychic, 138; of genesis, 102, 113, 127, 128; of heaven on earth, 41; insubstantiality of, 103; masturbatory, 145; narcissistic, 105; nostalgic, 113; of origin, 1–27, 42; of prior identity, 2; psychotic, 135; reality and, 3; realization of, 1–27; representation of, 2, 133; re-substantiating, 103; of resurrection, 41; sexual, 102; space of, 133; transgressive, 156; wish-fulfilling, 20; of the witch, 144
Father, the Imaginary, 7, 12, 20, 193*n18*; identification with, 41
Father, the Symbolic, 7, 12, 18, 19, 22, 42
Faustus, 153, 155
Felman, Shoshana, 27

"Fern Hill" (Thomas), 30, 94, 102, 103, 104, 105, 106, 107, 108, 109, 110–117
Ferris, Paul, 149
Fragmentation, 13, 15, 28; melancholic, 3, 41; psychic, 16
Freud, Sigmund, 12, 73, 149, 193*n18,* 198*n82*; affirmation and, 76; endopsychic myths and, 26; instinct and, 138; on melancholia, 16, 93, 95–97; mourning and, 14; notions of advent and, 2; repetition compulsion and, 102

Gadamer, Hans Georg, 5
Gaze: desiring, 113; projective, 113; in time, 115
Genesis: aborted, 52; ambivalent, 42; of consciousness, 126; fall of, 82; fantasy of, 102, 113, 127, 128; introduction to, 39–43; preoccupation with, 25; return to, 52; of speaking subject, 1–27; textual, 2
Genesis, Book of, 29, 71, 73, 74, 78, 81, 82, 153, 159
Green, André, 25, 79, 192*n14,* 193*n18,* 198*n75,* 198*n76,* 206*n63*
Guilt, 13, 77, 80

Hallucinations, 104, 132, 142, 144, 145; phobic, 57
Holbrook, David, 22, 32, 173, 174, 175, 176, 177, 178, 179, 180, 181, 182, 184, 185, 186, 203*n9,* 204*n22*

"I, in my Intricate Image" (Thomas), 78
Identification: with child's perception, 122; dynamics of, 32; eucharistic, 48; identity and, 8; with Imaginary Father, 41; imaginative, 64; melancholic, 16; narcissistic, 8; positive, 88; primary, 11, 12, 15, 20, 193*n18*; processes of, 42; redemptive oral function of, 51–59; regenerative oral dynamics of, 48; self, 88, 119, 123; *semiotic* dynamics of, 57; in symbolic functioning, 6; transferential, 21; unconscious, 97; with the Word, 40
Identity: antithetical, 206*n61*; confirmation of, 180; defamiliarizing sense of, 144; destruction of, 100; essentialist notion of, 8; establishing, 8; identifications and, 8; loss of, 131; provisional, 88; reality and, 144; self, 65, 198*n77*; subjective, 4, 7, 198*n77*
Illusion: generative function of, 11
Images: allusive, 40; anatomical, 28; birth, 22; conception, 22; destruction of, 100; idealizing, 94; maternal, 104; mnemic, 95, 96; movement of time and, 113; oppositional, 23; poetic, 28; projective, 44; recuperative, 94; vaginal, 99; visceral, 22, 42
Imaginary, [the], 3, 8, 10, 29, 41, 54, 63, 68, 91, 95, 105, 132, 140, 150, 154; autistic bounds of, 103; the Christian, 197*n64*; dying process, 41; faith in, 9; as formative force, 8; the infantile, 135; the maternal, 131; the melancholic, 3; mistrust in, 26; poetic, 4, 9; space of, 44, 134; subjectifying role of, 31; transformative role of, 63, 68; truth of, 63
Imagination, 141; adult, 30, 94, 102, 104, 105, 106; cohesive use of, 63; disjunctive, 85; integrative, 85; limits of, 30, 94, 102, 104, 105, 106; memory and, 106; mnemonics of, 106; narcissistic, 15; nostalgic, 15. *See also* Nostalgia; recuperative function of, 93
"Incarnate Devil" (Thomas), 28, 29, 70–92, 93, 94, 97, 98, 100, 134

Integration, 61, 62; actuality of, 63; defamiliarization and, 95–96; eucharistic process of, 81; of the feminine/masculine, 105; of maternal function, 95; object relations and, 6; parental environment and, 68; processes of, 2, 61; provisional moments of, 7, 8; psychosomatic, 63; self, 8, 194*n22*; self-identification and, 123; suspension of, 68; symbolization and, 79; transformative effect of, 95–96
Intentionality: relational motion of, 26
Intersubjectivity: illusion of, 104; theories, 4, 5
Intertextuality, 1, 192*n14*; orality and, 28
"In the Direction of the Beginning" (Thomas), 22
Intimacy, 18, 19
Introjection, 6, 192*n14*

Jakobson, Roman, 24, 203*n8*
Jeanson, Francis, 64
Jung, Carl, 102, 105, 108, 126

Klein, Melanie, 13; defensive mechanism and, 14; ego organization and, 194*n22*; paranoid-schizoid position, 13; primary ambivalence and, 13; splitting and, 13, 14; strategies of reparation and, 13, 14, 29; sublimation and, 14; symbol-formation and, 14
Kristeva, Julia, 4, 107, 178, 193*n18,* 195*n42,* 197*n64,* 198*n76,* 198*n77*; on fertility and grains, 49; manic-depression and, 14; melancholia and, 16, 17; modes of representation in text and, 9; narcissism and, 6–7, 11, 16; object relations theory and, 2; on poetic dynamics, 2; poetic symbolization and, 89–90; primary identification and, 11; subjectivity and, 11; sublimation and, 14; symbolization and, 3, 64; truth of the real and, 63

Lacan, Jacques, 2, 7, 27, 96, 100, 102, 202*n4*; concept of "Real," 64; the Imaginary and, 9; the impossible "Real" and, 29; notion of self, 8; order of language and, 17; paternal law and, 17
Language: abuse of, 178; alienating effect of, 18; as alienating symbolic order, 17; archaic origins of, 20; Benjamin's notion of, 29, 30, 73, 74; blasphemous, 83; bodies of, 27; of Christianity, 44; conditions of, 67; conflictual attitude toward, 17; creation of, 64; dynamics of, 1; Edenic, 98; of enchantment, 124; expressive properties, 3; fallen, 29, 71; frustration with, 17; function of, 18, 19; historical conception of, 30, 98; imaginary origin of, 72–76; inadequacy of, 69; language/reality, 29; limitations of, 69, 196*n62*; magic function of, 24, 31, 151; "of Man," 73, 76; materiality of, 9, 21, 69; meaning/subjectivity, 48; melancholic disbelief in, 20; metaphorical function, 24, 69; mistrust in, 69; name, 74, 75, 76, 83, 85; normative, 18; object, 68; origin of, 98, 206*n51*; paternal function, 18; perverse, 179; phatic function of, 203*n8*; poetic, 1, 17, 18, 19, 20, 123, 124, 138, 151; of poetry, 76; of prayer, 41; predicative, 9, 20; pure, 99, 108; recuperative function of, 93; relational properties, 3; relation to reality, 29; religious, 196*n62*; scriptural, 24; *semiotic,* 18; signifier and signified, 20; solipsism of,

29; speech/writing, 205*n48*; subjectifying dynamics of, 2; symbolic boundaries of, 31; syntactic, 18; of things, 73, 83, 84; transcending, 18; of translation, 98; transsymbolic cohesiveness of, 20; truths and, 63
Law of the Father, 64
Logic: of Christian sacrifice, 42; of desire, 10; devil's, 79; disjunctive, 85; fusional, 23; of language, 196*n62*; redemptive, 57; of sacrifice, 57; of self-identity, 198*n77*; of the supplement, 205*n48*
Logos: metaphor for, 46; oral-aural nature of, 47; psychosomatic, 50; search for, 159
Longing: nostalgic, 2
Loss: affective meaning of, 14; of ambivalent archaic object, 16; anticipated, 116; chronotopos of, 146; control of, 14; denial of, 93, 97; displacement of, 3; eroticization of, 94; of faith, 43; of identity, 131; mastery of, 95; melancholic, 2, 22; narcissistic, 93, 102; negativity of, 66, 96; nostalgia and, 94; obsession over, 94; past, 66; prospective, 66; reality of, 93, 97, 100, 115, 131, 146; reenactment of, 95; repetition of, 94; signifiers of, 30; signs of, 93–95, 94
Love: maternal, 7, 8, 20, 193*n18*; possibility of, 39; *semiotic* signification of, 46

Magic, 23, 24, 31, 151
"The Map of Love" (Thomas), 126
Masochism: primary, 79
Maternal: abjection, 15, 17, 20, 23, 57; absence, 95, 207*n8*; affect, 20; affect of the "Thing," 16; ambiguous, 41, 134, 142; beginning, 136; castration, 135, 146, 159; configuration, 13; destructive aspect of, 137; devouring/castrating, 54, 55; enchantment, 132; environment, 102, 103, 134; figure of time, 113; function, 104, 193*n18*; idealization of, 13, 150; images, 14, 104; Imaginary, 131; love, 7, 8, 20; mirroring function, 108; object, 18, 19, 39, 52; peace with, 105, 127–130, 135; pre-object, 195*n42*; remembered, 127; reparation of, 62; return of, 141, 144; seduction of, 133; sexualized, 132, 134, 140; space, 108, 134, 139; sublimation, 44; symbiosis, 2, 6; symbolic configuration of, 133; "Thing," 44; violence, 15
Meaning, 59; abortion of, 54; affective, 5; articulation of, 5; depletion of, 54; desire for, 10; destruction of, 177; facilitation by abjection, 30; indeterminacy of, 9; meaningfulness of, 48; of metaphor, 200*n20*; of mystical experience, 44; of parables, 49; as plenitude, 20; poetic, 9, 20, 70, 183; space, 44; subjective, 2, 25, 27, 48; subversion of, 63; support of, 63; suspension of, 177; symbolic, 45; in time, 43
Melancholia, 16, 95–97; ambivalence and, 3; denial of object in, 100; desire and, 16; destination of, 135; as disintegrative state, 14; mourning and, 4, 30, 97; narcissistic, 16; negation of image in, 94; negativity and, 51; object of, 2; origin of, 100; as revolt, 93; splitting and, 15, 17; sublimation of, 22; suicidal object of, 106; time and, 94; transformation to desire, 12
Memory, 123; of death by separation, 26; dialectic of, 148; imagination

and, 106; journeys through, 102; of light of old, 45, 52, 59; mythical, 98; negation by melancholia, 94; nostalgic, 30; pure, 108, 123, 124; reparative, 30; returning, 122; seasons of, 124
Metaphor, 18, 40, 115, 194*n34*, 203*n13*; as act in time, 125; audio-visual, 47; change of weather/mood, 119, 124, 125; collapse of, 57; of conversion, 40; dead, 67; decondensation of, 57, 58; deictic function of, 200*n20*; Edenic, 86; eucharistic, 22; indeterminacy of, 9; intimation and, 200*n20*; limit language of, 196*n62*; literalization of, 137, 155; live, 113, 135; for Logos, 46; meaning of, 200*n20*; of metaphors, 109, 210*n74*; mustardseed sun, 40, 43; of origins, 115; phenomenology of, 30; for projective gaze, 113; scriptural, 24, 67; *semiotic* signification of, 50, 56; superimposition of opposites and, 126; symbolic boundaries of, 137; theories of, 69; as transverbal signifier, 200*n20*
Moses, Stéphané, 98, 208*n26*
Mourning, 14, 93, 96; melancholia and, 4, 30, 97; nocturnal, 41
"The Mouse and the Woman" (Thomas), 131, 132, 133, 150–169, 186
Moynihan, William, 77, 78, 100, 173
Mustardseed: as metaphor, 40; poetics in, 43–50
Myth, 40; biblical, 72, 79; Celtic, 143; Christian, 57, 196*n62*; cloven, 77, 83; of creation, 22, 78; endopsychic, 26, 39–43, 198*n82*; heretical, 78; nostalgic, 99; ontological foundation of, 99; original integrity, 71; Orphic, 39, 40, 96, 178; of regeneration, 22; of subject's genesis, 40

Name of the Father, 64
Narcissism, 25, 41; aggressive aspect, 100; autistic aspect, 11; autoeroticism and, 11, 12; benign, 31, 104, 127; erotic, 11, 198*n77*; fragility of, 15; identification and, 8; infantile, 102; negative center of, 26; omnipotence and, 22–23; primary, 6–7, 15; productive, 104; psychic life and, 11; solipsism and, 70; subjectivity and, 11, 103; as symbolic disposition, 11
Negation: of death, 44, 55; of negation, 55; of object, 94; of signifier, 55, 94, 100
Nostalgia, 15, 95–97; childhood and, 105–108; desire and, 44; function of, 93; longing and, 2; loss and, 94; of nostalgia, 106; phenomenology of, 94; rage and, 77; redoubled, 106, 115; re-presenting object in, 100; role in poetic text, 30; role in signification, 93–94; serial, 102; subjectivity and, 97; symbolization and, 30; time and, 94

Object: aesthetic, 66; ambiguous, 15, 17, 53; annihilation of, 14; archaic, 3; assimilation of, 195*n43*; bad/good, 15, 65, 74; control of, 14; denial of, 93; of desire, 113; displacement of, 46; fragmentation of, 14; imaginary, 29, 91, 95; limits of, 11; loss, 56, 97; maternal, 3, 13, 14, 18, 19, 39, 52, 151; negation of, 94; persecutory, 13; pre-, 3; real, 65; renunciation of, 195*n43*; representation, 6; sense of, 95; somatic-symbiotic, 15; sublimation of, 15, 94; symbiotic, 3; undifferentiated, 15

Object relations theory, 7, 57, 68, 95, 210*n57*
Oedipal themes, 6, 7, 14, 18, 19, 20, 24, 25, 27, 28, 31, 64, 102, 105, 131–135, 139–142, 154, 155
Oedipus, 108, 134
Origin: abject, 22, 42; of ambiguity, 81, 84; of being, 20; of consciousness, 108; of creativity, 30, 94–95; of desire, 95, 97; of evil, 76, 84; fantasy and, 2, 42; idealized, 30; imaginary, 72–76; internal knowledge of, 163; of language, 98, 206*n51*; metaphor of, 115; mythologized, 77; of reverie, 106; of signification, 95, 97; Symbolic, 97, 98, 100; traumatic, 22, 28, 42
Orpheus, 39, 40, 96, 178
the Other, 5; alienated, 19; metaphorical, 40, 67–68; nameless, 89; negation of, 89; *One,* 81; procuring, 67; scriptural, 25; secret, 87; self-identification with, 88; subjectivity and, 26; symbolic relation toward, 2; symbolization and, 26; unnamed, 87

Parables, 49, 69, 136
Paternal function, 7, 12, 15, 18, 19, 20, 40, 76, 80, 81, 131, 160; of language, 18; pre-oedipal, 12; of the Symbolic, 28
Pleasure principle, 30, 31, 136, 195*n42*
"Poem in October" (Thomas), 30, 94, 102, 104, 105, 106, 108, 109, 117–130, 185, 186
"Poem on his Birthday" (Thomas), 29, 35–60, 38–39, 61, 62, 72, 78, 79, 81, 83, 125, 128, 129, 184, 185
Poetic mimesis, 29, 67, 182; aesthetic effect of, 62; intensity of, 66; reality effect of, 62
Poetic(s), 46, 52, 62, 67, 68; authenticity, 182; defamiliarization, 66; discourse, 67; imaginary, 4; performance, 41; performance/representation, 42; signification, 24, 182; speech-act, 49; subjectivist, 1, 2; symbolization, 30, 61
Poetry: language of, 17, 18, 19, 20, 76; magic of, 23; manic-depressive and obsessional models, 62; meaning in, 2, 20; psychosis and, 31; redemption through, 76; signification of absence in, 20; theories of, 21, 69
Pratt, Annis, 126, 137, 138, 143, 159
Projection, 6, 68, 192*n14*; narcissistic, 82; processes of, 42; regenerative oral dynamics of, 48, 51–59; *semiotic* dynamics of, 57; wish-fulfilling, 113
"A Prospect of the Sea" (Thomas), 102, 126, 131, 133, 135–150, 186
Proust, Marcel, 30, 121, 122, 141
Psychosomatic: body, 50, 52, 63; enchantment, 48; integration, 63; logos, 50; threshold of existence, 52

Rage, 86–88, 89, 206*n56*; nostalgia and, 77
the Real, 132. *See also* Lacan, Jacques; impossibility of, 63, 64, 65, 161, 202*n4*; meaning of, 202*n4*; object, 65; possibility of, 61–70; sense of being, 61; symbolic order of, 64; symbolic origin of, 72–76; truth, 62
Reality, 74; aesthetic, 66; being in, 61; boundaries of, 158; of castration, 132, 202*n4*; cognizance of, 73; continuity of, 62; of death, 96; defamiliarizing sense of, 144; denial of, 185; effect, 62; escape from, 57; experience of, 63–64, 65; fantasy and, 3; imaginary,

150; of infantile imaginary, 135; inner, 57, 63, 182; inside/outside, 6, 82; of instincts, 138; intense, 66; interdependent aspects of, 61; intimate, 70; judgment, 74; knowledge and, 73; of loss, 93, 97, 100, 115, 131, 146; me/not-me, 6; origin of, 81; in poetry, 62; psychic, 10, 14, 94; of reality, 65; relation to language, 29; of sex, 136; of signified, 70; of subject, 5, 26, 61, 103; Symbolic, 74, 145–146; temporal, 145–146; testing, 74, 156; textual, 9, 29; of time, 132, 146; trust in, 62; unbearable, 57; verbal mastery of, 151
Recuperation, 93–130
Redemption: cathartic, 79; of primal sin, 79; through poetry, 76
"Refusal to Mourn the Death, by Fire, of a Child in London" (Thomas), 96
Regeneration: as desiring subject, 39; motifs of, 22; myths, 22; perpetual, 40; of speaking subject, 2, 3; transformative, 48
Regression, 20
Reparation, 13, 14
Repetition: of archaic separation, 102; compulsive and transformative, 94, 102; double determination of, 93–101, 97–101, 135, 136, 142, 208*n26*; obsessive-tautological, 94; *semiotic* effect of, 144; in time, 97
Representation: of abjection, 57; of beginning, 148; imaginary, 3, 63, 132, 154; object, 6; performance and, 42; poetic, 10; reproduction of the conditions of, 62; *semiotic,* 62, 63, 65, 141; symbolic, 3, 10, 65, 132, 136; of the world-to-be, 67
Repression, 13, 52, 54; consciousness and, 3; failed, 75; lifting of, 143; limitations of, 75; primal, 12, 15; primary, 15; return of, 143; undermining, 52; willed, 143
Resistance: dynamics of, 32
Resurrection, 22, 40, 41, 72; Christian topos of, 22; fantasy of, 41
Retribution, 84–86
Reverie, 104, 105, 106, 107, 108, 137; childhood, 107, 120, 124, 135, 140, 144; nostalgic, 121; perception in, 135; poetic, 106, 120, 124
Rhiannon, 199*n1*

Sacrifice, 84–86
Self: abjection, 72; absorption, 25; affirmation, 39; analysis, 149; annihilation, 154; authentication, 88, 151; autonomous, 206*n61*; consciousness, 21, 28, 72, 78, 79, 122, 135, 143; denial, 74, 179; deprecation, 173; dramatization, 149; enchantment, 156; expression, 177; externality of, 8; false, 177, 178, 182; generation, 21, 39, 146, 154; identification, 88, 119, 123; identity, 65, 198*n77*; integration, 8, 194*n22*; judgment, 76; negation, 100; psychology, 5; realization, 11; redemption, 71; reflexivity, 21, 26, 70, 75, 88, 132, 149, 154, 157, 175; sacrifice, 196*n62*; signification, 7, 69, 90; subject and, 7, 8
Separation, 64, 65; abjection as, 15; agonies of, 80; archaic, 102; into being, 94; as castration, 7; death by, 26; inside/outside, 82; irrepressible, 69; maternal, 12; from maternal symbiosis, 6; negativity of, 15; premature, 22, 56; primoridal, 6; psychic mark of, 3; re-birth and, 39; repetition of, 102; of subject, 6; sublimation of, 12; traumatic, 3, 56

Sexual: ambiguity, 91; boundaries, 133; differentiation, 20, 193*n18*; fantasy, 102
Sexuality, 140; awakening, 143; conflict and, 143; consciousness of, 133; reality of, 132, 136; repressed, 102; textuality and, 31, 145
Signification, 1, 6, 7, 8, 55, 123; binding motion of, 13; of body, 9; boundaries of, 131–135; empty, 71; integrative properties of, 183; levels of, 90; metonymic, 18; nostalgia and, 93–94; oral dynamics of poetic, 24; orders of, 85; origins of, 95, 97; poetic, 2, 9, 12, 24, 182; self, 69, 90; *semiotic,* 17, 18, 28, 42, 46, 56, 151, 160; subjectifying, 124; *symbolic,* 17, 18; textual, 17; transferential dynamics of, 7–9, 8
Signified: defamiliarization of, 70; perception of, 70; reality of, 70; re-familiarization of, 70; solidarity with signifier, 69; unmediated vision of, 69; verbal, 56
Signifier: divine, 49; empty, 43, 47, 51, 53, 57, 69; literalness of, 49; of loss, 30; negation of, 55, 57; opaque, 67; reception of, 49; sacramental, 161; scriptural, 25; *semiotic,* 158; silence and, 57; solidarity with signified, 18–19, 69; *symbolic,* 19
Space: absolute, 52; appropriation of, 140; as-if, 72; autarchic, 104; for being, 9, 10, 11; chaotic, 134; common, 10; condensation of, 113; containing, 140; devouring, 23; differential, 18, 19; empty, 44; existence in, 66; of fantasy, 133; germinative, 52; heterogeneous, 9, 10, 24; imaginary, 44, 72, 134; intermediary, 11; of intimacy, 43; intrapsychic, 61; maternal, 108, 134, 139; metaphorical, 135; modes of representation in, 9; negative, 20; paranoic, 134; performative, 10; potential, 11, 104; projective, 57, 103; psychic, 12, 21, 59; redeeming, 57; relational, 11; representational, 52; *semiotic,* 123, 140; between signifier and signified, 18, 19, 20; subjective, 61; symbolic, 52; temporal, 111; textual, 9, 10, 11, 51; of the "Thing," 59; transitional, 10, 43, 51, 102, 104, 105, 106, 135, 185; undifferentiated, 105; utopian, 52
Speech: alienated, 57; disanimated, 44; full, 44; futility of, 43; mechanical, 57
Subject, 53, 191*n3*; accommodation of, 9; aggression and, 13, 14; ambiguity of, 57; ambivalent, 13; being of, 21; coming into being of, 13; decentered, 26; emergent, 21; fragmentation and, 3; genesis of, 1–27; history of, 94; identity of, 4; integrated, 89; integrity of being of, 8; lived experience of, 5; manifest melancholia of, 17; meaningful being of, 48; original advent, 2; positioning of, 61; post-Freudian, 25; presence in text, 63; psychic life of, 3; psychoanalytic, 4; reality of, 26, 61; re-enactment of separation of, 6; reentry into the Symbolic order, 18, 19; regeneration of, 2; reification of, 4; self and, 7, 8; self-realization of, 11; self-signifying, 7; semiological being of, 2; signifying, 2, 9; split, 23, 43, 69; subjectivity of, 39
Subject and process, 77, *198*n76
Subjective: being, 7, 8, 106; identity, 7, 198*n77*; meaning, 25, 27; ontology, 29; space, 61

Subjectivity: of analyst, 5; antithetical, 88–91, 153; beyond narcissism, 103; boundaries of, 6, 31, 131–135; crisis of, 25; dialectic of, 82; dynamics of, 61; experience of, 1, 28; limits of, 198*n76*; meaning and, 2, 48; narcissism and, 11; nostalgia and, 97; objective aspect of, 174; the Other and, 26; poetics and, 2; potential, 103; provisional, 88; reciprocally interacting, 4; split, 81; of subject, 39

Sublimation, 16, 39, 192*n14*; of abjection, 22; aesthetic, 14, 40; archaic, 44, 52; castrated, 18; cathartic, 57; collapse of, 54; of death, 52, 57; fragility of, 53–54; maternal, 17, 44; of melancholia, 22; of object, 94; poetic, 102; primary, 15; regenerative, 22; religious, 40; sacrificial, 53; of separation, 12; symbolic, 3, 15

Super-ego, 76, 80, 86

Symbolization, 6, 158; advent of, 14; cathartic negation of loss and, 14; communicative functions of, 61; death-negating, 44; effective, 63; infant's access to, 207*n8*; integrative, 79, 88; intersubjective dynamics of, 192*n14*; of maternal abject, 57; mechanisms, 178; negativity, and of, 77, 93–95; nostalgia and, 30; origin of, 3; the Other and, 26; poetic, 28, 30, 61, 89–90, 132; psycho-semiological processes of, 28; relational gestalt of, 68; strategies of, 61; subversion of, 63; support of, 63; textual, 61

Text: affective experience and, 4; authenticity of tone in, 61; being in, 9, 29; as chronotopos of wish fulfillment, 9; desire in, 3; dialogical interpretation of, 27; dissociated, 100; faith and, 24; generative properties of, 1, 28; heterogeneous space of, 10, 24; as heterogeneous utterance, 9; imaginative experience and, 4; as intersection between nostalgia and melancholia, 13; intersubjective dimension of, 1; melancholic, 94; nostalgia and, 30, 94; as performance, 2; poetic, 1–27, 28, 174; as process of becomming, 9; projective space of, 103; psychoanalytical interpretation of, 27; psycho-symbolic mechanisms in, 4; reality of, 9; self-generation and, 21; self-reflexivity of, 21; signification of, 17; as space for being, 11; subject's presence in, 63; transitional space of, 10, 43, 51, 102, 105, 106, 135, 185

Textual: discourse, 62; performance, 88; space, 9, 10, 11, 51; symbolization, 61

Textuality: boundaries of, 31, 142; sexuality and, 31, 145

Thanatos, 39, 138, 139

Theories: intersubjectivity, 4, 5; of metaphor, 69; object relations, 2; of poetry, 21, 69; psychoanalytical, 2, 21; psycho-semiological, 1

"Thing," 195*n42*; archaic, 15; assimilation of, 68; concept of, 68; maternal, 16, 44; melancholic, 195*n42*; narcissistic, 52; nostalgic, 15, 17, 52, 64; space of, 59

Thomas, Dylan: "Before I knocked," 22; dialectical method, 57; eucharistic poetics of, 27, 28; faith and, 43–50; "Fern Hill" and, 30, 94, 102, 103, 104, 105, 106, 107, 108, 109–117; "I, in my Intricate Image," 78; "Incarnate Devil" and, 134; "In the Direction of the Beginning," 22; letter to Marguerite Caetani, 171–172;

melancholia and, 94–130; motif in abortion, 27; "The Mouse and the Woman" and, 132, 133, 150–169; nostalgia and, 30; "Poem in October" and, 30, 94, 102, 104, 105, 106, 108, 109, 117–130; "Poem on his Birthday" and, 35–60, 125, 128, 129; preoccupation with genesis, 25; "A Prospect of the Sea" and, 133, 135–150; reader responses to, 31–32, 70, 171–190; regressive-sublimative movement in, 23; "Refusal to Mourn the Death, by Fire, of a Child in London," 96; "To-Day, This Insect," 100; use of Christian motif in, 22, 24, 25, 39, 42, 79; use of oppositional images, 23; "Vision and Prayer," 26, 99; "When I Work," 67; works on childhood/adolescence, 101–130

Time: acts in, 51; anxiety over, 43, 59; axes of, 148; being in, 94, 105, 107; condensation of, 113; corrosiveness of, 43; dead end of, 52; destructive, 44, 52; entrance into, 51; existence in, 66; faith in, 113; falling out of tune with, 116; manipulation of, 113; maternal figure of, 113; meaning in, 43; melancholia and, 94; movement of, 113; negativity of, 52, 65; nostalgia and, 30, 94; reality of, 132, 146; recalled, 119; redemptive, 44, 115; spatialized, 107, 115; transitional space of, 10, 43, 51, 102, 104, 106, 135

"To-Day, This Insect" (Thomas), 100

Transference, 5, 174; intersubjective dynamics of, 32

Transubstantiation, 25, 133

Trust: basic, 204*n15*; breach of, 74; ontological, 74; in reality of reality, 65; Symbolic, 74

Truth, 63, 123; of abjection, 78; of created world, 78; of illusion, 101–105; nameless, 79; nonexistent, 67; in nostalgic myth, 99; obsession with, 26; real, 62, 63; value, 45

Unity: of being, 26; creation of, 64; Edenic, 85, 96; imagination and memory, 106; internal, 2; nostalgic, 18; potential, 108; primordial, 102, 108; psychosomatic, 63; sense of, 2; symbiotic, 18, 76

"Vision and Prayer" (Thomas), 26, 99

"When I Woke" (Thomas), 67

Winnicott, Donald W., 4, 11, 30, 68, 94–95, 102, 104, 105, 107, 108, 204*n15*, 210*n57*, 210*n70*; creativity and, 30, 94–95, 104; "doing" and "being" in, 107, 116, 139–142, 210*n57*; phenomenological approach to self, 10; subjectivity and, 11; transitional spaces and, 10, 11, 43, 51, 102, 104, 105, 106, 135, 185